Your All-in-One Resource

On the CD that accompanies this book, you'll find additional resources to extend your learning. The CD interface resembles the one shown here:

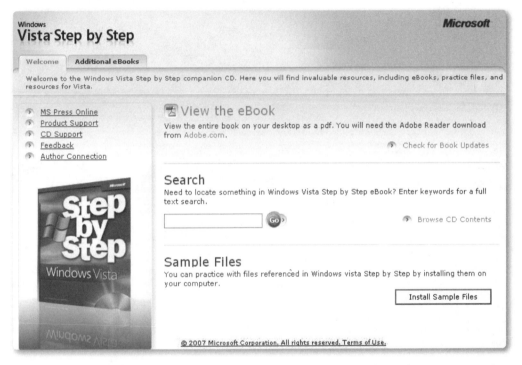

From the Welcome tab of the CD interface, you can access a variety of resources on the CD or online, including the following:

- Search or view the electronic version of this book.
- Install the book's practice files.
- Check for book updates.*
- Get product support or CD support.*
- Send us feedback.

* Requires Internet access

From the Additional eBooks tab of the CD interface, you can access electronic books and reference materials on the CD, including the following:

- *Microsoft Computer Dictionary, Fifth Edition*
- *Windows Vista Product Guide*

Microsoft® Expression® Web 2
Step by Step

Chris Leeds

PUBLISHED BY
Microsoft Press
A Division of Microsoft Corporation
One Microsoft Way
Redmond, Washington 98052-6399

Library of Congress Control Number: 2008929792

Printed and bound in the United States of America.

1 2 3 4 5 6 7 8 9   QWT   3 2 1 0 9 8

Distributed in Canada by H.B. Fenn and Company Ltd.

A CIP catalogue record for this book is available from the British Library.

Microsoft Press books are available through booksellers and distributors worldwide. For further information about international editions, contact your local Microsoft Corporation office or contact Microsoft Press International directly at fax (425) 936-7329. Visit our Web site at www.microsoft.com/mspress. Send comments to mspinput@microsoft.com.

Acquisitions Editor: Juliana Aldous Atkinson
Developmental Editor: Sandra Haynes
Project Editor: Kathleen Atkins
Editorial Production: Online Training Solutions, Inc.
Technical Reviewer: Dan Maharry; Technical Review services provided by Content Master, a member of CM Group, Ltd.

Body Part No. X15-04057

Contents

What do you think of this book? We want to hear from you!

Microsoft is interested in hearing your feedback so we can continually improve our books and learning resources for you. To participate in a brief online survey, please visit:

www.microsoft.com/learning/booksurvey/

What do you think of this book? We want to hear from you!

Microsoft is interested in hearing your feedback so we can continually improve our books and learning resources for you. To participate in a brief online survey, please visit:

www.microsoft.com/learning/booksurvey/

Introducing Expression Web 2

Microsoft Expression Web 2 is the newest Web editing and management application from Microsoft. It is a professional design tool used to create modern, standards-based sites that deliver superior quality on the Web.

Expression Web 2 can be purchased alone or as part of Microsoft Expression Studio 2, which is an integrated group of applications that, besides Expression Web 2, includes the following:

- **Expression Blend 2.** A professional design tool used to create engaging, Web-connected multimedia experiences for Windows.

- **Expression Design 2.** A professional illustration and graphic design tool used for building compelling elements for both Web and desktop application user interfaces. Expression Design 2 is available only as part of Expression Studio. It is not available as a stand-alone application.

- **Expression Media 2.** A professional asset management tool for visually cataloging and organizing all your digital assets, and that provides for effortless retrieval and presentation, and can be used to create compelling and customizable Web galleries.

- **Expression Encoder.** A professional encoding tool that offers enhancement, encoding, conversion, and publishing of video. It's also the fastest way to produce video experiences using Microsoft Silverlight.

From the perspective of a designer or developer, the modern Web bears only a slight resemblance to the Web of as little as five years ago. Expression Web 2 is an effort by Microsoft to provide a tool that helps designers attain modern Web design standards and practices.

Expression Web 2 includes features that help ensure your output keeps within the World Wide Web Consortium (W3C) validity standards, and that help you to cleanly separate content from presentation by taking advantage of the functionality and capabilities in cascading style sheets (CSS).

As you drill deeper into Expression Web 2, you will find tools to make working with Microsoft ASP.NET much more comfortable than ever before, such as the ASP.NET Development Server that installs with Expression Web and the ASP.NET Controls group in the Toolbox task pane.

Expression Web 2 helps you to easily use some of the new features in ASP.NET 2.0, which are just the ticket for designers interested in validity, accessibility, and a best practices type of workflow. Specifically, ASP.NET Master Pages, Navigation Controls, and Data Controls spring to mind. It's refreshing that tools with this type of power are available in a user-friendly "designer's" application like Expression Web 2 as opposed to being relegated to a very "programmer-oriented" tool such as Microsoft Visual Web Developer or Microsoft Visual Studio.

Upgrading from FrontPage

Former Microsoft Office FrontPage devotees may be dismayed at first glance to find that many of the familiar "Web Bots" and components are not present in Expression Web 2. Not to worry. Firstly, even if you install Expression Web 2 as an upgrade to FrontPage, you will still be able to retain the FrontPage application on your system, so you can always use FrontPage with your previous work that relied heavily on FrontPage features. Secondly, everything that was in FrontPage that didn't make its way into Expression Web 2 stayed behind for a reason. The feature wrote W3C-invalid code, relied on browser-specific rendering, required proprietary server software, or suffered a combination of those shortcomings.

You should feel comfortable using your existing copy of FrontPage to maintain previous work that relies on its proprietary features, but be sure to move forward with Expression Web 2 by creating and maintaining your new work with it; the program provides too many benefits not to.

What's New in Expression Web 2

Just a quick look at the "what's new" section of the F1 Help manual in Expression Web 2 will give you an idea of how much went into this new version. It's far from a simple update or service pack. (There's even a service pack available for Expression Web 1 to prove it.)

This newest build really shows the direction that Microsoft and the Expression Web team have decided to pursue—not just a standards-based mind-set, but the application becoming "technology agnostic." For instance, rather than limiting server-side scripting capabilities to ASP.NET, this release includes PHP features such as Intellisense and code completion, PHP includes that render in Design view, and even the ability to preview PHP files from any folder location by using the Expression Web Development Server that installs with Expression Web 2, rather than needing to resort to publishing your PHP files just to test them.

Beyond the collection of additional features included by virtue of the PHP support, you'll find that the ability to use Adobe Flash, Windows Media, and Silverlight in your pages is just a click or two away on the Insert menu.

Expression Web 2 continues this development direction with a new ability to import and use Adobe Photoshop files in your Web pages, with extensive layer and Web-ready file options.

The development direction spills over even into the ways the product is made available. Firstly, buying the application as an upgrade isn't limited to users of just Expression Web 1 but also any version of Adobe Creative Suite, Adobe/Macromedia Dreamweaver, Adobe GoLive, Microsoft Office, or even QuarkXPress.

Beyond that, you can get Expression Studio as part of the Microsoft Partner program, at *partner.microsoft.com/40043719*. Expression Web 2 is also available as part of the Microsoft Expression Professional Subscription, which includes Expression Studio as well as Visual Studio Standard, Office Standard, Microsoft Office Visio Professional, Windows XP, Windows Vista Business Edition, Microsoft Virtual PC, Parallels Desktop for Mac, and even preconfigured virtualized server environments all in the same package.

And if you're a student, you can get Expression Studio 2, and a huge collection of other Microsoft development software through DreamSpark, at *downloads.channel8.msdn.com/Default.aspx*. With Microsoft DreamSpark, students can download Microsoft developer and design tools at no charge, making it easier for them to learn the skills they need to excel both during school and after graduation.

Information for Readers Running Windows XP

The graphics and the operating system–related instructions in this book reflect the Windows Vista user interface, but you can also use a computer running Windows XP with Service Pack 2 (SP2) or Service Pack 3 (SP3) installed.

Most of the differences you will encounter when working through the exercises in this book on a computer running Windows XP relate to appearance rather than functionality. For example, the Windows Vista Start button is round rather than rectangular and is not labeled with the word *Start*; window frames and window-management buttons look different; and if your system supports Windows Aero, the window frames might be transparent.

In this section, we provide steps for navigating to or through menus and dialog boxes in Windows XP that differ from those provided in the exercises in this book. For the most part, these differences are small enough that you will have no difficulty in completing the exercises.

Managing the Practice Files

The instructions given in the "Using the Companion CD" section are specific to Windows Vista. The only differences when installing, using, uninstalling, and removing the practice files supplied on the companion CD are the default installation location and the uninstall process.

On a computer running Windows Vista, the default installation location of the practice files is *Documents\Microsoft Press\Expression Web 2 SBS*. On a computer running Windows XP, the default installation location is *My Documents\Microsoft Press\Expression Web 2 SBS*. If your computer is running Windows XP, whenever an exercise tells you to navigate to your *Documents* folder, you should instead go to your *My Documents* folder.

To uninstall the practice files from a computer running Windows XP:

1. On the Windows taskbar, click the **Start** button, and then click **Control Panel**.

2. In **Control Panel**, click (or in Classic view, double-click) **Add or Remove Programs**.

3. In the **Add or Remove Programs** window, click **Microsoft Expression Web 2 Step by Step**, and then click **Remove**.

4. In the **Add or Remove Programs** message box asking you to confirm the deletion, click **Yes**.

> **Important** If you need help installing or uninstalling the practice files, please see the "Getting Help" section later in this book. Microsoft Product Support Services does not provide support for this book or its companion CD.

Using the Start Menu

Folders on the Windows Vista Start menu expand vertically. Folders on the Windows XP Start menu expand horizontally. However, the steps to access a command on the Start menu are identical on both systems.

To start Microsoft Expression Web 2 on a Windows XP computer:

→ Click the **Start** button, point to **All Programs**, click **Microsoft Expression**, and then click **Microsoft Expression Web 2**.

Navigating Dialog Boxes

On a computer running Windows XP, some of the dialog boxes you will work with in the exercises not only look different from the graphics shown in this book but also work differently. These dialog boxes are primarily those that act as an interface between Expression Web 2 and the operating system, including any dialog box in which you navigate to a specific location.

For example, to navigate to the *My Pictures* folder in Windows XP:

→ On the Places bar, click **My Documents**. Then in the folder content pane, double-click *My Pictures*.

To move back to the *My Documents* folder in Windows XP:

→ On the toolbar, click the **Up One Level** button.

Features and Conventions of This Book

This book has been designed to lead you step by step through all the tasks you are most likely to want to perform in Microsoft Expression Web 2. If you start at the beginning and work your way through all the exercises, you will gain enough proficiency to be able to create complex Web sites and pages. However, each topic is self contained. If you have worked with another Web editor, such as Microsoft Office FrontPage, or if you completed all the exercises and later need help remembering how to perform a procedure, the following features of this book will help you locate specific information:

- **Detailed table of contents.** Scan this listing of the topics and sidebars within each chapter to quickly find the information you want.
- **Chapter thumb tabs.** Easily locate the beginning of the chapter you want.
- **Topic-specific running heads.** Within a chapter, quickly locate the topic you want by looking at the running head of odd-numbered pages.
- **Detailed index.** Look up specific tasks and features and general concepts in the index, which has been carefully crafted with the reader in mind.
- **Companion CD.** Install the practice files needed for the step-by-step exercises, and consult a fully searchable electronic version of this book and other useful resources contained on this CD.

In addition, we provide a glossary of terms for those times when you need to look up the meaning of a word or the definition of a concept.

You can save time when you use this book by understanding how the *Step by Step* series shows special instructions, keys to press, buttons to click, and other functionality.

> **Important** Whether you are using Windows XP or Windows Vista, you may notice that the screen shots of the Expression Web 2 interface differ from the default gray theme that you may be using. The application was set to use the default Windows color scheme in an effort to provide greater readability of the various interface elements. If you want to change the color scheme of Expression Web 2, on the Tools menu, click Application Options, and then on the General tab of the Application Options dialog box, select the Use Your Current Windows Color Scheme check box.

Convention	Meaning
	This icon indicates a reference to the book's companion CD.
USE	This paragraph preceding a step-by-step exercise indicates the practice files or programs that you will use when working through the exercise.
BE SURE TO	This paragraph preceding or following an exercise indicates any requirements you should attend to before beginning the exercise or actions you should take to restore your system after completing the exercise.
OPEN	This paragraph preceding a step-by-step exercise indicates files that you should open before beginning the exercise.
CLOSE	This paragraph following a step-by-step exercise provides instructions for closing open files or programs before moving on to another topic.
1 **2**	Large numbered steps guide you through hands-on exercises.
1 2	Small numbered steps guide you through procedures in sidebars and expository text.
→	An arrow indicates a procedure that has only one step.
Tip	These paragraphs provide a helpful hint or shortcut that makes working through a task easier, or information about other available options.
Important	These paragraphs point out information that you need to know to complete a procedure.
Troubleshooting	These paragraphs explain how to fix a common problem that might prevent you from continuing with an exercise.
See Also	These paragraphs direct you to more information about a given topic in this book or elsewhere.
Save	The first time you are told to click a button in an exercise, a picture of the button appears in the left margin. If the name of the button does not appear on the button itself, the name appears under the picture.
Enter	In step-by-step exercises, keys you must press appear as they would on a keyboard.
Ctrl + Tab	A plus sign (+) between two key names means that you must hold down the first key while you press the second key. For example, "Press Ctrl + Tab" means "hold down the Ctrl key while you press the Tab key."
Program interface elements and user input	In steps, the names of program elements, such as buttons, commands, and dialog boxes, are shown in bold characters. Text that you are supposed to type is shown in bold characters.
Glossary terms	Terms explained in the glossary are shown in bold italic type.
Paths and emphasized words	Folder paths, URLs, and emphasized words are shown in italic characters.

Using the Companion CD

The companion CD included with this book contains the practice files and sample sites you'll use as you work through the book's exercises, as well as other electronic resources that will help you learn how to use Microsoft Expression Web 2.

> Digital Content for Digital Book Readers: If you bought a digital-only edition of this book, you can enjoy select content from the print edition's companion CD.
>
> Visit *go.microsoft.com/fwlink/?LinkID=127011* to get your downloadable content. This content is always up-to-date and available to all readers.

What's on the CD?

The following table lists the practice files and sample sites, as well as sample sites depicting the results of completed exercises, that are supplied on the companion CD.

Chapter	Files and sites
Chapter 1: Understanding How Expression Web 2 Works	*Sample Sites\CH1* *Sample Sites\Publish\CH1*
Chapter 2: Moving from FrontPage to Expression Web 2	*Files\Microsoft_FrontPage_to_ Expression_Web.doc* *Sample Sites\CH2* *Sample Sites\CH2-Done* *Sample Sites\FrontPageExample* *Sample Sites\FrontPageExample-Done*
Chapter 3: Becoming Familiar with Modern Web Site Standards	*Sample Sites\CH3* *Sample Sites\CH3-Done*
Chapter 4: Presenting Information on a Web Page	*Sample Sites\CH4* *Sample Sites\CH4-Done*
Chapter 5: Enhancing a Web Site with Images	*Files\CH5-Import* *Files\PSImport.psd* *Sample Sites\CH5* *Sample Sites\CH5-done*
Chapter 6: Creating a Web Site from a Template	*Files\BGlogo.jpg* *Files\logo.jpg* *Sample Sites\CH6-done*

Chapter	Files and sites
Chapter 7: Creating a Web Site from Scratch	*Files\CH7template* *Sample Sites\CH7-done*
Chapter 8: Taking It to the Next Level	*Files\CH8.fwp* *Files\Flash.swf* *Files\silverlightsample* *Files\WindowsMedia.wmv* *Sample Sites\CH8* *Sample Sites\CH8-done*
Chapter 9: Publishing a Web Site	*Sample Sites\CH9* *Sample Sites\Publish\CH9*
Chapter 10: Managing a Web Site	*Sample Sites\CH10* *Sample Sites\Publish\ CH10SelectivePublish*
Chapter 11: Using ASP.NET Features	*Sample Sites\CH11* *Sample Sites\CH11-Done*
Chapter 12: Using PHP Features	*Sample Sites\CH12* *Sample Sites\CH12-Done*

In addition to the practice files and sample sites, the CD contains some exciting resources that will enhance your ability to get the most out of using this book and Expression Web 2, including the following:

- *Microsoft Expression Web 2 Step by Step* in eBook format
- *Microsoft Computer Dictionary, Fifth Edition* eBook
- *Windows Vista Product Guide*

> **Important** The companion CD for this book does not contain the Expression Web 2 software. You should purchase and install that software before using this book. See the "What's New in Expression Web 2" section in "Introducing Expression Web 2" earlier in this book to learn about new ways to acquire the software.

Minimum System Requirements

To perform the exercises in this book, your computer should meet the following requirements:

- **Processor.** Pentium 700 megahertz (MHz) or higher; 2 gigahertz (GHz) recommended.
- **Memory.** 512 megabytes (MB) of RAM; 1 gigabyte (GB) or more recommended.
- **Hard disk.** For the eBooks and downloads, we recommend 3 GB of available hard disk space with 2 GB on the hard disk where the operating system is installed. Expression Web 2 requires a minimum of 1.5 GB of hard drive space.

> **Tip** Hard disk space requirements will vary depending on configuration; custom installation choices might require more or less hard disk space.

- **Operating System.** Windows XP with Service Pack 2 (SP2), or Windows Vista.
- **Drive.** DVD drive.
- **Display.** Monitor with 1024 × 768 or higher screen resolution and 16-bit or higher color depth.
- **Software.** Windows Internet Explorer 7 or Microsoft Internet Explorer 6 with service packs.

Step-by-Step Exercises

In addition to the hardware, software, and connections required to run Expression Web 2, you will need the following to successfully complete the exercises in this book:

- Microsoft Expression Web 2
- 24 MB of available hard disk space for the practice files

Installing the Practice Files

Some exercises in *Microsoft Expression Web 2 Step by Step* use the Web site templates included when you install Expression Web 2. For other exercises, there are practice files and sample sites that come on this book's accompanying CD.

To install the files from the CD:

1. Remove the companion CD from the envelope at the back of the book, and insert it into the CD drive of your computer.

The Step By Step Companion CD License Terms appear. Follow the on-screen directions. To use the practice files, you must accept the terms of the license agreement. After you accept the license agreement, a menu screen appears.

> **Important** If the menu screen does not appear, click the Start button and then click Computer. Display the Folders list in the Navigation Pane, click the icon for your CD drive, and then in the right pane, double-click the StartCD executable file.

2. Click **Install Practice Files**.

3. Click **Next** on the first screen, and then click **Next** to accept the terms of the license agreement on the next screen.

4. If you want to install the practice files to a location other than the default folder (*Documents\Microsoft Press\Expression Web 2 SBS*), click the **Change** button, select the new drive and path, and then click **OK**.

> **Important** If you install the practice files to a location other than the default, you will need to substitute that path within the exercises.

5. Click **Next** on the **Choose Destination Location** screen, and then click **Install** on the **Ready to Install the Program** screen to install the selected practice files.

6. After the practice files have been installed, click **Finish**.

7. Close the **Step by Step Companion CD** window, remove the companion CD from the CD drive, and return it to the envelope at the back of the book.

Using the Practice Files

When you install the practice files and sample sites from the companion CD, the files are stored on your hard disk in chapter-specific subfolders under *Documents\Microsoft Press\ Expression Web 2 SBS*. Each exercise is preceded by a Housekeeping segment that lists the sample Web site needed for that exercise and any extra tasks you need to complete before you start working through the exercise, as shown here:

> **USE** the *CH3* sample site. This site is located in the *Documents\Microsoft Press\Expression Web 2 SBS\Sample Sites* folder.
>
> **BE SURE TO** start Expression Web before beginning this exercise.
>
> **OPEN** the *CH3* site by clicking Open Site on the File menu, and display the *default.htm* page in Split view.

Wherever possible, we made the exercises independent of each other. However, if you choose to do exercises in a sequence other than that presented in the book, be aware that there are exercises in some chapters that depend on other exercises performed earlier in the book. If this is the case, we will tell you where in the book the prerequisite exercises are located.

You can browse to the practice files in Windows Explorer by following these steps:

1. On the Windows taskbar, click the **Start** button, and then click **Documents**.

2. In your *Documents* folder, double-click *Microsoft Press*, double-click *Expression Web 2 SBS*, double-click *Sample Sites* or *Files*, and then double-click a specific chapter folder, file, or site.

Removing the Practice Files

You can free up hard disk space by uninstalling the practice files that were installed from the companion CD. The uninstall process deletes any files that you created in the *Documents\Microsoft Press\Expression Web 2 SBS* folder while working through the exercises.

Follow these steps:

1. On the Windows taskbar, click the **Start** button, and then click **Control Panel**.

2. In **Control Panel**, under **Programs**, click the **Uninstall a program** task.

3. If the **Programs and Features** message box asking you to confirm the deletion appears, click **Yes**.

See Also If you need additional help installing or uninstalling the practice files, see the "Getting Help" section later in this book.

> **Important** Microsoft Product Support Services does not provide support for this book or its companion CD.

Getting Help

Every effort has been made to ensure the accuracy of this book and the contents of its CD. If you run into problems, please contact the appropriate source, listed in the following sections, for help and assistance.

Getting Help with This Book and Its CD

If your question or issue concerns the content of this book or its companion CD, please first search the online Microsoft Press Knowledge Base, which provides support information for known errors in or corrections to this book, at the following Web site:

www.microsoft.com/mspress/support/search.aspx

If you do not find your answer in the online Knowledge Base, send your comments or questions to Microsoft Learning Technical Support at:

mspinput@microsoft.com

Getting Help with Expression Web 2

If your question is about Microsoft Expression Web 2, and not about the content of this Microsoft Press book, please search the Microsoft Help and Support Center or the Microsoft Knowledge Base at:

support.microsoft.com

You can also visit the following Web site, where you can ask Chris Leeds, the author of this book, any specific questions you may have about Expression Web 2, and find other Expression-related resources.

www.ExpressionWebStepByStep.com

In the United States, Microsoft software product support issues not covered by the Microsoft Knowledge Base are addressed by Microsoft Product Support Services. The Microsoft software support options available from Microsoft Product Support Services are listed at:

support.microsoft.com/

Outside the United States, for support information specific to your location, please refer to the Worldwide Support menu on the Microsoft Help and Support Web site for the site specific to your country:

support.microsoft.com/common/international.aspx

Another source of help is the Expression product team, who maintain an online community that fosters user-to-user assistance:

www.microsoft.com/expression/community

Chapter at a Glance

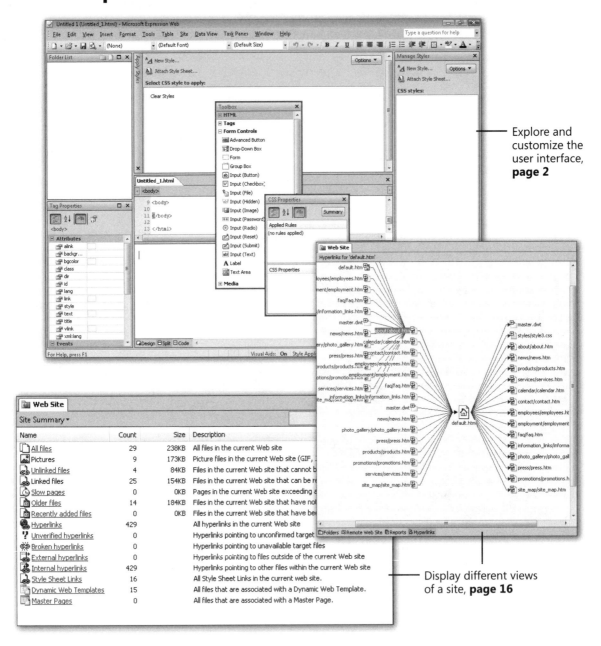

Explore and customize the user interface, **page 2**

Display different views of a site, **page 16**

1 Understanding How Expression Web 2 Works

In this chapter, you will learn to

- ✔ Explore and customize the user interface.
- ✔ Open an existing site.
- ✔ Display different views of a site.
- ✔ Explore an individual Web page.
- ✔ Understand basic Expression Web 2 concepts.

Microsoft Expression Web 2 is a new program that allows you to easily build *standards-compliant* and *accessible* Web sites. Expression Web 2 also has features that allow you to build components on your site that previously required significant hand coding or a code editing application such as Microsoft Visual Studio or Microsoft Visual Web Developer. Whether you're simply interested in building a standards-based Web site or bringing your existing site up to current standards—that is, to follow the latest versions of *XHTML\HTML*, *CSS*, and accessibility standards as laid out by the *World Wide Web Consortium* (*W3C*)—Expression Web 2 is a great tool to choose. As a bonus, by using Expression Web 2, you are also creating a Web site that has valid code that is based on *cascading style sheets*.

Basing a site on current W3C standards aids in ease of long-term maintenance, *cross-browser compatibility*, and accessibility by both *search engines* and nonvisual browsers such as *screen readers* that are used by vision-impaired visitors.

Users of Microsoft Office FrontPage, Adobe Dreamweaver, or Adobe GoLive will find the transition to Expression Web 2 fairly easy. Though Expression Web 2 ignores most *proprietary editor features*, it allows the full capability of editing and managing sites that were originally created by using FrontPage or other HTML editors. The goal for Expression Web 2 is to make the transition to standards-compliant, modern Web sites as painless as possible.

In this chapter, you will explore and customize the *user interface* and open an existing site. You will also use the views in Expression Web 2 to explore an individual Web page. Finally, you will learn some basic Expression Web 2 concepts.

Important   Before you can use the practice files in this chapter, you need to install them from the book's companion CD to their default location. For more information about practice files, see "Using the Companion CD" at the beginning of this book.

Troubleshooting   Graphics and operating system–related instructions in this book reflect the Windows Vista user interface. If your computer is running Windows XP and you experience trouble following the instructions as written, please refer to the "Information for Readers Running Windows XP" section at the beginning of this book.

To improve the readability of the graphics in this book, Expression Web 2 was set to use the Windows color scheme instead of the default Expression Studio 2 color scheme.

Exploring and Customizing the User Interface

The user interface in Expression Web 2 closely matches the interfaces of the other applications in Expression Studio 2. Almost everything you might need to do within Expression Web 2 is available to you from the 12 menus on the menu bar. These menus are "intelligent," in that the items you use most often move up the list that appears when you open a menu, and items that you use less frequently are moved down. If an item can't be used, that particular menu item will be unavailable and indicated by a grey color instead of black. In addition to the menu bar and toolbar, Expression Web 2 includes additional panes that are part of your workspace. You can resize, move, *dock*, and *undock* these panes.

Pane   Menu bar   Code pane   Common toolbar   Pane

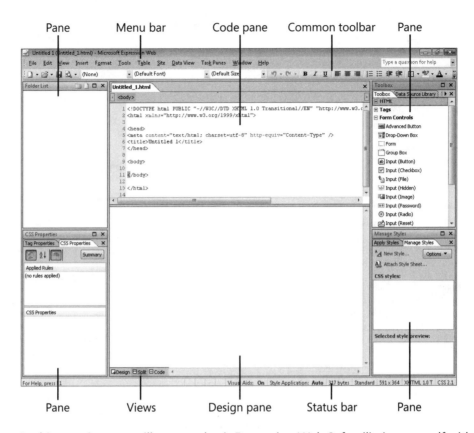

Pane   Views   Design pane   Status bar   Pane

In this exercise, you will start and exit Expression Web 2, familiarize yourself with the toolbar commands, and manipulate the panes that are available to you. There are no practice files for this exercise.

 BE SURE TO install Expression Web 2 before beginning this exercise.

Start

1. Click the **Start** button, point to **All Programs**, point to **Microsoft Expression**, and then click **Microsoft Expression Web 2**.

A page named *Untitled_1.htm* opens when you start Expression Web 2 for the first time. You may also be prompted as to whether you want to make Expression Web 2 your default HTML editor.

> **Troubleshooting** If you previously had a site open with Expression Web 2, that site will open automatically by default. If that's the case, click Close Site on the File menu, click Exit on the File menu, and then restart Expression Web 2.

2. On the menu bar, click the **File** menu to reveal its contents.

3. On the **File** menu, point to **New**.

The New submenu displays commands for creating a new page; a Web site; an HTML, an *ASPX*, or a *PHP* file; or a cascading style sheet.

> **Troubleshooting** Notice that the command for creating a new folder is unavailable. You do not have a site open, and folders can be created only within a site.

4. Continue to explore the commands on the **File** menu. Then explore the **Edit**, **View**, **Insert**, **Format**, **Tools**, **Table**, **Site**, **Data View**, **Task Panes**, **Window**, and **Help** menus.

There's a large array of items available on these menus. Don't let the number of items overwhelm you. The point of this exercise is not to learn each and every one of them, but to become familiar with the contents of the menus and to understand the logical groups in which items are arranged.

> **Tip** As you're exploring, don't forget to explore the menu items that have an arrow so that you can see what is available in their submenus.

Below the menu bar is the Common toolbar. This toolbar contains the most commonly used tools that you'll need when designing pages.

5. Using the mouse pointer, point to each of the buttons on the **Common** toolbar to reveal its *tooltip*.

> **Tip** Toolbar buttons with small downward-pointing arrows indicate that a subgroup is available for that particular button. You'll want to explore these subgroups to become familiar with the available options.

Toolbar Options

6. At the end of the toolbar is the **Toolbar Options** button, a downward-pointing arrow with a small horizontal line above it. Click this button to reveal the **Add or Remove Buttons** option.

7. Click **Add or Remove Buttons** to display two commands: **Common** and **Customize**.

By default, all buttons are present on the Common toolbar.

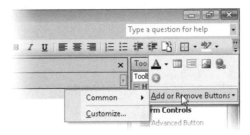

8. Click **Customize** to open the **Customize** dialog box. Then explore the three tabs of the dialog box—**Toolbars**, **Commands**, and **Options**—to find out what you can add and remove from the toolbars.

When the Customize dialog box is open, you can move toolbar buttons by dragging them to a new position on the toolbar, remove them by dragging them off the toolbar, and resize some of them by selecting them and then click-dragging their edges.

All the toolbars that are available in Expression Web 2 can be dragged over your workspace or docked against any side of the workspace.

9. Drag the **Common** toolbar by the handle on its far-left side and drop it in the middle of your workspace.

This is called a *floating toolbar*.

> **Tip** In addition to placing a floating toolbar wherever you want it, you can resize it.

10. Drag the toolbar again, to the right edge of your workspace.

Now the Common toolbar is docked to the right side of your workspace.

11. Drag the toolbar back to its original location.

12. Right-click anywhere on or next to the **Common** toolbar to see a menu that shows the available toolbars.

You can click one of the toolbars in the menu to quickly make the toolbar available for an immediate task at hand, such as adding and managing content regions in a Microsoft .NET master page.

> **Tip** The whole idea of all these different toolbars, and the ability to add or remove buttons and customize them, is that Expression Web 2 is designed to enable you to lay out your workspace the way that works best for you. Every designer works differently, and every project has a slightly different work flow; so keep the flexibility of these toolbars and buttons in mind when you begin a new project. Spending 10 minutes customizing and arranging your toolbars can result in hours of time savings over the course of a sizable project. Trust me, the good folks at Microsoft didn't spend all the time required to make these toolbars so flexible just to show you what they can do. They did it so that you could save yourself time and have a workspace that meets your needs.

Toolbars, no matter how flexible or well thought out, are limited by their very nature. What happens if you have some kind of functionality that requires a level of complexity that simply can't be handled by a button? Enter the pane.

> **Tip** Eleven toolbars are available for display in the workspace, including the default Common toolbar and the menu bar. Each of the additional toolbars can help you work faster; but they do occupy screen space, so you probably won't want to have them open all the time.

13. On the menu bar, click **Task Panes**.

A long list of available panes is displayed.

The groups of panes are separated by horizontal lines. Each group of panes between the horizontal lines will appear in the same pane area.

14. On the **Task Panes** menu, click **CSS Properties**.

The CSS Properties task pane opens in the lower-left corner of your workspace.

15. Open the **Task Panes** menu again.

The CSS Properties command has a check mark but the Tag Properties command doesn't.

16. Click **Tag Properties** to reverse the check marks. The Tag Properties task pane is now active in your lower left workspace.

Manipulating which panel is visible within a task pane isn't solely limited to the Task Panes menu. You can also click the tabs near the top of the task pane. If there are a number of tabs open, you can use the directional icon to scroll through the tabs.

These tabs represent the various panes that are available within that particular group.

17. On the **Task Panes** menu, click **Data Source Library**, **Data Source Details**, and **Conditional Formatting** to add these task panes to the **Toolbox** task pane group. Examine each of these panes, and then click **Toolbox** on the **Task Panes** menu to bring that pane to the top of the group.

18. Look at the **Toolbox** task pane (located by default in the upper-right section of your workspace).

There are several tabs and buttons at the top of the pane. You can click the arrow next to the tab on the right to scroll through the different tabs within the pane. You can click the Maximize button to maximize the pane and click the Close button to close the pane.

19. Drag one of the tabs and release it over the center of your workspace so that it floats.

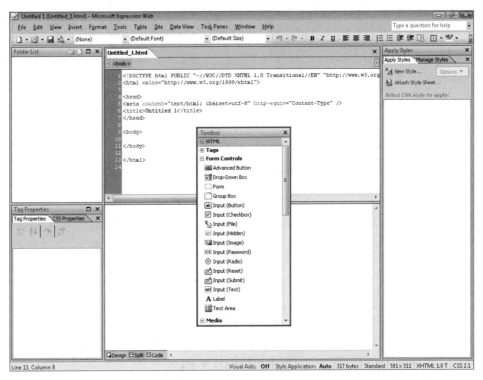

20. Drag the tab to any side of the workspace so that it is docked.

21. Repeat steps 19 and 20, using a few of the task panes. Give some thought to how you might like your workspace to be laid out.

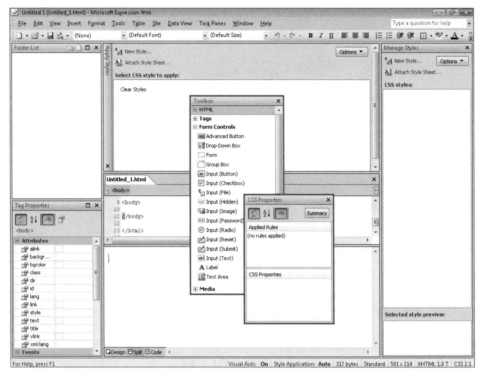

22. On the **Task Panes** menu, click **Reset Workspace Layout** (at the bottom of the menu) to reset the panes to their original state.

23. On the **File** menu, click **Close** to close the *Untitled_1.html* file that was created when you opened Expression Web 2 in step 1 of this exercise.

You have now seen all of the options that are available to you in Expression Web 2 to modify the graphical user interface (GUI). Keep in mind that all of these available tools are there to help you to set up the workspace so that it suits your workflow or a specific task.

> **Tip** With all of the customizations and options in the toolbars alone, the choices can become overwhelming. When you add the pane groups and all the possible panes they can contain, the sheer volume of available tools can compound this issue. A third-party application that provides a greatly enhanced level of control over all of the panes in Expression Web 2 is available from *www.panemanager.com*.

Expression Web 2 contains two important additional methods for deeper customization: the *Application Options* and *Page Editor Options* dialog boxes.

To open the Application Options dialog box, on the Tools menu, click Application Options.

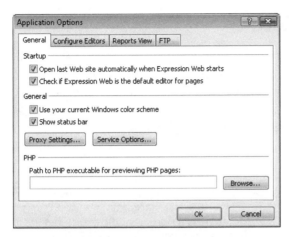

This dialog box contains four tabs in which you can set options for how the editor behaves on a global level. The options here are self explanatory and well documented in the application's F1 Help manual.

To open the Page Editor Options dialog box, on the Tools menu, click Page Editor Options.

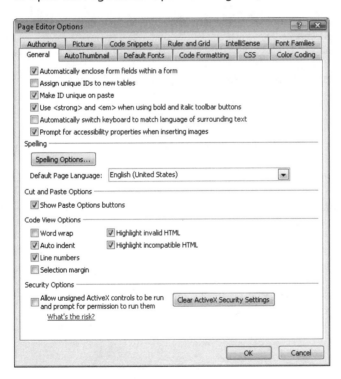

This dialog box contains 12 tabs in which you can set virtually limitless options. The options here offer much more fine-grained control of the editor's specific behavior and preferences. You'll find them well documented in the application's F1 Help manual.

Opening an Existing Site

An *Expression Web site* consists of a logical grouping of folders that contain all of the pages, images, and other files that make up the site. In most cases, the site also contains *metadata* that Expression Web 2 uses to recognize when files were changed, to update references to files you might have renamed or replaced, the location to which the site has been published, and an array of other data the program can use for behind-the-scenes management.

In this exercise, you will open and examine an entire site by using Expression Web 2.

> **Troubleshooting** On the File menu, there is a significant difference between clicking Open and clicking Open Site. Clicking Open Site opens an entire site within Expression Web 2, thereby enabling automatic hyperlink updates, publishing capabilities, and so on.
>
> Clicking Open opens only a single file. Any changes that are made to this file do not affect any other files. In most cases, clicking Open Site will be the preferred action.

 USE the *CH1* sample site. This sample site is located in the *Documents\Microsoft Press\ Expression Web 2 SBS\Sample Sites* folder.

1. On the **File** menu, click **Open Site**. In the **Open Site** dialog box, browse to *Documents\Microsoft Press\Expression Web 2 SBS\Sample Sites*, and then click *CH1*.

2. Click **Open** to open the site in Expression Web 2.

   The site contains one of the Small Business Web site templates that come with Expression Web 2.

   With a site open, the Folder List on the left side of your workspace lists all the files and folders that make up your site. The main window is set in Folders view.

> **Tip** Folders view is very convenient for examining, managing, and modifying site structure. If you rename a folder, Expression Web 2 automatically updates all of the internal links and references to it (as long as you're using metadata to manage the site). When you're designing a site from scratch, it is a good idea to use Folders view for designing the overall architecture and folder structure for the site.

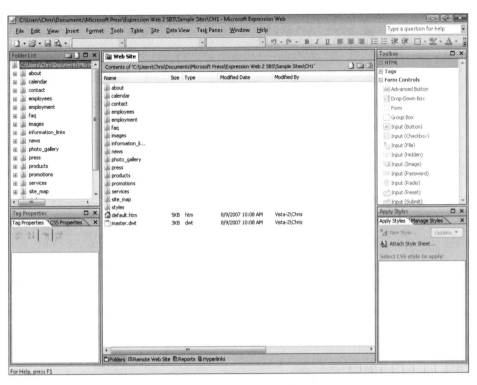

3. Click one of the subfolders in the **Folder List**.

In the main window, Folders is highlighted at the bottom, indicating the window is in Folders View. Folders View shows the contents of the folder clicked in the Folder List.

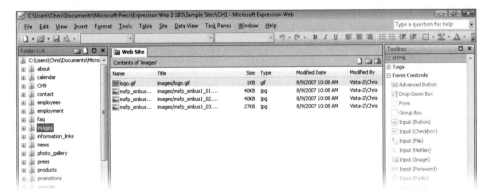

4. Click the *root folder*, the folder at the very top of the **Folder List**.

All of the site's files and subfolders reappear in your main workspace.

BE SURE TO leave the *CH1* site open for use in the next exercise.

Displaying Different Views of a Site

In addition to the default Folders view, Expression Web 2 provides a number of other views to assist in designing and managing a site.

In Expression Web 2, when a site is open but no individual files are open, four views are available at the bottom of your main workspace: Folders, Remote Web Site, Reports, and Hyperlinks.

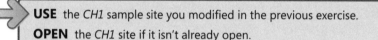

In this exercise, you will set up a remote Web site and examine it on a folder level.

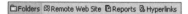
USE the *CH1* sample site you modified in the previous exercise.
OPEN the *CH1* site if it isn't already open.

1. Click the **Web Site** tab at the top of the workspace to ensure that you're in **Web Site** view.

> **Tip** Right-click the white space below the list of files and folders in your main workspace. A shortcut menu opens, displaying the New and Arrange commands, both of which have submenus.

> **Tip** The commands in the shortcut menu are those which are most often needed when working in this view. From the New submenu, you can select various types of new files or even a new folder. From the Arrange submenu, you can select many different ways to arrange the files that you see in Folders view. When you are working on a large site, using these different criteria to arrange the files in your workspace makes it easier for you to navigate and to find particular files quickly.

2. Click **Remote Web Site View** at the bottom of your main workspace.

An empty view and a prompt to set up a *remote Web site* opens.

3. In the upper-right corner of the workspace, click **Remote Web Site Properties**.

The Remote Web Site Properties dialog box opens.

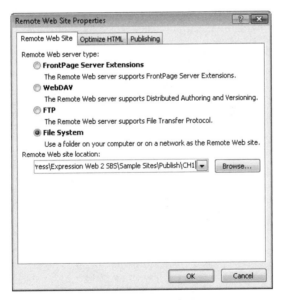

4. Click **File System** as your remote Web server type.

5. Click **Browse**, and browse to *Documents\Expression Web 2 SBS\Sample Sites\ Publish\CH1*, which will be your remote site. Then click **Open**, and in the **Remote Website Properties** dialog box, click **OK**.

6. At the bottom of your main workspace, click **Reports**.

Expression Web 2 displays the default Site Summary report containing a variety of statistical information about your site.

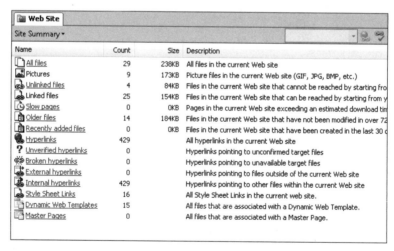

7. Above your main workspace, click the **Site Summary** arrow.

All of the various reports are available from the menu that opens. The reports are segregated into three logical groups: Files, Shared Content, and Problems, to make it easier for you to find the specific report view you need.

8. Click each available report on the menu and examine it.

9. At the bottom of your main workspace, click **Hyperlinks**.

10. In the **Folder List**, click **default.htm** to display the page and its linked files in the main workspace.

> **Tip** Files that show in Hyperlinks view with a plus sign (+) can be clicked to expand them and show all the files they link to. The file names can be double-clicked to open them within Expression Web 2.

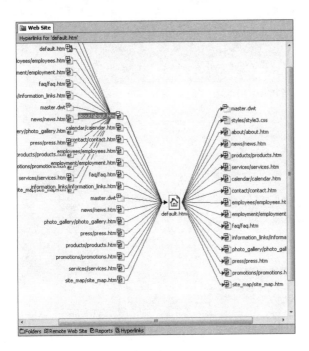

> **Tip** Hyperlinks view is very useful for figuring out where a file is used within a site, understanding how the site's overall navigation works, and other situations where you need either a big-picture overview of an entire site or a tight view of a particular file's purpose within a site.

 BE SURE TO leave the *CH1* site open for use in the next exercise.

Exploring an Individual Web Page

In the previous section, you opened a site and examined it on a folder level. In this exercise, you will open a page within this site, examine it at a page level, and use Expression Web 2 for editing files.

> **USE** the *CH1* sample site you modified in the previous exercise.
>
> **OPEN** the *CH1* site if it isn't already open.

1. In the **Folder List**, double-click **default.htm**.

   The home page of the sample site opens in the Expression Web 2 workspace.

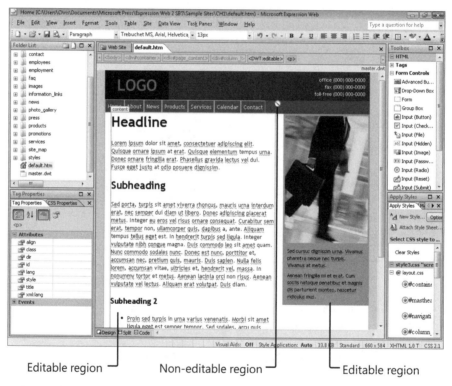

   Editable region — Non-editable region — Editable region

2. Point to the page header and page footer.

   The pointer changes from an insertion point to a no-insertion-point icon, because the page is attached to a *Dynamic Web Template (DWT)*.

> **Tip** In Expression Web 2, DWTs are the preferred method of keeping static pages within pages unified under a common look. In fact, every site template that comes with Expression Web 2 uses DWTs to control the content pages. DWTs work when you save files on your local computer, so there are no specific server requirements.

Save

3. There are two editable regions that you can work within on this page. Change the text in each of them, and then click the **Save** button.

At the bottom of the design surface are three view buttons: Design, Split, and Code.

4. Click **Split**.

Split view shows both Code and Design views simultaneously.

5. Adjust the size of each view by dragging the separator between them up or down.

6. Select some text in the Design pane at the bottom of your workspace.

Notice how the Design view selection is also selected in the Code view pane.

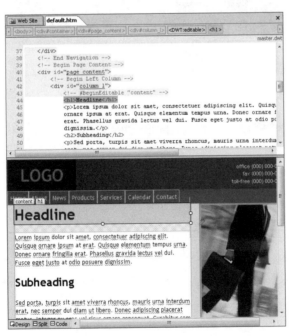

7. In the **Folder List**, double-click the *master.dwt* file to open it. Delete the fax number in the header.

Along the top of your Code pane is the quick tag selector bar. Notice the arrow on the tag when you pause the mouse pointer over it.

8. Click the arrow to display some options you can use.

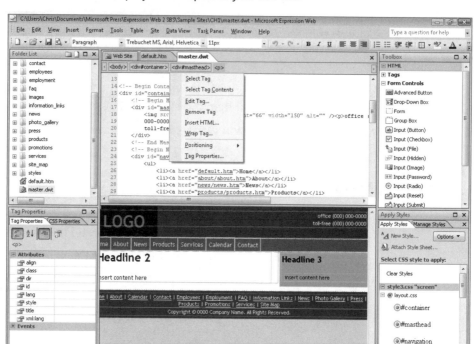

9. Save the page.

You are asked whether you want the pages that are attached to the DWT to be updated.

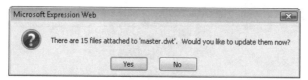

10. Click **Yes**, and then click **Close** on the confirmation box.

11. Set the mouse pointer in the navigation bar in the Design surface by clicking the **Home** link.

From right to left on the quick tag selector bar, the Home link is inside of an <a> tag that's inside an <li> and <ul> tag, which is inside a series of nested <div> tags.

> **Tip** The quick tag selector bar, Split view, and the CSS Properties task pane are indispensable tools for deeply exploring a complex document. With these tools, you can accurately and quickly find an exact place in a document's code structure, which is useful for designing, repairing, or modifying pages.

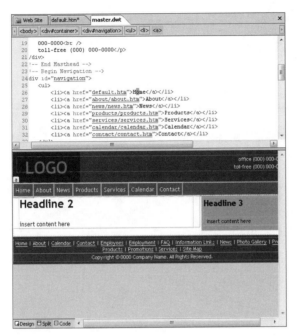

12. Point to each of the tags on the quick tag selector bar slowly from left to right.

Notice that when you point to a tag, a blue border appears around the corresponding element in the Design pane.

13. In the quick tag selector bar, click **div#navigation** to select that page element.

Notice that the containing element is a <div> tag.

> **Tip** All of the templates supplied in Expression Web 2 use completely *table-free* cascading style sheet layouts in addition to being based on a DWT. Expression Web 2 provides a number of tools to work with the cascading style sheets that control the layout and presentation of the page.

14. Click the **Home** link in the page's navigation bar.

Show set
properties
on top

15. On the **Task Panes** menu, click **CSS Properties**. On the **CSS Properties** task pane, ensure that the **Show set properties on top** button is selected in order to show all of the CSS elements pertaining to that link stacked at the top of the **CSS Properties** task pane.

16. Expand the **font** item in the **CSS Properties** task pane by clicking the plus sign (+) beside the item.

From here, you can quickly change the whole cascading style sheet presentation of an element. All elements that are styled are highlighted in the CSS Properties task pane.

 CLOSE the *CH1* site. If you are not continuing directly to the next chapter, exit Expression Web 2.

You've now seen how Expression Web 2 works with pages on an individual level, from both a code and design standpoint, and you've had a chance to work with the Expression Web 2 tools. You've also seen how the Expression Web 2 site templates rely on DWTs and cascading style sheets for layout and style.

Understanding Basic Expression Web 2 Concepts

With Expression Web 2, you have virtually limitless possibilities for setting up your workspace, and you can chose to use or not use *proprietary technology* such as meta-files. The overriding predisposition of Expression Web 2 is to write W3C-valid code and produce accessible sites, all while not forcing you to wade through HTML code.

You will also find DWTs to be an efficient way to manage Web sites and keep them uniform and uniformly updated.

Expression Web 2 makes a distinction, and so should you, about what is an individual file and what is a file that's part of a logical grouping: an Expression Web site.

Although Expression Web 2 is an excellent tool for working on documents at any level, from presentation to their code structure, if you understand and make use of the Expression Web "site" concept, you can use the excellent site management capabilities of Expression Web 2.

Key Points

- Expression Web 2 is the Web design component of *Microsoft Expression Studio 2*.
- The tools in Expression Web 2—toolbars, panes, and various Site views—can be easily customized to match your workflow.
- There is a distinct difference between a single file that exists or is opened from outside of an Expression Web site and a file that's opened from within an Expression Web site.
- With the Expression Web 2 tools, you can easily find the exact place in a document's structural code by using synchronized design and code panes.
- There are multiple views for sites and pages, which provides greater workspace efficiency.
- Dynamic Web Templates aid in keeping Web sites uniform and in keeping common content areas on pages attached to them in perfect synchronization.
- Expression Web 2 is not only a great design and editing tool, but also a great site management tool.

Chapter at a Glance

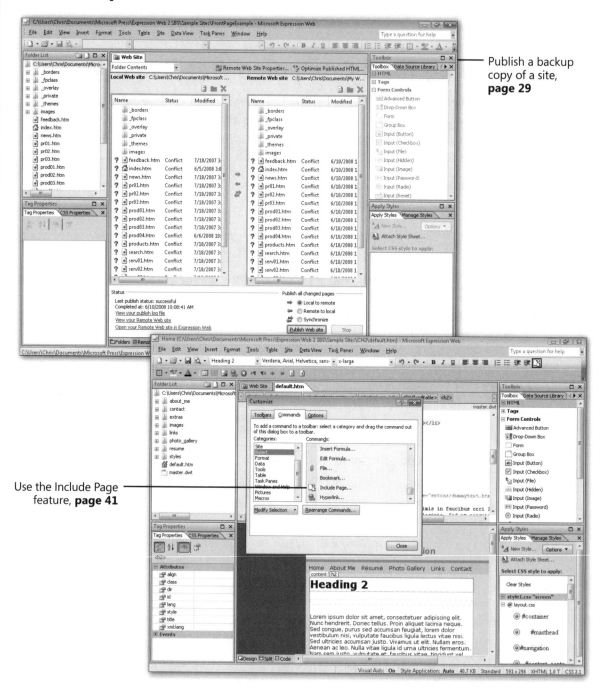

Publish a backup copy of a site, **page 29**

Use the Include Page feature, **page 41**

2 Moving from FrontPage to Expression Web 2

In this chapter, you will learn to

✔ Understand the differences between Expression Web 2 and FrontPage.

✔ Publish a backup copy of a site.

✔ Manage FrontPage sites by using Expression Web 2.

✔ Use the Include Page feature.

✔ Convert FrontPage sites to Expression Web 2.

Microsoft Office FrontPage was developed a decade ago, and 10 years is a long lifetime for a technology product. In its lifetime, FrontPage has gained many users, and this book would be remiss if it didn't give some serious and specific help to former FrontPage users. Even if you were never a FrontPage user, you may, at some time, need to convert, modify, or manage a FrontPage Web site.

In this chapter, you will learn about some of the differences between Microsoft Expression Web 2 and FrontPage. Next you will learn how to manage and protect sites that were created in FrontPage. Then you'll learn how to implement some FrontPage features in Expression Web 2 and how to convert a site developed in FrontPage.

> **Important** Before you can use the practice files in this chapter, you need to install them from the book's companion CD to their default location. For more information about practice files, see "Using the Companion CD" at the beginning of this chapter.

> **Troubleshooting** Graphics and operating system–related instructions in this book reflect the Windows Vista user interface. If your computer is running Windows XP and you experience trouble following the instructions as written, please refer to the "Information for Readers Running Windows XP" section at the beginning of this book.
>
> To improve the readability of the graphics in this book, Expression Web 2 was set to use the Windows color scheme instead of the default Expression Studio 2 color scheme.

Understanding the Differences Between Expression Web 2 and FrontPage

Expression Web 2 is designed to enable you to continue to manage and make minor edits to FrontPage sites, but Expression Web 2 is also designed so that you will no longer use outdated FrontPage features. Expression Web 2 abandons old and proprietary FrontPage features, and provides tools for current techniques supported by the World Wide Web Consortium (W3C), with *cross-platform* capabilities.

If you used FrontPage as only an editing, management, or publishing tool, you'll have an easier time moving forward than those who relied more heavily on FrontPage features such as FrontPage *themes*, *navigation components*, or other "*Web Bots*" provided by FrontPage.

One of the first things you'll notice is that many items that might be familiar to you as a FrontPage user do not appear in the Expression Web menus.

Here's a partial list of the items that do not appear:

- FrontPage themes
- Shared borders
- Web components, including:
  - Dynamic effects
  - Hit counter
  - Photo gallery
  - Link bars
  - Other items that were found in the Web Component dialog box
- Navigation and Task views
- Database Results Wizard

You'll undoubtedly find that other items do not appear in their familiar menu locations.

The rationale behind the disappearance of many of these menu items is simple: They inserted non-W3C compliant code, required FrontPage Server Extensions, or both. Professional Web developers will not miss most of the absent menu items, and the replacement techniques and tools that Expression Web 2 provides produce a much better Web site.

Publishing a Backup Copy of a Site

When you need to work on a FrontPage site, you should first protect it by creating a backup copy of the site. The best way to make the backup copy is by using the publishing feature.

> **Tip** If you were previously a FrontPage user, it's a good idea to retain an installation of FrontPage. Situations might arise, for example, in which a customer doesn't want to move away from FrontPage navigation components or a theme and needs you to do some work on an existing FrontPage site.
>
> If you don't have FrontPage installed, you can't easily do various FrontPage proprietary tasks such as modifying FrontPage themes, manipulating pages in *Navigation view*, or working with the *Database Results Wizard*. Though Expression Web provides appropriate ways to perform all of these tasks, not all site owners will want to invest the time that would be required to carry out the improvements, or perhaps they like the simplicity of working with some of these proprietary FrontPage features.

In this exercise, you will use Expression Web 2 to back up a FrontPage site.

> **USE** the *FrontPageExample* site. This sample site is located in the *Documents\Microsoft Press\Expression Web 2 SBS\Sample Sites* folder.
>
> **BE SURE TO** start Expression Web 2 before beginning this exercise.
>
> **OPEN** the *FrontPageExample* site by clicking Open Site on the File menu.

1. In Windows Explorer, create a folder location for publishing your backup, such as *Documents\My Web Sites\FPbackup.*

2. Switch to Expression Web 2. On the **File** menu, click **Publish Site**.

The Remote Web Site Properties dialog box opens.

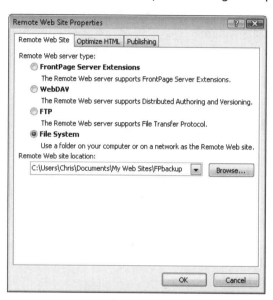

3. On the **Remote Web Site** tab, click **File System**, and then click **Browse**. Browse to the folder you created in step 1, and then click **Open**. Then in the **Remote Web Site Properties** dialog box, click **OK**. When Expression Web 2 prompts you to confirm that you want to create a Web site at that location, click **Yes**.

The *Remote Web Site* view is displayed in Expression Web 2.

4. In the lower-right corner of the workspace, click **Publish Web site**.

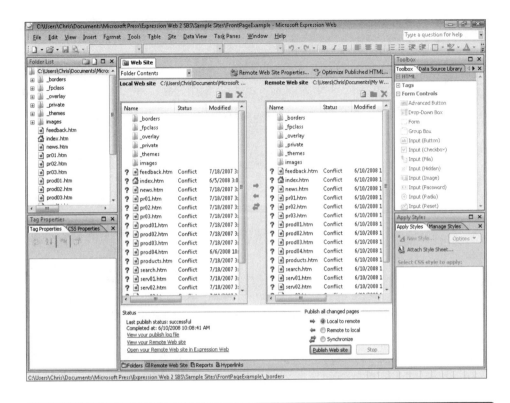

Troubleshooting If you attempt to publish a site that has FrontPage features that rely on server-side code execution or *FrontPage Server extensions* to a disk-based location, you will get a warning alert. Because you're publishing to a disk-based location as a form of backup, click Ignore And Continue.

Expression Web 2 publishes the site, thereby creating a backup copy of the original FrontPage site on your computer.

5. At the bottom of the work area, click the **Folders** button to view the files in the *FrontPageExample* site.

You can now do whatever you want with the open site in full confidence that it is a copy of the original site, and no harm can come to the original FrontPage site.

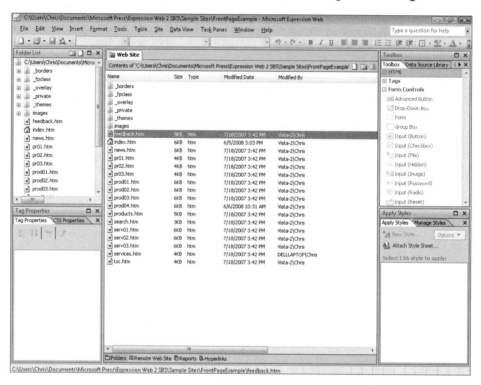

> **Important** The preceding process is the preferred method of moving, copying, or backing up any FrontPage Web site. You should use the publish method whether you are publishing from your server to your local computer or another server, or from a local file location to the server, or to another file location. There are *metafiles* and hidden folder structures that must stay intact for continued reliability, and the publish method guarantees the best result.

BE SURE TO leave the *FrontPageExample* site open for use in the next exercise.

Managing FrontPage Sites by Using Expression Web 2

Expression Web 2 is a great tool for managing any kind of site, including those that were created in FrontPage.

Virtually any FrontPage feature can still be used through Expression Web 2. Most of the absent FrontPage features were simply removed from the user interface but are present beneath the surface. The logic here is that the Expression development team wanted former FrontPage users to be able to open pages, change text and images, and make other page-level modifications, but not necessarily to continue using the original features.

Even though Expression Web 2 is nondestructive to Web sites that were created in FrontPage, it's still a good idea to back up FrontPage sites before modifying them.

If you need to make significant modifications to FrontPage components or themes, the best method is to use FrontPage.

However, when you manage and publish FrontPage sites with Expression Web 2, you'll get the benefits of better syntax highlighting (based on the *DOCTYPE*), much better style sheet creating and editing capabilities, the ability to easily insert media files such as Adobe Flash, Microsoft Windows Media, and Microsoft Silverlight applications, as well as many other standards-based improvements.

The following exercises will acquaint you with using Expression Web 2 to maintain and manage an existing FrontPage site.

Changing Shared Border Content

Here's the scenario: You need to change the content in a *shared border* in a FrontPage-created Web site. You don't want to do a full conversion to the site; you simply want to change some common content and then publish it.

In this exercise, you will replace FrontPage content in a shared border.

> **USE** the *FrontPageExample* site you modified in the previous exercise.
>
> **OPEN** the *FrontPageExample* site if it isn't already open.

1. Open the *index.htm* page in Split view, and display the **shared border** at the bottom of the page.

For this example, you will change the e-mail address at the bottom of the page from *someone@microsoft.com* to *Mail@Example.com*.

> **Tip** Not only is the content you want to change inside a shared border, but it is also a **FrontPage substitution**. You simply want to replace it with a normal e-mail address and mailto hyperlink.

2. Click the **someone@microsoft.com** hyperlink to select it, and then press the [Del] key to remove both the hyperlink and the FrontPage substitution.

3. Type **Mail@Example.com** to replace the original hyperlink. Select the text you typed, right-click the selection, and then click **Hyperlink**. In the **Insert Hyperlink** dialog box, click **E-mail Address**.

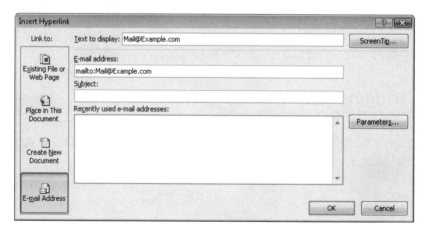

4. Type the e-mail address and a message subject, and then click **OK**.

Save

5. On the toolbar, click **Save**.

Expression Web 2 saves the changes to the page.

Preview

6. On the toolbar, click the **Preview** button to preview how visitors will see your change.

7. Click a few links and check the footer area of those pages to be sure that your change to the shared border updated the pages that receive that content.

You've just successfully changed a FrontPage proprietary feature from within the design surface of Expression Web 2. In the next exercise, you'll make a change to an even more FrontPage-centric element from a less than apparent facility in Expression Web 2.

BE SURE TO leave the *FrontPageExample* site open for use in the next exercise.

Adding a Page

Here's the scenario: You need to create a new page and add it to your existing Navigation view and link bars that were originally created in FrontPage. The best method would be to open the relevant site in FrontPage, create the new page, and add it to the Navigation view. However, this exercise assumes that FrontPage isn't available to you.

> **Important** Navigation view does not appear in the Expression Web 2 interface. It has been removed to discourage continued use because the link bars it generates are not valid HTML. In the following exercise, you'll temporarily bring back the Navigation view to add a page so that it will be included in the site's existing link bars. It is strongly recommended that you use this method very sparingly and only in situations where it is absolutely necessary.

In this exercise, you will create a page and add it to your existing Navigation view and link bars.

1. In the **Folder List**, right-click **prod03.htm**, click **Copy**, right-click the root folder, and then click **Paste**.

   Expression Web 2 creates a file named *prod03_copy(1).htm* in the root folder.

2. Right-click the **prod03_copy(1).htm** file, click **Rename**, type **prod04.htm**, and then press Enter.

   The Folder List displays the *prod04.htm* file in the list.

3. In the **Folder List**, double-click **prod04.htm** to open it for editing. Right-click the Design surface of the page, whether in Design or Split view, and then click **Page Properties**.

4. In the **Title** box of the **Page Properties** dialog box, change the page title to **Adventure Works Product 4**.

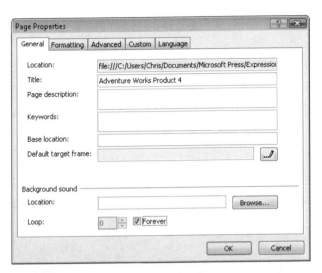

5. Click **OK** to close the **Page Properties** dialog box.

6. On the toolbar, click **Save**.

Save

You have now created, renamed, and changed the page title of a *very* FrontPage proprietary site. You'll notice that many of the page elements are showing notices about adding them to Navigation view to display the **link bars** and page banners.

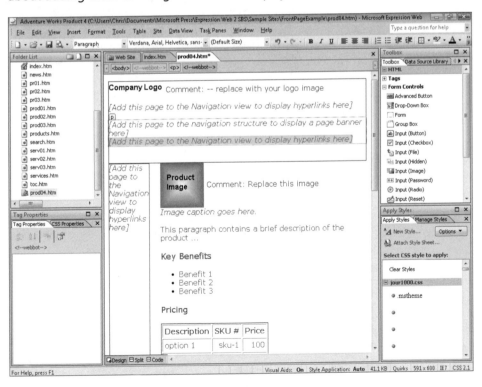

In order to use your newly created page, you'll need to get Navigation view back temporarily.

7. On the **Tools** menu, click **Macro**, and then click *Visual Basic Editor*.

The Microsoft Visual Basic Editor starts.

8. In the Visual Basic Editor, click **View**, and then click **Immediate Window**. In the **Immediate** window pane, type the following code:

```
ActiveWebWindow.ViewMode = WebViewNavigation
```

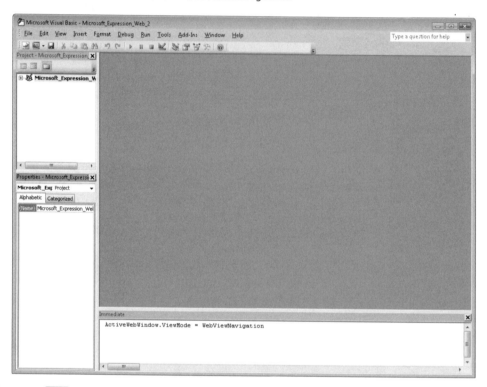

9. Press ⎡Enter⎤ to run the code. Then switch to Expression Web 2.

A representation of Navigation view is displayed.

10. Drag the **prod04.htm** page you created in step 2 into the **Navigation** pane, and drop it immediately to the right of Product 3. Select the page icon, click its name to make it editable, and then type **Product 4**.

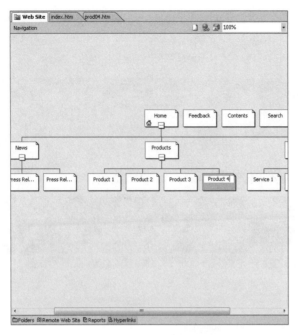

11. In the **Navigation** pane, double-click the **Product 4** page icon to open the page for editing.

Notice that the page has the same elements as its sibling pages.

12. On the toolbar, click the **Preview** button to view this page as a visitor would see it. In the browser, navigate to a few of the other product pages to verify that your changes in the preceding steps have created a uniform page.

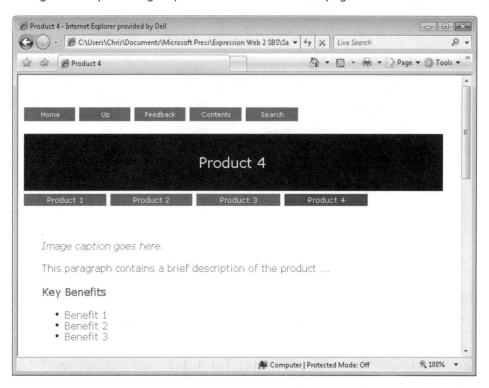

 CLOSE the *FrontPageExample* site and the Visual Basic Editor.

By using the preceding method, you can make minor changes to sites that rely heavily on the FrontPage navigation structure for elements such as navigation bars, *page banners*, and other elements that require the now obsolete FrontPage Navigation view.

It's important to use the method for only quick changes to a site that isn't ready for a full conversion. It would be counterproductive to use discontinued features such as Navigation view on new sites, especially because Expression Web 2 has so many tools to make use of superior techniques. For example, the *ASP.NET Navigation controls* would be a great replacement for a FrontPage navigation bar of a relatively high level of complexity, and a series of *Interactive Buttons*, whether in a Dynamic Web Template, an Include Content section, or simply on the face of a standard HTML page, can easily replace a simple graphical FrontPage navigation bar.

Using the Include Page Feature

Though the majority of FrontPage proprietary features are absent from Expression Web 2 because they don't create valid code, there might be a few occasions when you will want to use one or two of these features. For example, one that doesn't have any negative aspects, such as not being cross-browser compatible or requiring anything special on the server, is the FrontPage Included Content Web component. This Web component simply copied all of the content between the <body> and </body> tags of one page in a Web site and wrote it into another page or set of pages. It was similar to a server-side include but worked at *save time* instead.

This feature was good for actions such as inserting a menu into a number of pages. By using a FrontPage Include, you'd need to maintain or modify the code in only one page, and its changes would be reflected in all pages that used its content.

In this exercise, you will customize the Expression Web 2 toolbar so that you can access the Include Page feature.

USE the *CH2* sample site. This sample site is located in the *Documents\Microsoft Press\ Expression Web 2 SBS\Sample Sites* folder.

OPEN the *CH2* site by clicking Open Site on the File menu.

1. Open the *default.htm* page. If you're not in Split view, click **Split** at the bottom of the workspace.

2. On the Tools menu, click **Customize** to open the **Customize** dialog box. Click the **Commands** tab.

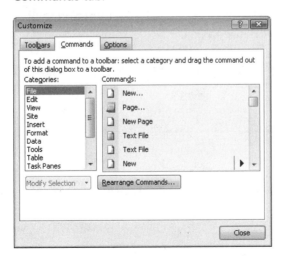

3. Below **Categories**, click **Insert**, and then below **Commands**, scroll down to **Include Page**. Drag **Include Page** to the **Common** toolbar, and then close the **Customize** dialog box.

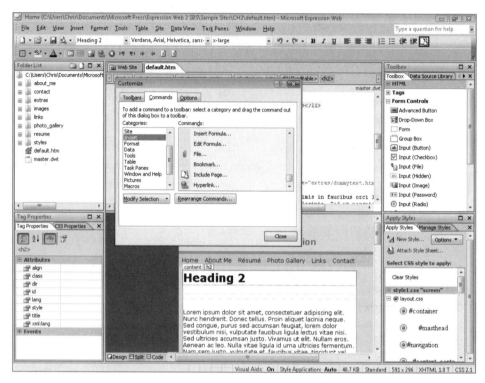

4. In the Design pane, click to place the *insertion point* just after the *2* in **Heading 2**, and then press ⌈Enter⌋ to create a new paragraph.

Include Page

5. Click the **Include Page** button you added to the **Common** toolbar, to open the **Include Page Properties** dialog box.

6. Click **Browse**, and then browse to the file *dummytext.htm* inside the site's *Extras* folder. Select the file, and then click **OK**.

Expression Web writes the content from *dummytext.htm* into the home page of the site.

 CLOSE the *CH2* site.

The preceding exercises showed you an example of a FrontPage feature that is worth keeping. It doesn't require anything special on the server and doesn't do anything invalid from a W3C validity point of view, but it makes updating common content very easy. Here's the way it works: when you put an Include Page into your site, Expression Web 2 copies all of the code between the <body> and </body> tags and simply writes that content into the places you've included it. Expression Web 2 takes care of updating the paths to images and other files, as well as recognizing changes to the include page and updating all the pages that use its content.

Converting FrontPage Sites to Expression Web 2

The first thing you need to consider when converting a FrontPage site to Expression Web 2 is strategy. You need to plan what you will do to replace FrontPage link bars, shared borders, and themes. After these decisions are made, it will be fairly easy work.

See Also For more information about converting a FrontPage site, see the *Microsoft_FrontPage_to_Expression_Web* document in the *Documents\Microsoft Press\Expression Web 2 SBS\Files* folder.

Interactive buttons in Expression Web are a good replacement for FrontPage link bars. DWTs can be used instead of ***FrontPage shared borders***, and cascading style sheets are the obvious choice for replacing FrontPage themes. All of these Expression Web features are easy to use, and you'll reap benefits of HTML validity and accessibility, in addition to cross-browser and cross-platform usability.

There are a number of ways to convert a FrontPage site to a standards-based Expression Web site.

In this exercise, you will learn the conversion method that's most efficient from a workflow point of view, and you will dispose of all the old FrontPage content with a single click.

> **Important** If you try to open a FrontPage site that contains themes and shared borders, every new page you create will inherit those elements. Trying to convert a FrontPage site this way is, at worst, a recipe for frustration and at best, just not a very efficient way to work. The most efficient way to do a conversion is to create a new site with Expression Web 2 and copy into it only the text and images from the FrontPage site.

> **USE** the *FrontPageExample* site you modified earlier in this chapter.
> **OPEN** the *FrontPageExample* site by clicking Open Site on the File menu.

1. On the **File** menu, click **New**. In the **New** dialog box, click the **Web Site** tab. Click **Templates** in the left pane, and then click **Small Business 1** in the center pane.

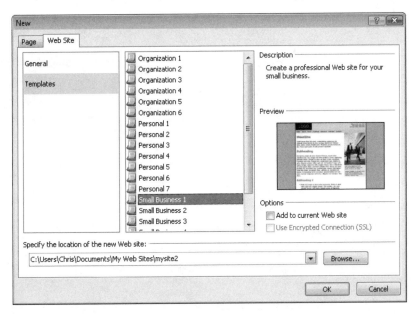

2. Browse to the location where you want to locate the site, and then click **OK** to create it.

3. Arrange the pages and navigation of the site as you want, modify the style attributes if necessary, and generally build a new Web site for the old FrontPage site's content.

   When you have the Web site template in Expression Web configured to your liking, you're just about ready to start migrating text, images, and other assets from the original FrontPage site.

   > **Tip** To make things easier, you should have a copy of the old FrontPage site within the structure of the new site you created in step 1.

4. Open Windows Explorer and locate the *FrontPageExample* site that will provide the content. Drag the folder containing the site from Windows Explorer into the root folder of your newly created Web site in Expression Web 2.

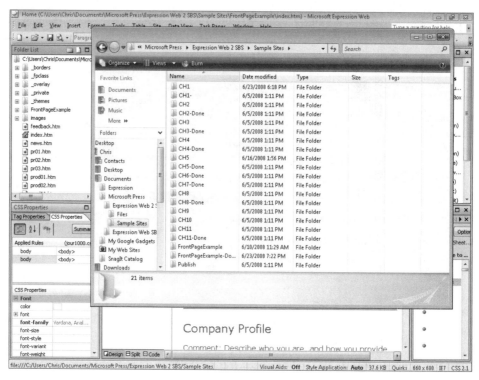

5. In the message box warning you that directories containing Web site configuration will not be imported, click **OK**.

   The FrontPage site's files are moved into your Expression Web 2 site, and you can easily copy content and provide easy access to the other assets you might still need.

6. As you use images from the old site's folder structure, simply drag them into the *images* folder of your Expression Web 2 site. Do the same for any other asset you want to reuse from the old site.

7. After you migrate all of your content into the new pages, delete the old FrontPage folder structure, and you're ready to publish your Expression Web 2 site.

 CLOSE the open Web site. If you are not continuing directly to the next chapter, exit Expression Web 2.

Important Assuming that your previous FrontPage site was published to a server, it's highly recommended that you delete the files in that Web site before publishing the Expression Web 2 site to the same location. This removal can be accomplished by opening the live site with Expression Web 2 and deleting all of the files and folders from your old FrontPage site or by asking your hosting provider to remove all of the files and folders from your hosting space.

Key Points

- Many FrontPage features are absent, but everything that's gone can be replaced in a better, more efficient, and standards-based way.

- Some FrontPage features that are absent from Expression Web can be brought back with minimum effort.

- You can convert an old, inefficient FrontPage site to take advantage of the new standards-based, cross-browser, and cross-platform type of site that Expression Web 2 was designed to build.

- You can protect an original FrontPage site by publishing it to a *local folder*.

- Though not all FrontPage features can be added to new sites created in Expression Web 2, all existing FrontPage sites can be managed and published by using Expression Web 2.

- Elements that require proprietary FrontPage features should not be used; they should be fondly remembered relics.

Chapter at a Glance

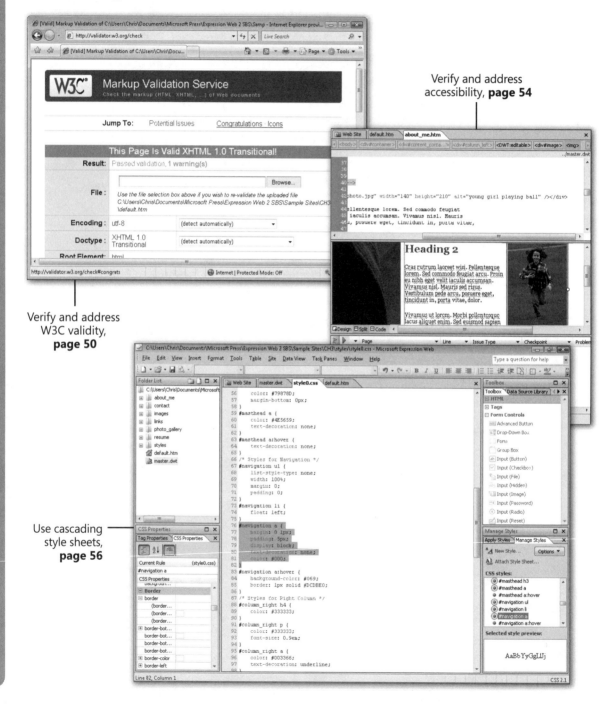

Verify and address
accessibility, **page 54**

Verify and address
W3C validity,
page 50

Use cascading
style sheets,
page 56

3 Becoming Familiar with Modern Web Site Standards

In this chapter, you will learn to

✔ Verify and address W3C validity.

✔ Verify and address accessibility.

✔ Use cascading style sheets.

✔ Choose and use the right DOCTYPE.

✔ Verify and improve cross-browser rendering.

Today's modern Internet emphasizes several key principals: validity, accessibility, cross-browser compatibility, and a clean separation of content and presentation. These principles pave the way for richer Web pages that are more easily indexed by search engines and more predictably rendered by browsers, among other things. You will be glad to know that Microsoft Expression Web 2 provides you with the tools you'll need to accomplish Web site development based on modern Web standards and best practices, and actually makes development easy.

For most of the key principals, you don't need to be an expert in behind-the-scenes code, because Expression Web 2 will either automatically ensure these principals are followed, or provide you with a visual interface.

In this chapter, you will learn to verify that your site's HTML and cascading style sheets are valid according to the World Wide Web Consortium (W3C) standards, and to check and address accessibility. You will also learn to use cascading style sheets and to choose and use the right Document Type Declaration (DOCTYPE). Finally, you will learn to check and improve cross-browser rendering.

Important Before you can use the practice files in this chapter, you need to install them from the book's companion CD to their default location. For more information about practice files, see "Using the Companion CD" at the beginning of this book.

Troubleshooting Graphics and operating system–related instructions in this book reflect the Windows Vista user interface. If your computer is running Windows XP and you experience trouble following the instructions as written, please refer to the "Information for Readers Running Windows XP" section at the beginning of this book.

To improve the readability of the graphics in this book, Expression Web 2 was set to use the Windows color scheme instead of the default Expression Studio 2 color scheme.

Verifying and Addressing W3C Validity

You can visit the W3C Web site at *w3c.org*. One of the functions of W3C is to maintain a set of standards that define valid code. Expression Web 2 is predisposed to meet those standards by writing valid HTML/XHTML code.

In this exercise, you will verify the validity of code, and you will set up a problem and fix it.

USE the *CH3* sample site. This sample site is located in the *Documents\Microsoft Press\ Expression Web 2 SBS\Sample Sites* folder.

BE SURE TO start Expression Web 2 before beginning this exercise.

OPEN the *CH3* site by clicking Open Site on the File menu, and display the *default.htm* page.

Preview

1. On the toolbar, click the **Preview** button to open the page in Windows Internet Explorer (or your default Web browser). Open another tab in your browser or open another browser window and go to *validator.w3.org*. Click the **Validate by File Upload** tab, click **Browse**, navigate to and double-click the local copy of this page, and then click **Check**.

A copy of your local page is uploaded to the W3C's validation engine, which reports that the page is fully valid.

See Also You may notice a warning when you validate your page, that references a Byte Order Mark (BOM). For more information about including or excluding a BOM from your documents, see "Converting an HTML Page to PHP" in Chapter 12, "Using PHP Features."

> **Tip** To save time, instead of browsing to the page on your local system, you can copy the URL from the address bar in the browser preview you opened and paste it into the file field.

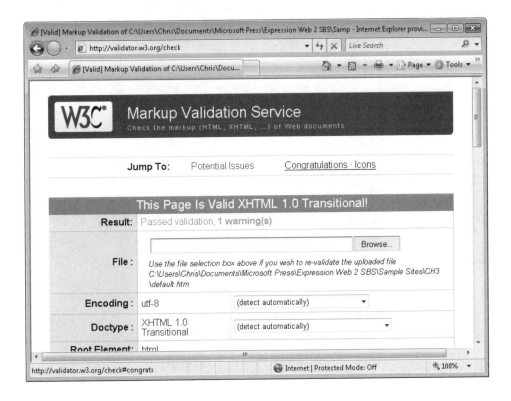

2. Close the browser or browsers, and return to Expression Web 2. Click **Split** at the bottom of the workspace to display the page in Split view.

Because Expression Web 2 won't let you make validity mistakes through Design view, you need to make a mistake manually in the code.

3. Set the insertion point in front of the first **<p>** tag in the main editable region, and add an erroneous extra **<p>**. Expression Web 2, in an effort to maintain validity, will automatically close the <p> tag (or any open tag, for that matter). Delete the </p> tag it inserts, to create the error.

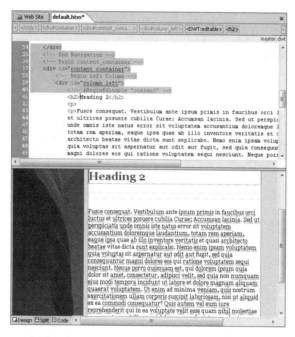

Error

Validity rules dictate that you can't have nested <p> tags and must close the open tag before adding another. Besides the red underline on your errant <p> tag, there's another warning in the lower area of your main workspace. If you hover over the icon, you'll see text relating to the incompatibilities that it's encountering.

4. Save the page, and then preview it once more. Again, open another tab in your browser or open another browser window and go to *validator.w3.org*. Click the **Validate by File Upload** tab, click **Browse**, double-click the local copy of this page, and then click **Check**.

The page now fails because of the extra <p> tag. This illustrates how a single broken HTML element can cause a cascade of errors within a document.

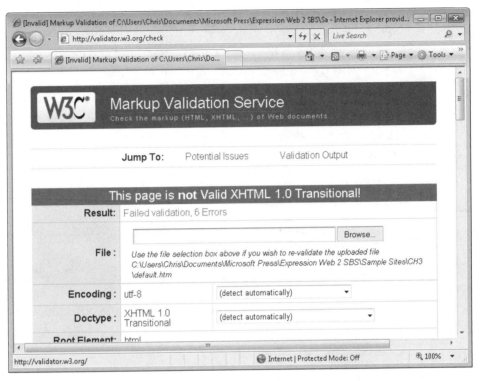

5. Close the browser window or windows and return to Expression Web 2.

The second <p> tag has a red line beneath it. When you have code in Expression Web 2 that violates the standards of the document's DOCTYPE declaration, you'll see this red line under the invalid tags. If you pause the mouse pointer over one of these underlined tags, Expression Web 2 displays a tip that explains what's wrong with the underlined tag.

6. Delete the extra <p> tag to bring your page back into validity again.

> **Tip** To see this validation process in effective use, visit the W3C validation engine at *validator.w3.org*, and test a page from a popular Web site, such as YouTube. You'll be shocked by how badly some popular sites fail validation.

BE SURE TO leave the *CH3* site open for use in the next exercise.

CLOSE the open browser windows.

Verifying and Addressing Accessibility

Accessibility relates to the way a page is structured and how it will render in devices that are used by people who have vision problems or who need other special browser considerations.

Good HTML/XHTML practices such as using valid code and meaningful *alt tags*, and not relying on JavaScript or Flash for key elements such as navigation, will prevent most accessibility problems.

In this exercise, you will create code that violates accessibility standards, and then you will repair the error.

USE the *CH3* sample site you modified in the previous exercise.

OPEN the *CH3* site if it isn't already open, and display the *default.htm* page.

1. On the **Tools** menu, click **Accessibility Reports** to open the **Accessibility Checker**.

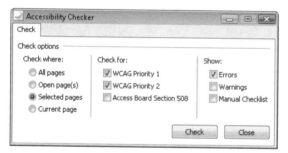

2. Using the default **Accessibility Checker** settings, click **Check**.

   The Accessibility task pane opens below the Design pane and shows errors that exist in the open page.

3. Close the **Accessibility** task pane.

   Because you're not going to find any errors in this Expression Web 2 template, you need to create an error.

4. In the **Folder List**, expand the *about_me* folder, and then open the *about_me.htm* page. If your screen is not in Split view, click **Split** at the bottom of the workspace.

5. Select the image that is in the Design pane, and find the code for the image in the Code pane. In the tag for that image, remove the *alt* attribute (*alt=""*).

   Accessibility rules dictate that every image must have an *alt* attribute even if the attribute is empty, as shown in this page.

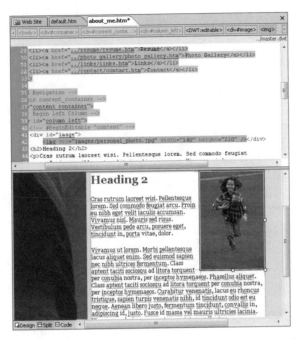

Save

6. On the toolbar, click the **Save** button. On the **Tools** menu, click **Accessibility Reports** to open the **Accessibility Checker**, and then click **Check**.

An error is now visible in the Accessibility task pane.

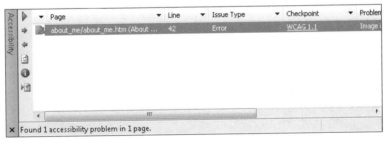

Rather than simply replacing the previously removed, empty *alt* attribute, let's put something meaningful there.

7. Set the insertion point immediately in front of the closing image tag that you modified in step 5, type **alt="Young girl playing ball"**, and click **Save**.

8. In the **Accessibility** task pane, click the **Refresh** button.

Refresh

The error no longer appears.

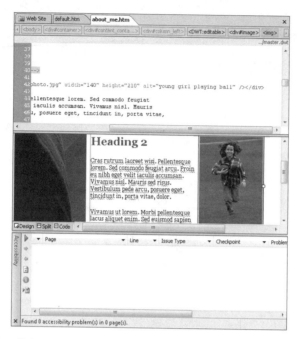

9. Click the **Close** button on the **Accessibility** task pane to close it.

Close

BE SURE TO leave the *CH3* site open for use in the next exercise.

Tip You can generate a report by clicking Generate HTML Report in the Accessibility task pane. Expression Web 2 generates a new page that has the errors reported. This report can be generated for a page, for a selection of pages, or for a site, and is a valuable tool when redesigning or analyzing a site. You can save or print the report for your own records or for your customer.

Using Cascading Style Sheets

A cornerstone of modern Web standards and practices is the separation of content from presentation. Expression Web 2 helps you with this separation by leaning strongly toward cascading style sheets for presentational tasks such as formatting text and creating visual elements for your layout.

In this exercise, you will modify some of the cascading style sheet elements in the Dynamic Web Template (DWT), which is a feature of Expression Web 2 that you can use to create and include global elements that attach to your content pages. This feature greatly aids in creation, modification, and management of Web sites.

> **USE** the *CH3* sample site you modified in the previous exercise.
>
> **OPEN** the *CH3* site, if it isn't already open, and display the *master.dwt* page.

1. Click **Split** at the bottom of the workspace to display the page in Split view. Select the navigation bar at the top of the page. If necessary, set your insertion point in the navigation bar, and then click the **<div #navigation>** entry on the quick tag selector.

The entire <div id="navigation"> element is selected.

2. In the **CSS Properties** task pane on the left, click the **CSS Properties** tab if it's not already active in the pane. Under **Applied Rules**, click **#navigation** for style0.css, and then in the **CSS Properties** task pane, note the gray style (#DCDBE0) next to **background-color**.

> **Important** When working in the CSS Properties task pane, it's important to click the Show Set Properties On Top, Sort Alphabetically, and Summary buttons. By doing this, you'll stack all of the properties that have been specifically styled at the top of the list and you won't have to search through the entire list to find the style you're looking for.
>
>
>
> Show set properties   Sort Alphabetically   Summary
> on top

3. Click **background-color**, and then click the arrow that appears, to show the **Color Selector**. Click **More Colors**. Then in the **More Colors** dialog box, click **Select**.

4. Pause the eye dropper over the image to the left of the navigation bar in the page's design surface, and pick up the color of the image area that is adjacent to the navigation bar.

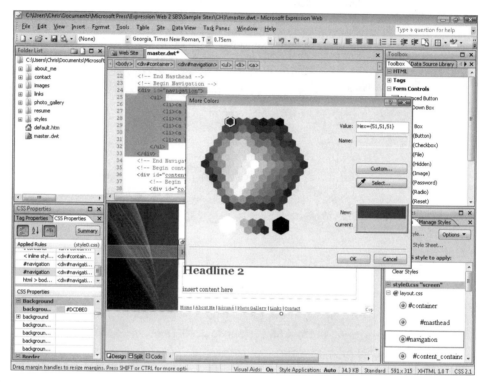

5. Click **OK** to accept your selection.

The background color of the navigation bar changes.

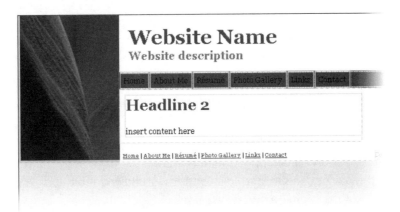

There are more style rules in play for that navigation bar than the color of the DIV element that contains it.

6. When the navigation DIV element is selected, point to the other elements on the quick tag selector bar to see how they relate to the irregular area within that DIV element: <ul>, <li>, and <a>.

Notice that when the pointer is over the <a> element, the culprit is visible.

7. On the quick tag selector bar, click **<a>** to display its properties in the **CSS Properties** task pane.

8. Delete the text to the right of the top entry for the **border** style to remove the borders and border colors for the **#navigation a** style.

The navigation bar is now starting to look more uniform.

Save

9. On the toolbar, click the **Save** button. Allow Expression Web 2 to update all of the pages that the Dynamic Web Template is attached to, and allow the style sheet to be saved.

10. Display the *default.htm* page, and view the presentation of this Dynamic Web Template's elements. Then preview the page in your browser. Notice that the navigation bar looks uniform. Now point to the links in the navigation bar. They don't look very uniform.

11. In Expression Web 2, open the *master.dwt* file. To remedy the consistency issues in the navigation bar, and for a better workflow, double-click the **#navigation a** entry in the **Manage Styles** task pane.

Your style sheet opens, with the selected style ID in focus.

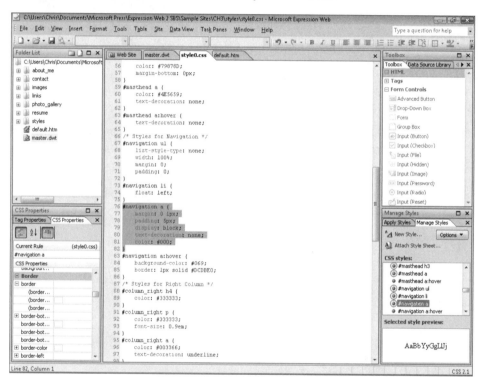

12. On the style sheet, look for the entry **#navigation a:hover.** This entry controls the link's appearance when you point to it. Remove the following line of code:

```
border: 1px solid #DCDBE0;
```

13. Save your style sheet, and then switch to *default.htm* to preview the file in your browser.

Notice that the navigation bar is starting to take shape and is looking more uniform. The borders are gone from the <a> element both when you point to it and when you don't.

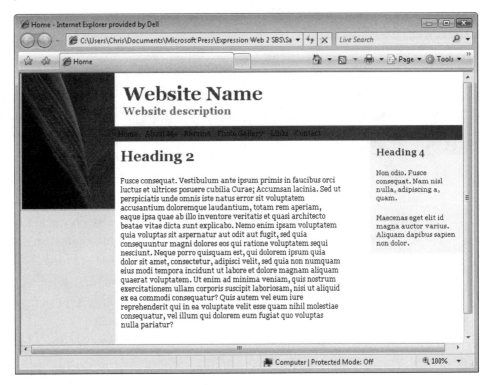

14. In Expression Web 2, switch to *master.dwt*. On the quick tag selector bar, in the navigation <div> element, click **<a>.** In the **CSS Properties** task pane, scroll down to **Color.**

Notice that the setting is a dark color.

15. Select the color entry to open the **Color selector**, and change the **color** attribute to a lighter color.

Preview

16. Save the Dynamic Web Template, and when prompted, save the style sheet. Switch to *default.htm*, and then click the **Preview** button to view the file in Internet Explorer. Point to the navigation links.

The navigation links now have a uniform appearance. They all have the lighter text color and lack the border.

17. Close your browser. In Expression Web 2, switch to *master.dwt*. In the Design pane, set the insertion point in the editable region on the right, and click the **<div #column_right>** tag on the quick tag selector.

18. In the **CSS Properties** task pane, scroll to **background**, and change the color value from **#F7F7F9** to **#D7DCDF**, which is more appropriate for this page.

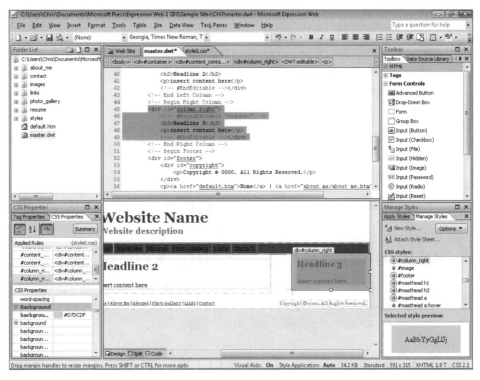

19. Click **Save** to save your changes to the Dynamic Web Template. Allow Expression Web 2 to update all of the pages that the Dynamic Web Template is attached to, and allow the style sheet to be saved.

20. Switch to *default.htm*, preview the page in a browser, and review your changes. Notice that there is now a silver background for the column on the right. Click the navigation links to review all of the pages.

BE SURE TO leave the *CH3* site open for use in the next exercise.

CLOSE the open browser windows.

During the preceding exercise, you made global changes to the presentation of every page in a site by simply editing a few lines on a style sheet. You edited the style sheet's code both directly and by using the Expression Web 2 user interface. Though it might seem trivial on such a small site, think about how effective this method would be on sites with thousands of pages!

Imagine changing the link colors or other elements in every single page by simply editing one line in one single file. In addition, imagine how much less code is required for this type of arrangement than endless <font> tags to control presentation within the page code itself.

This is the just tip of the iceberg in regard to separation of content and presentation.

Choosing and Using the Right DOCTYPE

A DOCTYPE is a declaration at the very beginning of an HTML/XHTML file that tells the browser what kind of document it's receiving. A valid DOCTYPE is the very first thing you need to make sure your page(s) will validate.

Expression Web 2 can work with any DOCTYPE; in fact, you'll find the following seven in the Code Snippets library:

```
<!DOCTYPE HTML PUBLIC "-//W3C//DTD HTML 4.01 Frameset//EN" "http://www.w3.org/
TR/html4/frameset.dtd">
```

```
<!DOCTYPE HTML PUBLIC "-//W3C//DTD HTML 4.01//EN" "http://www.w3.org/TR/html4/
strict.dtd">
```

```
<!DOCTYPE HTML PUBLIC "-//W3C//DTD HTML 4.01 Transitional//EN" "http://www.w3.org/
TR/html4/loose.dtd">
```

```
<!DOCTYPE html PUBLIC "-//W3C//DTD XHTML 1.1//EN" "http://www.w3.org/TR/xhtml11/
DTD/xhtml11.dtd">
```

```
<!DOCTYPE html PUBLIC "-//W3C//DTD XHTML 1.0 Frameset//EN" "http://www.w3.org/
TR/xhtml1/DTD/xhtml1-frameset.dtd">
```

```
<!DOCTYPE html PUBLIC "-//W3C//DTD XHTML 1.0 Strict//EN" "http://www.w3.org/TR/
xhtml1/DTD/xhtml1-strict.dtd">
```

```
<!DOCTYPE html PUBLIC "-//W3C//DTD XHTML 1.0 Transitional//EN" "http://www.w3.org/
TR/xhtml1/DTD/xhtml1-transitional.dtd">
```

For a complete list of DOCTYPES, see the W3C's list at *http://www.w3.org/QA/2002/04/ valid-dtd-list.html*.

In addition to making a page valid, there's an added benefit to a correct DOCTYPE: predictable browser rendering. To deliver consistent display in all browsers, the browser needs to be told what kind of file it's displaying.

> **Troubleshooting** By default, Expression Web 2 inserts an XHTML 1.0 Transitional DOCTYPE on every page it creates and ensures that the code is appropriate for the DOCTYPE. The only time you need to consider the DOCTYPE is when you're working on an existing site that was created by using another program or in a situation where you want to use a different DOCTYPE than the standard one that Expression Web 2 provides.

In this exercise, you will change the DOCTYPE of a file and then validate it.

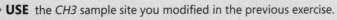

USE the *CH3* sample site you modified in the previous exercise.
OPEN the *CH3* site if it isn't already open, and display the *default.htm* page in Split view.

1. At the top of the Code pane, locate the following DOCTYPE information:

```
<!DOCTYPE html PUBLIC "-//W3C//DTD XHTML 1.0 Transitional//EN" "http://
www.w3.org/TR/xhtml1/DTD/xhtml1-transitional.dtd">
```

2. In the Code pane, select the entire DOCTYPE line, and then press [Ctrl]+[Enter] to open the **Code Snippets** list.

Notice the seven different DOCTYPEs that are available from the Code Snippets list.

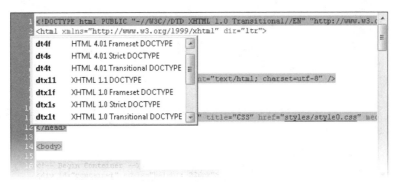

3. Click **HTML 4.01 Transitional DOCTYPE**, and then click **Save**.

Notice that the DOCTYPE is also shown on the status bar of Expression Web 2.

4. Preview the page in a browser.

The preview page appears to be the same as when you first opened it.

5. Open another tab in your browser or open another browser window and go to *validator.w3.org*. Click the **Validate by File Upload** tab, click **Browse**, double-click the local copy of this page, and then click **Check**. Instead of the previously valid page, a failing page with four errors is now displayed.

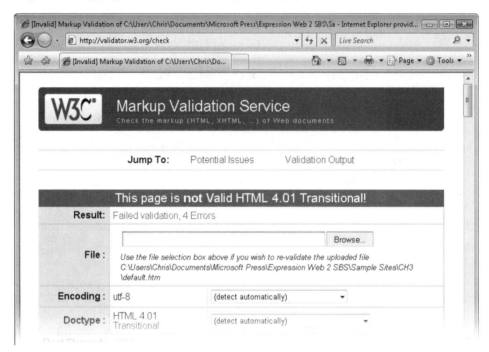

6. Close the browser, and in Expression Web 2, display the *default.htm* page.

In the Code pane, red underlines appear beneath items that don't match the DOCTYPE you selected in step 3.

7. In the Code pane, select the DOCTYPE, press Ctrl + Enter to open the **Code Snippets** list, and click **XHTML 1.0 Transitional DOCTYPE** to return the page to its original state.

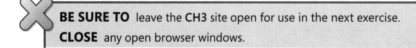

BE SURE TO leave the **CH3** site open for use in the next exercise.

CLOSE any open browser windows.

Setting the DOCTYPE

Besides manually setting the DOCTYPE in the source of your document, you can use the Page Editor Options dialog box of Expression Web 2. To open the dialog box and access the settings, on the Tools menu, click Page Editor Options, and then click the Authoring tab of the dialog box. You can set the default DOCTYPE for all new files, set .htm or .html file as the default extension, choose whether to use a *Byte Order Mark* with various file types, and an array of other options.

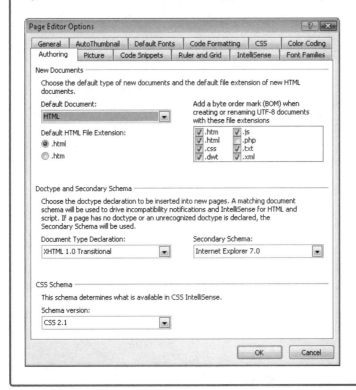

Troubleshooting The DOCTYPE of a file in Expression Web 2 dictates the IntelliSense, compatibility, validity, and accessibility testing rules. If you change a DOCTYPE, Expression Web 2 changes the way it treats the page code. Don't conclude, however, that using a looser or lower DOCTYPE is a cure for old sites that you're trying to clean up by using Expression Web 2. Generally, it's best to add a modern DOCTYPE and bring the code up to that standard.

Verifying and Improving Cross-Browser Rendering

Cross-browser rendering simply means how a page renders in different browsers. Generally, you want a Web page to render identically in all modern browsers. Sometimes, getting an absolutely identical rendering requires more work than it's worth, so what you should really concentrate on is getting an acceptable rendering across all common browsers.

Methods that you might use to obtain an absolutely identical rendering might cause problems when any of the browsers that are involved are updated or change versions, and you would need to repair whatever you did to obtain the identical rendering.

The solution is to make sure that your pages are valid and accessible, and that they render well across major browsers. This approach will stand the test of time.

> **Troubleshooting** In order to test your pages in browsers other than Internet Explorer, you must have the other browsers installed on your computer. For most testing, you can use Internet Explorer and Mozilla Firefox. Occasionally, you will want to also test in the Opera browser. Generally, if a page looks good in current versions of Internet Explorer and Firefox, it will look acceptable with most other browsers.
>
> Download at least one of the following browsers:
>
> ● Firefox: *www.getfirefox.com*
>
> ● Opera: *www.opera.com/download/*
>
> When you install a new browser, be sure to choose custom installation where offered. Ensure that the new browser does not become your default browser, and that you don't make any system changes unless that's what you truly want!

In this exercise, you will view a Web site in multiple browsers and address cross-browser inconsistencies.

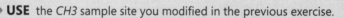

USE the *CH3* sample site you modified in the previous exercise.

BE SURE TO download and install the alternative browsers, as described in the preceding Troubleshooting paragraph, before starting this exercise.

OPEN the *CH3* site if it isn't already open, and display the *default.htm* page.

1. On the **File** menu, click **Preview in Browser**, and then click **Edit Browser List**. Make sure that your newly loaded browsers are displayed in the list, and select their check boxes to make them available in the **Preview** list.

> **Troubleshooting** If an installed browser is not displayed in the browser list, click Add. In the Add Browser dialog box, click Browse, browse to the Program Files folder to locate the browser you're looking for, and select it. Repeat the process for additional browsers as needed. When the browser list is as you want it, close all running instances of Expression Web 2, and then restart Expression Web 2.

2. On the **File** menu, click **Preview in Multiple Browsers**.

The *default.htm* page opens in all of the browsers you added in step 1. Compare the preview of the page in each of the browsers that opened. Be sure to point to links and navigate through the pages in each browser.

If you see an unacceptable inconsistency, you need to find that area in your page by using Design view and Split view, and use deductive reasoning to solve the problem. For example, if the problem is a deficient or excess application of padding on a certain element, then you'll probably need to find that element's style in the style sheet and remove or increase padding.

3. In Expression Web 2, with *default.htm* open for editing, on the **Tools** menu, click **Compatibility Reports**.

The Compatibility Checker dialog box opens.

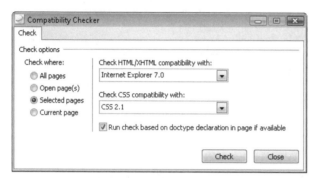

4. Click **All pages**, **Open page(s)**, **Selected pages**, or **Current page**. Select which browser you want the HTML/XHTML compatibility checked with, and which version of cascading style sheets you want the compatibility checked with, and then click **Check**.

The Compatibility Checker checks the code of the page and displays a report in the lower portion of your workspace.

The checker defaults to checking against Windows Internet Explorer 7. Using the Compatibility Checker is a good way to check for flaws that cause rendering problems in any browser.

CLOSE the *CH3* site and the open browser windows. If you are not continuing directly to the next chapter, exit Expression Web 2.

> **Tip** You can generate a report from the Compatibility task pane. Click Generate HTML Report in the Compatibility task pane, and Expression Web 2 generates a new page and reports the errors. This report is a valuable tool when you're redesigning or analyzing a site. You can save or print this report for your own records or for your customer.

Key Points

- Expression Web 2 helps you maintain W3C standards for validity.
- Expression Web 2 helps you check and address accessibility issues.
- Using cascading style sheets helps keep your page uniform and provides easy access to an entire site's presentation.
- Using the correct DOCTYPE is a requirement for a valid, accessible page.
- You can add browsers and configure the Preview menu options in Expression Web 2.

Chapter at a Glance

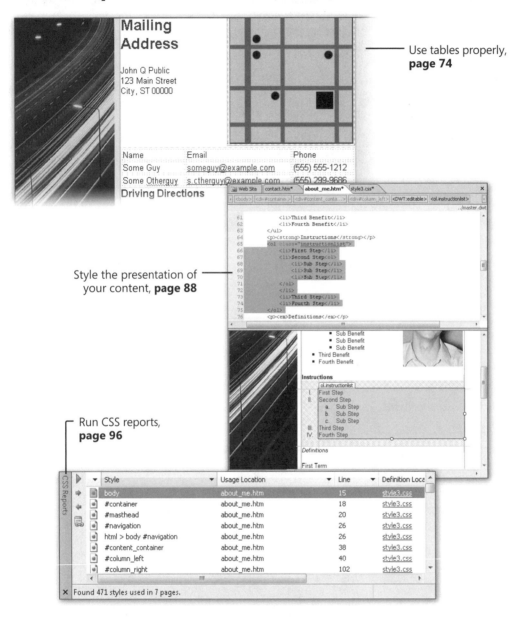

Use tables properly, **page 74**

Style the presentation of your content, **page 88**

Run CSS reports, **page 96**

4 Presenting Information on a Web Page

In this chapter, you will learn to

- ✔ Use tables properly.
- ✔ Use lists to group information.
- ✔ Use semantic markup.
- ✔ Style the presentation of your content.
- ✔ Run CSS reports.

At their most basic level, Web pages show information to visitors. Although this appears to be a simple concept, the modern Web adds some complexity. Page design should include considerations for accessibility regarding browsing devices of varied capability, for *search engines*, for *best practices*, and for *maintainability*.

Although it's beyond the scope of this book to provide an in-depth compendium on accessibility and search engine friendliness, the following exercises will help you form a good base of understanding of these considerations.

In this chapter, you will learn to use *tables* effectively on your Web page, and you will also learn to use *lists*. Then, you will learn to use *semantic markup*; and, finally, you will learn to use style sheets to control the presentation of the content on your page and check the compatibility of your style sheets with modern browsers by using the reporting features in Microsoft Expression Web 2.

> **Important** Before you can use the practice files in this chapter, you need to install them from the book's companion CD to their default location. For more information about practice files, see "Using the Companion CD" at the beginning of this book.

> **Troubleshooting** Graphics and operating system–related instructions in this book reflect the Windows Vista user interface. If your computer is running Windows XP and you experience trouble following the instructions as written, please refer to the "Information for Readers Running Windows XP" section at the beginning of this book.
>
> To improve the readability of the graphics in this book, Expression Web 2 was set to use the Windows color scheme instead of the default Expression Studio 2 color scheme.

Using Tables Properly

Now that Web developers are consistently using cascading style sheets for layout, check any of the templates that came with Expression Web 2. You won't find a single one that uses a table for *layout*. In the not so distant past, elements of a Web page were nested into a table or group of nested tables. Although that method provided a fair amount of precision, it was never the intended purpose of the <table> tag. As an unfortunate by-product of "table heavy" design, the source code of the page is always much more complex, which makes it less than ideal for screen readers to search engines, not to mention additional download time for browsers. The big question seems to be whether it's still acceptable to use tables. The answer is a definite Yes. Tables seem to have fallen out of favor for laying out pages; however, there are still plenty of good reasons to use tables, the most obvious of which is to present data in clear, *tabular* form.

In this exercise, you will use a properly coded and valid table structure to display some tabular data on your Web page.

> **USE** the *CH4* sample site. This sample site is located in the *Documents\Microsoft Press\ Expression Web 2 SBS\Sample Sites* folder.
>
> **BE SURE TO** start Expression Web 2 before beginning this exercise.
>
> **OPEN** the *CH4* site by clicking Open Site on the File menu, and display the *contact.htm* page.

1. On the **View** menu, point to **Visual Aids**, and then click **Show**. Ensure that **Block Selection** is the only selected visual aid.

   Visual Aids can help you see the various elements in a table.

2. In the Design pane, set the insertion point at the end of the ZIP Code in the address, and then press ⎆ Enter to create a new paragraph.

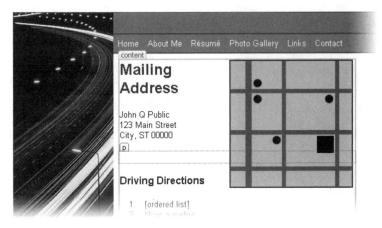

3. On the **Table** menu, click **Insert Table**. In the **Insert Table** dialog box, configure the table to have two *rows* and three *columns*, and accept the default settings.

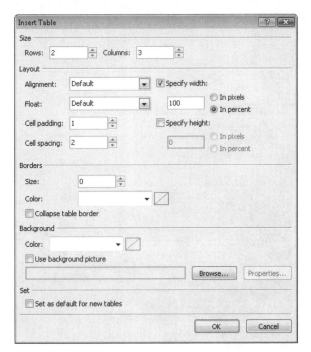

4. Click **OK** to insert the table. In the upper-left table *cell*, type **Name**. Tab to the next cell and type **Email.** Tab to the next cell, and type **Phone**. Press [Tab] again to move the cursor to the first cell in the next row. Type a name, an e-mail address, and a phone number into the cells in the second row.

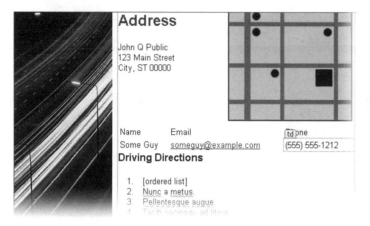

5. On the **View** menu, point to **Visual Aids**, and then click **Visible Borders** and **Empty Containers**.

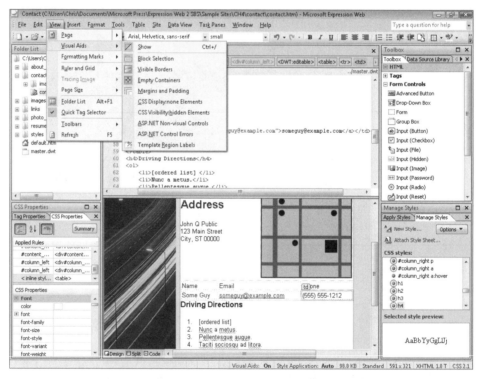

6. After you type a phone number in the last cell of the second row, press Tab to create a new, third row. Type a name, an e-mail address, and a phone number into the cells in this row.

7. Save the page, and preview it in a browser to make sure that the page appears as you want.

> **BE SURE TO** leave the *CH4* site open for use in the next exercise.
> **CLOSE** the *contact.htm* page.

Using Lists to Group Information

Among the essential tags for laying out information on a Web page are lists. There are three basic types of list, as shown in the following table.

List type	Tag	Purpose
Ordered list	<ol>	Numbered items
Unordered list	<ul>	Bulleted items
Definition list	<dl>	Term and definition arrangement (similar to the typical dictionary paradigm)

In this exercise, you will learn to insert all three types of lists and arrange information within them.

> **USE** the *CH4* sample site you modified in the previous exercise.
> **OPEN** the *CH4* site, if it isn't already open, and display the *about_me.htm* page.

Bullets

1. In the Design pane, set the insertion point immediately after **Heading 2**, and press `Enter` to create a new paragraph. Type **Benefits** as a title for the list that will follow. Press `Enter` to create another paragraph, and type **First Benefit**. On the toolbar, click the **Bullets** button.

In Split view, the <p> tag that previously surrounded the words *First Benefit* is now a <ul> tag, and the words are now wrapped in an <li> tag. The paragraph became an *unordered list*, and the text became a *list item*.

Increase Indent Position

2. Press `Enter` again to create a new list item line, and type **Second Benefit**. Press `Enter` once more to advance to the next list line; but before you type anything, click the **Increase Indent Position** button.

In the page code, a <ul> tag appears within the preceding <li> tag; there is now a list within a list.

3. Type three items here, pressing Enter between them, so that there will be three items in this inner list.

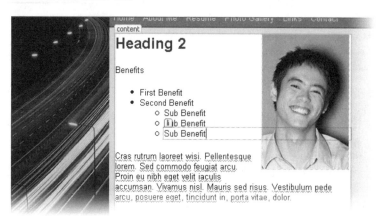

Decrease Indent
Position

4. When you reach the final list items in this inner list, press Enter, and then click the **Decrease Indent Position** button.

In Split view, the code for the inner list and list element closed and you're back out in the original list you inserted.

5. Type two more entries: **Third Benefit** and **Fourth Benefit**, pressing Enter between them to set them each as list items. After you type **Fourth Benefit**, press Enter twice to end the list and create a new paragraph.

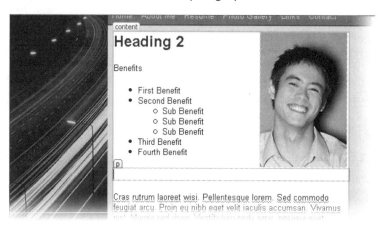

6. Save your page, and preview it in a browser to ensure that it appears as you want, and then switch to Expression Web 2.

7. In the Design pane, type **Instructions** in the paragraph immediately below your newly finished unordered list, and press Enter to create a new paragraph.

In this list example, we'll list instructions because they lend themselves by nature to an ordered, step-by-step type of list.

Numbering

8. Type **First Step**, and then click the **Numbering** button.

In Split view, the <p> tag that previously surrounded the words *First Step* is now an <ol> tag, and the words themselves are now wrapped in an <li> tag. The paragraph is now an ***ordered list***, and the text is a list item.

9. Press Enter to create a new list item line, and type **Second Step**. Press Enter once more to create one more list item line, but before you type anything, click the **Increase Indent Position** button.

In the page code, the <ol> tag within the preceding <li> tag. There is again a list within a list.

10. Type three items here, pressing Enter after each of them.

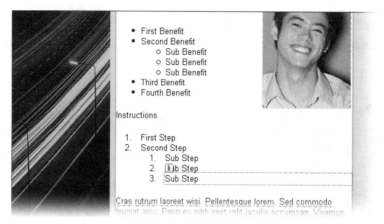

11. When you reach the final item in this inner list, click the **Decrease Indent Position** button. Then on the quick tag selector bar, click the **<ol>** entry to select the entire list you were working on.

In Split view, Expression Web 2 has closed the inner list and its final item, and returned to your original list.

12. Type two more entries: **Third Step** and **Fourth Step**, pressing ⌜Enter⌝ between them to set them each as list items. After you type **Fourth Step**, press ⌜Enter⌝ twice to end the list and create a new paragraph.

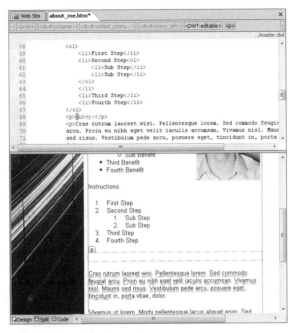

13. Save the page and preview it in a browser to ensure that it appears as you want.

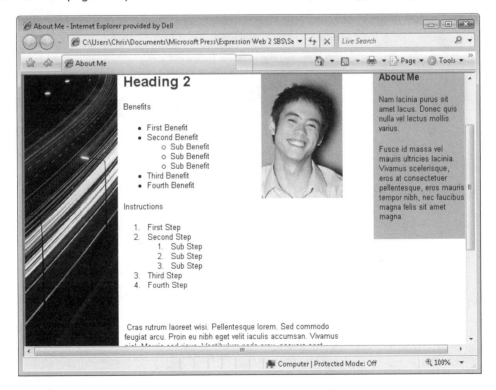

Definition lists aren't used as much as numbered and bulleted lists but are valuable for lists of terms and their definitions.

14. Switch to the Expression Web 2 interface. In the paragraph below the other lists, type **Definitions**, and press [Enter] to create a new paragraph. Type **First Term**. There is no button on the toolbar for **Definition** lists, so click the paragraph tag in the quick tag selector bar that contains *First Term* to select the entire tag. On the **Common** toolbar, in the **Paragraph** list, click **Defined Term <dt>**.

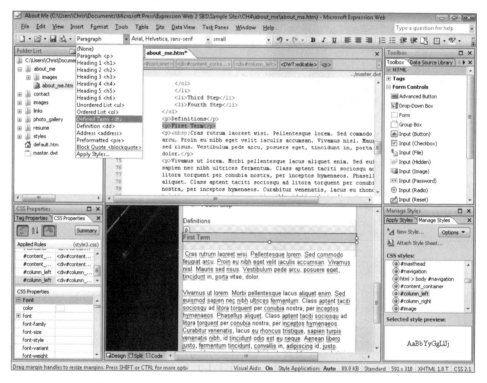

As in the other list examples, the <p> tag is replaced by a <dl> tag, and *First Term* is wrapped in a list item, this time a <dt> tag.

15. Press [Enter] to create a new line, which will be wrapped in a <dd> tag, and type a few sentences to describe *First Term*. Press [Enter] again to create a new line.

First Term is now set up for another <dd> definition.

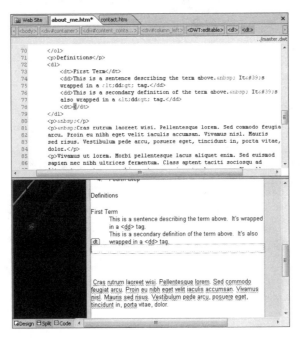

The Definition list functions slightly differently than the other two types of list. A Definition list provides an easy way to supply multiple definitions for a single term.

16. Type a secondary definition in this new line, and press Enter once more.

At this point, we want to add a term, not a definition on this new blank line.

17. In the Code pane, change the **<dd>** and **</dd>** tags to **<dt>** and **</dt>** tags.

18. Type **Second Term**.

The new term lines up under the first term.

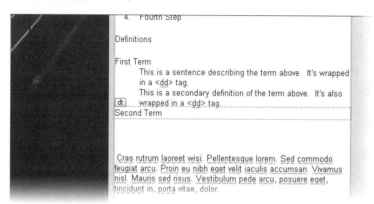

19. Press ⌷Enter⌷ to create a definition for this second term. Repeat this process a few times to become familiar with it. When you're done adding terms and definitions, press ⌷Enter⌷ twice to end the definition list and insert a new paragraph.

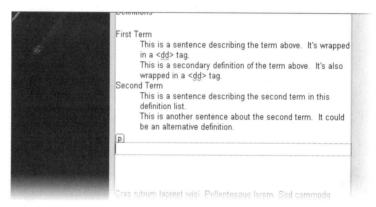

20. Save the page and preview it in a browser to ensure that it appears as you want.

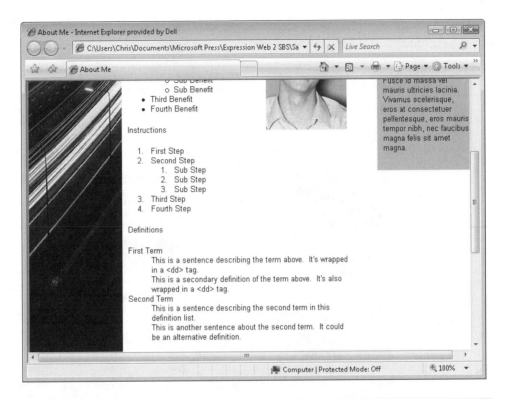

 BE SURE TO leave the *CH4* site open for use in the next exercise.

CLOSE the *about_me.htm* page.

Using Semantic Markup

Rather than thinking of HTML elements as ways to style your text, think of them as ways to describe what the text means and use cascading style sheets to style their appearance.

For instance, a list by nature groups similar elements together in a way that several paragraphs don't. An H1 element shows more importance than the same words marked up with a large font size, and an <em> (emphasized) or a <strong> tag adds additional meaning to a word where a <b> (bold) tag simply changes the font but doesn't add to the word's perceived importance.

In this exercise, you will learn to use HTML elements to enhance the meaning of the text and cascading style sheets to modify the appearance of the elements.

USE the *CH4* sample site you modified in the previous exercise.
OPEN the *CH4* site, if it isn't already open, and display the *contact.htm* page.

1. In the Design pane, scroll to the table of employee contact data.

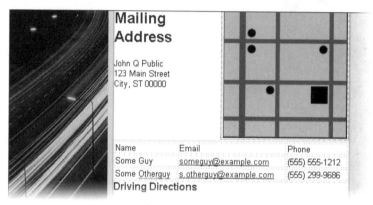

2. Select the top row of the table by clicking its **<tr>** button on the quick tag selector bar (the row that contains the words *Name, Email*, and *Phone*). In the Code pane, edit each of those table cell tags by replacing the **<td>** and **</td>** tags with **<th>** and **</th>**. Then save the page.

The Design view of the text that is contained in the cells changes slightly. This change occurred because you replaced a nondescript table cell with a *Table Head* cell. This tag indicates to search engines and non-visual browsers that this bit of data is different and is a heading for the columns below it.

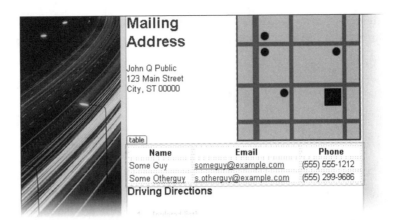

Bold

3. Open the *about_me.htm* page. In the Design pane, click in the word *Benefits*, which is being used as a title for your list of benefits, and then click the **Bold** button.

The page code now has the addition of a <strong> tag. This is much better than the old way: a <b> (bold) tag. Bold describes the look of the text, but Strong does more to describe its meaning.

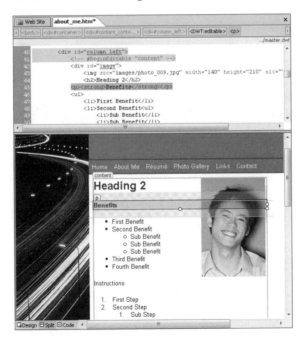

4. Repeat step 3 for the word *Instructions*.

Italic

5. Click in the final list name, **Definitions**. This time, instead of using the Bold button to wrap the word in a <strong> tag, click the **Italic** button.

Instead of the <i> tag for italic, the word is wrapped in an <em> tag, which means *emphasized*. The idea is that emphasized *means* something; italic only describes a font style.

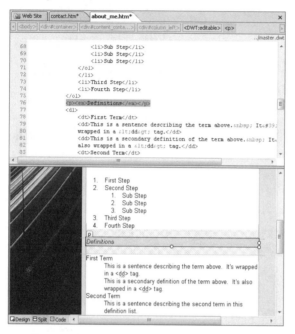

BE SURE TO leave the *CH4* site open for use in the next exercise.
CLOSE the *contact.htm* and *about_me.htm* pages after saving your changes.

The value of this shift from presentational markup (font tags, italic tags, bold tags, and so on) to semantic markup is clear. The old way simply applied a visual appearance to the text; the new way does something to lend a bit of description, which assists search engines and non-visual browsers to understand a level of meaning that font tag markup can't supply.

Styling the Presentation of Your Content

In the preceding exercises, we put some lists and tables on the page. They definitely serve the purposes for which they were intended: they contain the information they were designed to contain, and they keep it segregated from other information. Semantically, lists and tables are superior to using paragraph tags or one paragraph with line breaks between the relevant blocks. The only problem with them is their appearance.

This is another case of cascading style sheets to the rescue. You will now learn how to maintain the semantic value of these tags for search engines and non-visual browsers, but style them so that they look appealing to visitors.

In this exercise, you will learn to style the presentation of your content by using a class and by styling the base HTML element.

USE the *CH4* sample site you modified in the previous exercise.

OPEN the *CH4* site, if it isn't already open, and display the *contact.htm* page.

1. On the **View** menu, click **Visual Aids**, and then click **Margins and Padding**.

2. In the Design pane, scroll to the employee contact table, click in the top row, and select the table row that contains the table heads (<th>) by clicking the **<th>** entry on the quick tag selector bar.

3. In the **Apply Styles** task pane, click **New Style**. In the **New Style** dialog box, name the style **.tablehead**. Then select the **Apply new style to document selection** check box.

4. In the **Define in** box, click **Existing style sheet**, and in the **URL** list, click **../styles/ style3.css**.

5. Under Category, click **Font**. Then set **font-family** to **Courier New, Courier, monospace**; **font-weight** to **bold**; and **color** to **#FFFFFF**. In the **Block** category, set **text-align** to **left**, and in the **Background** category, set **background-color** to **#000000**.

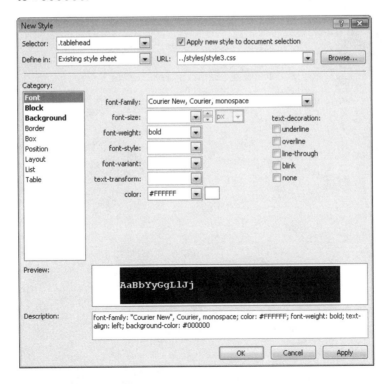

6. Click **OK** to close the dialog box.

> **Tip** In the Style Builder dialog box, when you make a specification within a category, the category title is bold.

You've modified the appearance of all of the <th> elements within that row by adding a style class (*class="tablehead"*) to the <tr> tag that contains them.

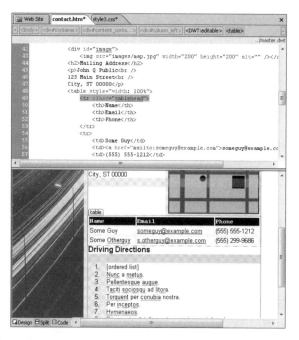

7. In the sample site, open the *about_me.htm* page, and in the Design pane, select the <ul> tag below *Benefits*.

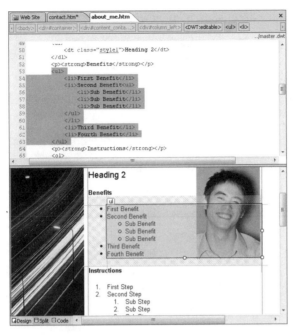

8. In the **Apply Styles** task pane, click **New Style**. In the **New Style** dialog box, name the style **.benefitlist**. Then select the **Apply new style to document selection** check box.

9. In the **Define in** box, click **Existing style sheet** and in the **URL** list, click **../styles/style3.css**.

10. In the **List** category, set **list-style-type** to **square**. Then click **Apply**.

The dialog box title changes from New Style to Modify Style.

The outer <li> elements now have a square bullet instead of the typical round bullet. The inner list items still have a round bullet.

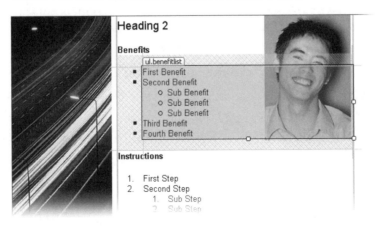

11. Change the *Selector* name from *.benefitlist* to **.benefitlist li**, and then click **Apply**.

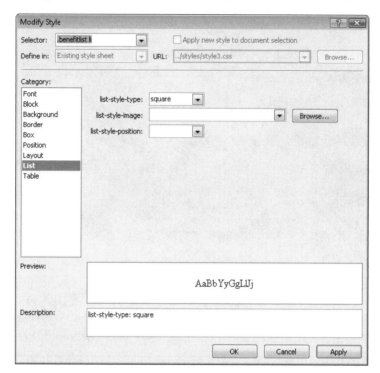

The inner list items now have a square bullet instead of a round bullet. This is because you classed the <ul> tag as *.benefitlist* but also added the <li> tag to that style specification in step 5. This procedure produces an identical effect for both the inner and outer lists.

12. Click **OK** to close the **Modify Style** dialog box.

13. In the Design pane, select **Instructions <ol>**, and in the **Apply Styles** task pane, click **New Style**. In the **New Style** dialog box, name the style **.instructionlist**. Then select the **Apply new style to document selection** check box.

14. In the **Define in** box, click **Existing style sheet (../styles/style3.css)**.

15. Select the **List** category, and set the **list-style-type** to **upper-roman**. Then click **OK** to close the **New Style** dialog box.

16. In the **Apply Styles** task pane, right-click **.instructionlist**, and then click **New Style Copy**, so that the inner list items do not have the same formatting as the parent element.

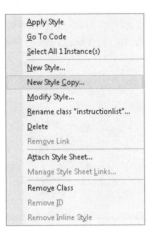

17. Give the new style the name **.instructionlist li li**, and in the **List** category, change
list-style-type to **lower-alpha**. Then click **OK**.

The inner list items now show lowercase alphabetic list items, and the outer list
items are uppercase roman numerals. The only code that has been added to the
page is the containing <ol> tag, which now has a class (*class="instructionlist"*)
applied to it.

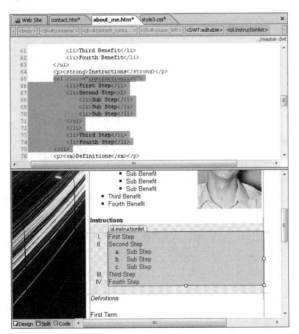

Another approach is to directly associate a style with one of the HTML elements,
such as <p>, <h1>, and <ol>.

18. In the **Apply Styles** task pane, click **New Style**, and type **dt** for **Selector**. In the **Font** category, set **font-family** to **Courier New, Courier, monospace**; **font-weight** to **bold**; and **text-transform** to **upper case**.

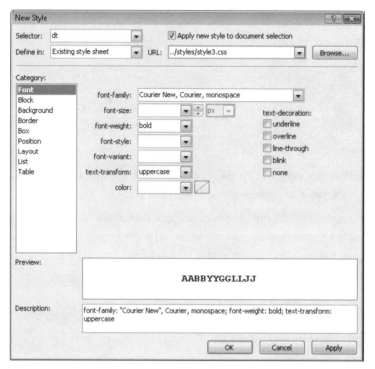

19. Click **OK**.

The Definition list terms are now in all capital letters and are in Courier bold font.

20. In the **Apply Styles** task pane, click **New Style**, and add a **Selector** of **dd**. In the **Font** category, set **font-family** to **Times New Roman, Times, serif**; **font-size** to **small**; and **color** value to **#808080**. Then click **OK**.

The definitions are now smaller and colored grey. These effects will apply to all Definition list terms and definitions in any page that has this style sheet linked to it. The code in the page hasn't changed at all. This style is applied to all Definition list items by default without the need to class them or mark them separately. This feature is a great advantage if you should want to change the appearance of a styled HTML element; all you would need to do is change its entry on the style sheet, and every instance of that element in dozens, hundreds, or even thousands of pages would instantly change!

BE SURE TO leave the *CH4* site open for use in the next exercise.

CLOSE the *contact.htm* and *about_me.htm* pages after saving your changes.

Cascading Style Sheets

When using cascading style sheets, several methods of altering the presentation of HTML elements are available, including the following:

- *CSS ID*: In the style sheet code, it will always begin with a number symbol (#). IDs are designed to be used only once in a page, and as such, are generally used for major page elements such as DIVs that make up major portions of a page.

- *CSS Class*: In the style sheet code, it will always begin with a period (.) and can be used multiple times in a page if necessary.

You can also specify a style for a basic HTML element itself, such as an ordered list or an anchor tag. This can be particularly useful because you define the HTML element only once on your style sheet, and every time that element appears in a page, it's styled in accordance with the style sheet's specification.

What is the real value of all this? Well, let's consider the worst-case scenario: you didn't use the list elements or the style sheet and classes to create these segments of information. You would have extensive *font tags* describing the appearance of every line, you would need to resort to paragraph indents and perhaps *block quotes* where they didn't even belong, and the file size of your code would be many times greater than it is now.

The best-case scenario: you've contained your information in a semantically valid element that adds to the meaning of the text itself, and you've given it the appearance that you want by creating styles on an external style sheet. You've prevented using a large amount of code, and you've given the text additional meaning beyond what can be seen. As a tremendous added bonus, an externally linked style sheet will be downloaded by the browser just once, cached, and used on any page that's linked to it. So, in addition to being cleaner and leaner, the code is also more efficient. Though this small example isn't as telling as a large site would be, the fact remains that these techniques can save space on your server, save page-load time for your site visitors, and add to content searchability.

Running CSS Reports

In the previous exercises, you used some of the style sheet features that Expression Web 2 makes easily available. This is a good time to take a look at your style sheet and compatibility reports to ensure that everything you just did is valid and will render well cross-browser.

In this exercise, you will use the CSS reporting and usage features in Expression Web 2. These reports will be helpful in both managing complex styles and in diagnosing and exploring how cascading style sheets are used and how they affect existing Web sites.

USE the *CH4* sample site that you modified in the previous exercise.
OPEN the *CH4* site if it isn't already open.

1. With the *CH4* sample site open, on the **Tools** menu, click **CSS Reports** to display the **CSS Reports** dialog box. Ensure that **All Pages** is selected and that each of the three error types—**Unused Styles**, **Undefined Classes**, and **Mismatched Case**—are selected. Then click **Check**.

Tip The first time you use the CSS Reports feature, Expression Web 2 may need to configure itself in order to allow the features to be used. A Configuration dialog box opens if this is the case, and you may need to restart your computer in order for the changes to take effect.

In the bottom of your workspace, the CSS Reports task pane is now open, and shows three unused styles.

2. Double-click the first error in the list: the h5 element.

In the Workspace above the CSS Reports task pane, the site's style sheet opens with the unused style highlighted.

3. Delete the highlighted style, and save the style sheet. Click the green arrow in the upper-left corner of the **CSS Reports** task pane to display the **CSS Reports** dialog box. Re-run your check, but this time, use the **Current Page** option.

The CSS Reports task pane displays two error reports.

4. Using the blue arrows on the left of the **CSS Reports** task pane, step through the errors and correct them if you want.

5. Click the green arrow again to redisplay the **CSS Reports** dialog box. In the dialog box, click the **Usage** tab. Ensure that **All Pages** and the three Usage options—**Class Selectors**, **ID Selectors**, and **Element Selectors**—are selected. Then click **Check**.

The CSS Reports task pane displays a list of styles used on the Web site.

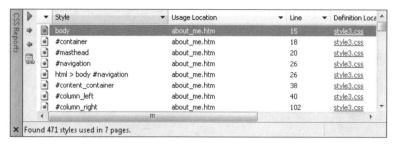

Using the same method as in the previous steps, you can step through the usage report and show the particular page and line where the usage occurs. This can be a very helpful tool when you're planning to make changes to a Web site's styles.

6. On the **Tools** menu, click **Compatibility Reports** to open the **Compatibility Checker** dialog box. In the dialog box, ensure that **All Pages** and **Run check based on Doctype declaration in page if available** are selected. Leave the Internet Explorer 7 and CSS 2.1 defaults selected. Then click **Check**.

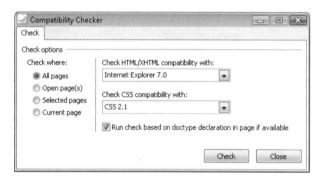

A new tab (Compatibility) is open in the pane where you were previously working with CSS Reports. In this case, there are no compatibility issues to report. This obviously won't be the case with all sites you encounter, but this feature is worth remembering, especially if you run into browser compatibility issues with a site.

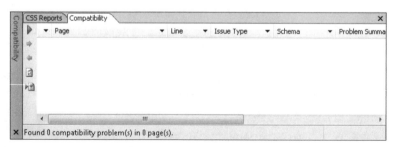

 CLOSE any open pages after saving them, and close the *CH4* sample site. If you are not continuing directly to the next chapter, exit Expression Web 2.

Although this exercise was run with a style sheet and didn't have many errors or compatibility issues, this tool is an excellent addition to your toolset for "fixing" existing sites and can save untold hours of trial-and-error testing, especially regarding problems like class and ID case issues, and cross-browser rendering.

Key Points

- Although using tables for layout is no longer a current best practice, tables still can be used effectively for tabular data.
- Lists are a cornerstone of displaying related information on Web pages.
- You can mark up your text as well as its semantic meaning.
- By using cascading style sheets to style text, you can gain easier maintenance of presentation while also reducing the overall code in the page itself.
- You can use cascading style sheet classes to style parent elements, copy classes to style inner elements, and even specify the default look of an HTML element through the cascading style sheet tools of Expression Web 2.
- Using cascading style sheets to style elements by selector or by their basic HTML container by name greatly aids in the efficiency of keeping a site uniform and changing the appearance of items globally.

Chapter at a Glance

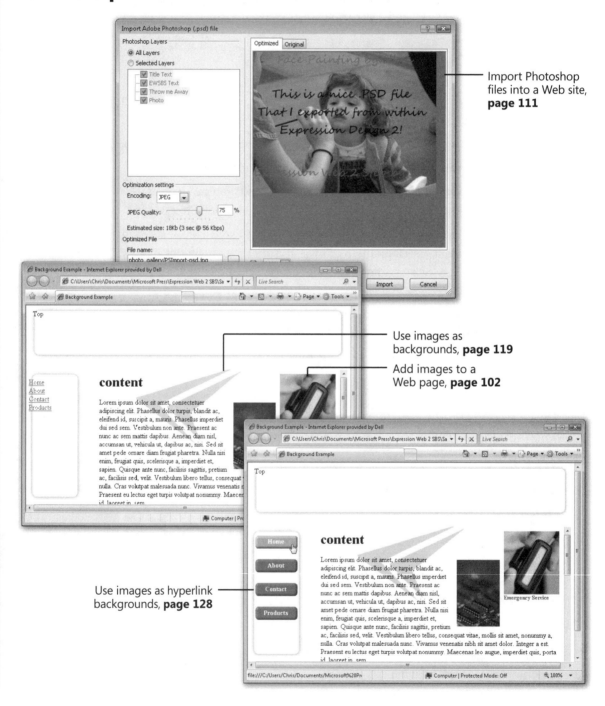

Import Photoshop files into a Web site, **page 111**

Use images as backgrounds, **page 119**

Add images to a Web page, **page 102**

Use images as hyperlink backgrounds, **page 128**

5 Enhancing a Web Site with Images

In this chapter, you will learn to

✔ Add images to a Web page.

✔ Edit images in Expression Web 2.

✔ Import Photoshop files into a Web site.

✔ Use images with a style sheet.

✔ Use images as backgrounds.

✔ Use images as bullets.

✔ Use images as hyperlink backgrounds.

It goes without saying that a Web page is quite uninteresting without images. Therefore, ensuring that the images on your site display as expected is an important part of designing your site. Whether you use images to show a product, to convey a thought, or simply to enhance the page's aesthetic appearance, you're going to be using them in your pages. You don't want to use a bunch of large-size images that don't have any *alt text* (descriptive text contained in an image's HTML tag) or semantic value on a page.

In this chapter, you will learn how to use images in your pages while maintaining their accessibility and validity, and you will learn how to edit images in Microsoft Expression Web 2. You will learn some new ways to use images in conjunction with cascading style sheets (CSS) to yield results that would otherwise be impossible, or at the very least, quite cumbersome. You'll learn how to import Photoshop (.psd) files, and use them in your pages. You'll learn how to use images in background areas and to use images as bullets. Then, you will learn to use images as hyperlink backgrounds.

> **Tip** To view the formatting marks and provide visual layout cues for this chapter, open any page and then, on the View menu, click Formatting Marks, and click Show.

> **Important** Before you can use the practice files in this chapter, you need to install them from the book's companion CD to their default location. For more information about practice files, see "Using the Companion CD" at the beginning of this book.

> **Troubleshooting** Graphics and operating system–related instructions in this book reflect the Windows Vista user interface. If your computer is running Windows XP and you experience trouble following the instructions as written, please refer to the "Information for Readers Running Windows XP" section at the beginning of this book.
>
> To improve the readability of the graphics in this book, Expression Web 2 was set to use the Windows color scheme instead of the default Expression Studio 2 color scheme.

Adding Images to a Web Page

Although putting images on a Web page may appear trivial at its core, there are key principles of modern Web design that you should understand to ensure that the site you build is fast loading, accessible, and meaningful to search engines. Key considerations are page file size and accessibility. Although images will "show" what you want, they don't do anything to "tell" their story or add to the value of the information they're related to. By understanding how to use images on a page correctly, you can universally enhance the point you're trying to make, providing impact, as well as making sure your image is accessible and search-engine friendly.

In this exercise, you will add a basic image to a Web page.

> **USE** the *CH5* sample site. This sample site is located in the *Documents\Microsoft Press\ Expression Web 2 SBS\Sample Sites* folder.
>
> **BE SURE TO** start Expression Web 2 before beginning this exercise.
>
> **OPEN** the *CH5* site by clicking Open Site on the File menu.

1. In the **Folder List**, click the **images** folder of the sample site. On the **File** menu, point to **Import**, and then click **File**.

   The Import dialog box opens.

2. In the **Import** dialog box, click **Add File**, and browse to the *Documents\Microsoft Press\Expression Web 2 SBS\Files\CH5-Import* folder.

3. In the *CH5-Import* folder, press Ctrl + A to select all of the files, and then click **Open**.

All the image file names appear in the Import dialog box.

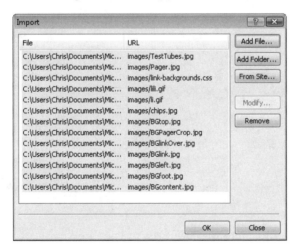

4. Click **OK** to close the **Import** dialog box and import the pictures into your site's *images* folder.

5. In the **Folder List**, double-click the *default.htm* page. Click just before the first letter of **Heading 2** in the content editable region. On the **Insert** menu, point to **Picture**, and then click **From File**.

The Picture dialog box opens.

> **Tip** In the Picture dialog box, you can click Views to choose one of several views: Thumbnails, Tiles, Icons, List, Details, Properties, or Preview. If the image names aren't intuitive, the most useful views will be Thumbnails and Preview.

6. In the *CH5\images* folder, click the *Pager* image, and then click **Insert** to close the dialog box.

The Accessibility Properties dialog box opens. This dialog box is intended to help you maintain your site's World Wide Web Consortium (W3C) validity and accessibility.

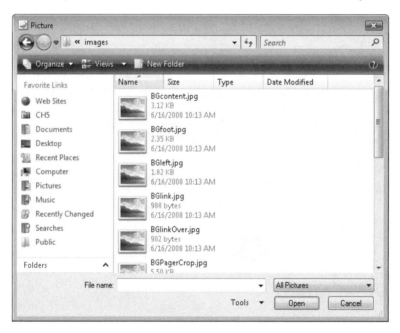

7. Enter a descriptive **Alternate text** value for the picture.

If you leave the text field blank, you will get an empty *alt* value (which is still valid but not descriptive).

> **Tip** The entry for *Long Description* is there to allow you to browse to a text file with a verbose description of a complex image or if you want to provide long descriptions for images in order to provide greater accessibility to visually impaired visitors using a screen reader browser.

8. Click **OK** to close the dialog box and insert the image.

Although your picture is now in the page, it's not doing a very good job of enhancing the text that's adjacent to it.

9. Double-click the image to open the **Picture Properties** dialog box, and then click the **Appearance** tab. Under **Wrapping style**, click **Right**, and then click **OK**.

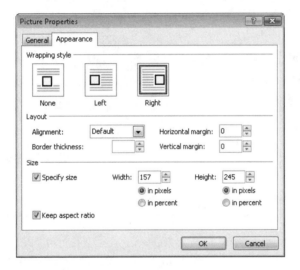

The image has now floated to the right of the text.

The text has come into contact with the image's edge. This is less than ideal because it can make the text difficult to read and just doesn't look very good.

10. Double-click the image to open the **Picture Properties** dialog box again. On the **Appearance** tab, type **5px** in the **Horizontal margin** box and in the **Vertical margin** box. Click **OK**.

The image margin is now five pixels. The text no longer touches the image.

11. Save the page and preview it in a browser.

 BE SURE TO leave the *CH5* site open for use in the next exercise.

Consider the result of the previous lesson: You imported a folder full of images into your site's existing *images* folder, inserted an image into your page and styled it to be complementary to the page and text. All the while, Expression Web 2 helped you maintain W3C validity and accessibility standards.

Editing Images in Expression Web 2

In general, a best practice is to prepare images in an ***image editor***, such as Microsoft Expression Design 2, or whatever image editor you're partial to, before importing them into your site. The operations you'd do in the image editor would include adjustment of ***physical size***, color adjustment, text overlay, and a host of other techniques, depending on the intended use of the image.

Although Expression Web 2 isn't intended to be used as your image editor, it does contain a number of tools you can use to make quick adjustments. Any professional will have his or her preferred graphics tool for a given job, but the ability to make an adjustment to an image while creating a new layout or in the course of maintaining an existing site is a time-saving feature.

In this exercise, you will edit an image within Expression Web 2.

USE the *CH5* sample site you modified in the previous exercise.
OPEN the *CH5* site if it isn't already open.

1. On the *default.htm* page, right-click the *Pager* image you inserted in the previous exercise, and then click **Show Pictures Toolbar**. Point to each button on the **Pictures** toolbar to view its tooltip.

Crop

2. On the **Pictures** toolbar, click the **Crop** button. Then drag the handles of the cropping box over the image to define the area of the image you want to keep.

Save

3. Press [Enter] to crop the graphic. Then on the Common toolbar, click **Save**. In the **Save Embedded Files** dialog box, click **Rename**, and then change the image name to **PagerCrop.jpg** (to preserve the original image).

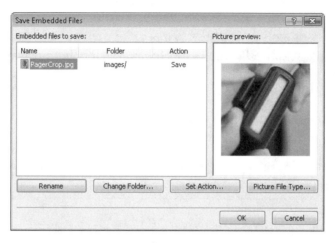

4. In the **Save Embedded Files** dialog box, click **OK**.

5. Double-click the image to open the **Picture Properties** dialog box, and then click **Edit**.

   The image opens in a Microsoft Paint window.

> **Troubleshooting** If Microsoft Paint is not your default image editor, you can right-click the image and then click Open With to select the image editor of your choice.

Text

6. Click the **Text** button, and draw a text box at the bottom of the image. In the text box, type **Emergency Service**.

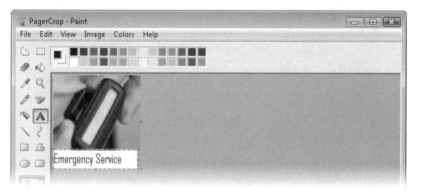

7. Save the picture as **PagerCropText.jpg**, and then close Paint.

8. On the *default* page, double-click the image to open the **Picture Properties** dialog box, and then click **Browse**. Navigate to the site's *images* folder, click the *PagerCropText* image, and click **Open**. Click **OK** to close the **Picture Properties** dialog box, and then save the page.

9. Click the end of the text paragraph in the **content** editable region, and then press
Enter to insert a new paragraph.

10. Insert the *TestTubes* image that you imported into the site earlier in this chapter.

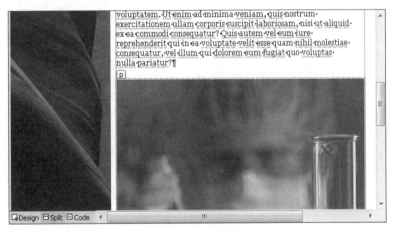

11. Double-click the image to open the **Picture Properties** dialog box, and then click
Picture File Type.

The Picture File Type dialog box opens. In this dialog box, you can choose different
file types: .jpeg, .gif, and .png. You can also change the image compression.

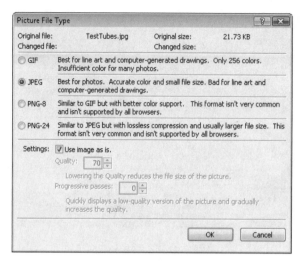

12. Clear the **Use image as is** check box, and change the **Quality** level to **60**.

The image file size is reduced significantly. You can also set the number of Progressive Passes for the image in the box below the Quality box, but this is generally only needed for purposely high file–size images such as high-quality artwork samples.

13. Click **OK** in the **Picture File Type** dialog box, and then click **OK** in the **Picture Properties** dialog box. Save the page and accept the default settings in the **Save Embedded Files** dialog box.

BE SURE TO leave the *CH5* site open for use in the next exercise.

Important Be careful when compressing images, whether through the facilities in Expression Web 2 or another image editor. As you compress them, the file size will get lower, along with the quality. For optimum image compression, you're looking for a balance between file size reduction and acceptable appearance.

Importing Photoshop Files into a Web Site

A great new feature in Expression Web 2 is the ability to import a .psd (Adobe Photoshop) file. Not only can you simply import the file, you can also convert it to a Web-ready .jpg, .gif, or .png file, open the original file in your default .psd editor, and easily re-import changes made to the source file.

In this exercise, you will use a Photoshop file in your site, and become familiar with the new features in Expression Web 2.

> **USE** the *CH5* sample site you modified in the previous exercise.
>
> **OPEN** the *CH5* site if it isn't already open.

1. Open the *photo_gallery.htm* page, and select the paragraph that contains the sentence *Insert your photo gallery here.*

2. With the paragraph selected, on the menu bar click **Insert**, pause your mouse pointer over **Picture**, and then click **From Adobe Photoshop (.psd)** to open the **Select Photoshop (.psd) file** dialog box.

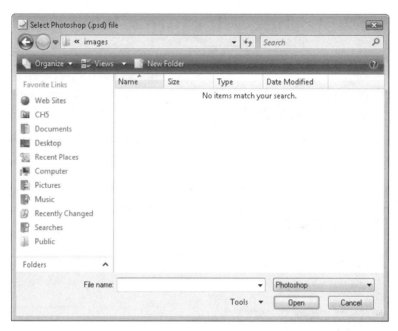

3. Browse to *Documents\Microsoft Press\Expression Web 2 SBS\Files\PSImport.psd*, and then click **Open** to open the **Import Adobe Photoshop (.psd) file** dialog box.

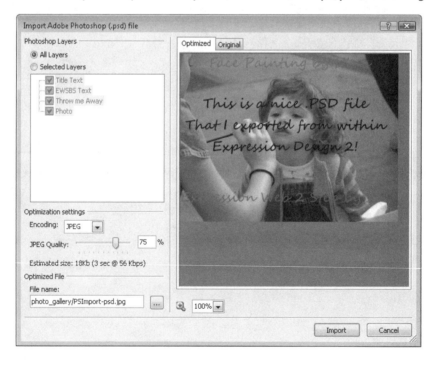

> **Tip** Expression Web 2 can import Photoshop .psd files that have all the following properties:
>
> - The color is 8 bits per channel (24 bits of color per pixel).
> - The color mode is RGB Color, Grayscale, or Indexed Color.
> - The resulting image size is 200 MB or less.
> - The file is saved with the Photoshop Maximize Compatibility format option turned on.
> - The file extension is .psd.
>
> The file doesn't need to be created in Adobe Photoshop. In this example, the .psd file was created in Expression Design 2 and exported as a .psd file.

4. In the **Import Adobe Photoshop (.psd) file** dialog box, under **Photoshop Layers**, click **Selected Layers**. Clear the **Throw me Away** check box to exclude this layer and its text. Leave the default encoding and quality settings as they are, and then click **Import**.

The Accessibility Properties dialog box opens.

> **Tip** In the Import Adobe Photoshop file dialog box, you can adjust the compression ratio of the resulting image, choose whether you want to save it as a .gif, .jpg, or .png, and set the file name and folder location you want the imported Web-ready image to occupy.

5. Give the image a description, and then click **OK**.

The image is now inserted into the page, as specified in step 4. Save your changes and preview the page in a browser.

6. Switch to the Expression Web 2 interface. Right-click the image you just imported, point to **Adobe Photoshop (.psd)**, and then click **Edit Source** or **Update from Source**.

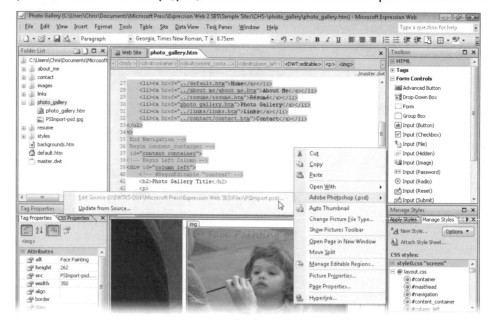

> **Tip** If you don't have an editor assigned to .psd files, Edit Source will be unavailable.

 BE SURE TO leave the *CH5* site open for use in the next exercise.

Consider the results of this exercise; without leaving the Expression Web 2 interface, you were able to use the Import Adobe Photoshop file feature to create a Web-ready, lightweight .jpg image and insert it directly into your page. You also retain the ability to quickly open the source file in your default .psd editor from within Expression Web 2 and easily update the resulting Web-ready image in your page, based on the changes made to the original Photoshop file.

> **Tip** If you elect to keep original files within your Expression Web site you may find it useful to right-click the files in the Folders List pane and then click Do Not Publish. Although you may find it convenient to keep original artwork and other files within your Web site, you'll most likely not want to waste hosting space or publishing bandwidth by publishing the original files to the live Web site.

Using Images with a Style Sheet

With the advent of cascading style sheets (CSS), some capabilities that were previously unavailable or that required significant hand coding are now made easy through the various CSS interfaces of Expression Web 2. In the upcoming exercise, you will manipulate an image's presentation by using CSS. Doing so keeps unnecessary code out of your page and ensures that the code that is there is modern, in keeping with W3C standards, and easily maintainable.

In this exercise, you will learn a few things that you can do with your style sheet and a simple image inserted into your page within the text content.

> **Important** In each of the following exercises, you will be adding and changing CSS code that's directly entered onto the page itself rather than on an attached style sheet. In each of these exercises, be sure to select the Apply New Style To Document Selection check box and select Current Page for the Define In value.

> **USE** the *CH5* sample site you modified in the previous exercise.
>
> **BE SURE TO** enable Visual Aids for Block Selections, Visible Borders, and Margins And Padding before beginning this exercise.
>
> **OPEN** the *CH5* site if it isn't already open, and display the *backgrounds.htm* page.

1. In Design view, click the page just before the first letter of the first paragraph in the **content** DIV.

2. On the **Insert** menu, point to **Picture**, and then click **From File**. In the **Picture** dialog box, navigate to the site's *images* folder, click the *chips* image, and then click **OK** to close the dialog box and insert the picture. Give the picture a meaningful **Alternate text** description when prompted, and then click **OK** again.

3. In Design view, click the image you just inserted, and then click **New Style** in the **Apply Styles** task pane. Change the **Selector** name to **.chippic**, and then specify the following settings:

Category	Option	Value
	Apply new style to document selection	Selected
Box	padding	10px (Same for all selected)
Layout	float	left

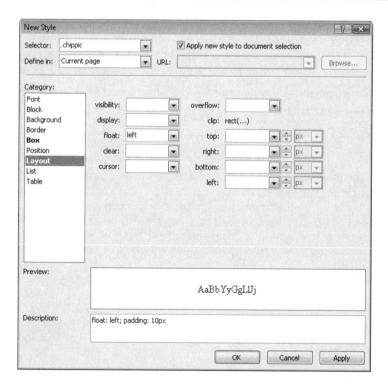

4. Click **OK** to close the dialog box and create your new style.

5. In the **Apply Styles** task pane, right-click **.chippic**, and then click **Modify Style**. In the **Category** list, click **Layout**, and then change **float** to **right** to see an alternative to the initial setting. Click **OK** to save your changes and to close the **Modify Style** dialog box. Review your changes in Design view.

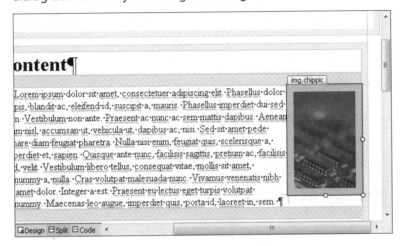

> **Tip** To find the style for an item more easily, select it in your page. Then in the Apply Styles task pane, click Options, and click Show Styles Used On Selection.

6. Click the image again in Design view. Right-click its style in the **Apply Styles** task pane, and then click **Modify Style** to open the **Modify Style** dialog box. Click **Layout** in the **Category** list again, and then in the **cursor** box, click **help**. Click **OK** to close the dialog box and return to Design view. Save your page and preview it in a browser.

7. With the page open in your browser, point to the image you just worked on.

    The cursor changes to a *Help cursor* (question mark and pointer).

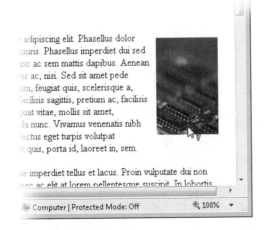

This technique of specifying the cursor for an image element can be helpful in giving your visitor a visual cue that there's additional information available about an image via its alt text that will pop up when hovered over.

8. Switch to Expression Web 2 and display Split view. Click the image you just styled in the Design pane, and examine its representation in the Code pane.

No code is added to the image tag other than *class="chippic"*.

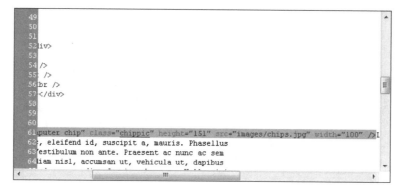

9. Press the Ctrl key, and then in the Code pane, click the underlined style.

This is known as a ***code hyperlink***. It focuses your editor on that style and shows the style in question as highlighted. You can easily see the styles that are used on this particular image.

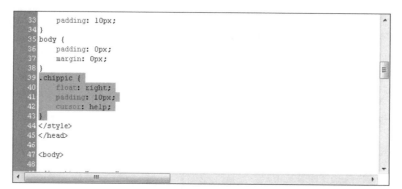

 BE SURE TO leave the *CH5* site open for use in the next exercise.

Consider what you accomplished in this exercise; using just the style sheet facilities in Expression Web 2, you modified the layout of a picture on the page and caused it to show the visitor a different cursor when it's hovered over, and all of this without writing any code by hand.

Using Images as Backgrounds

One of the best things about using CSS mark-up and images together is the ability to use the images as backgrounds. You can use CSS to style background images in tables and table cells, but for maximum flexibility, you can use CSS to style the background images by using DIV elements.

The flexibility to repeat or not repeat (generally known as *tiling*), keep the image as a static background so that it doesn't scroll with the page elements, and even layer images over each other are simply not things you can accomplish through any other method.

Expression Web 2 contains some of the best CSS interface tools ever available to a designer. Through the various panels and interfaces of Expression Web 2, you can not only take advantage of the benefits of CSS and images to style backgrounds with minimal learning required, if you have an interest in digging deeper under the hood of how CSS works, you can simply see the code results in the attached .css file or embedded styles that occurred from your actions within the Expression Web 2 interface. So in this way, Expression Web 2 is a great tool to learn how to use CSS. Expression Web 2 also brings significant advancements in CSS reporting and usage features.

See Also For more information about using CSS reporting, see "Running CSS Reports" in Chapter 4, "Presenting Information on a Web Page."

In this exercise, you will use images as backgrounds on various page areas.

> **USE** the *CH5* sample site you modified in the previous exercise.
>
> **OPEN** the *CH5* site, if it isn't already open, and display the *backgrounds.htm* page in Split view.

1. In the Design pane, click the <div> (*class="top"*). In the **Apply Styles** task pane, right-click **.top**, and then click **Modify Style**.

2. In the **Modify Style** dialog box, click **Background** in the **Category** list, then click **Browse** beside the **background-image** box. Navigate to the site's *images* folder, double-click the *BGtop* image, and click **no-repeat** in the **background-repeat** list. Then click **OK** to close the dialog box and return to your page.

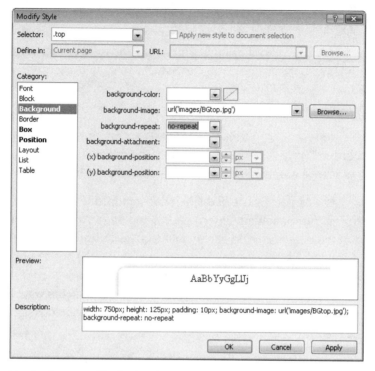

You've just specified a background image for the top <div> by using the interface.

3. In the Design pane, click the <div> (*class="left"*), below where you were just working. In the **Apply Styles** task pane, right-click **.left**, and then click **Modify Style**. Repeat step 2 to insert the *BGleft* image.

4. In the Design pane, click the <div> (*class="foot"*) at the bottom of the page. In the **Apply Styles** task pane, right-click **.foot**, and then click **Modify Style**. Repeat step 2 to insert the *BGfoot* image.

5. In the Design pane, click the <div> (*class="content"*) that contains the main content. In the **Apply Styles** task pane, right-click **.content**, and then click **Modify Style**. Navigate to the site's *images* folder, double-click the *BGcontent* image, but don't set any other values. Click **OK** to close the dialog box and return to your page. Save the page and preview it in a browser.

Tiles of the image you just specified fill the entire area of the DIV element.

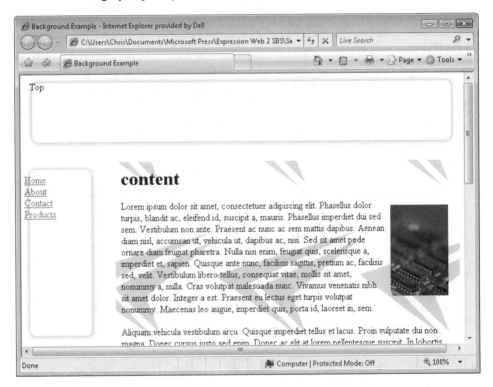

6. Switch back to Expression Web 2. In the Code pane, click the content <div> tag again. In the **Apply Styles** task pane, right-click **.content**, and then click **Modify Style**. Click **Background** in the **Category** list, click **no-repeat** in the **background-repeat** list, click **center** in the **(x) background-position** list, and then click **center** in the **(y) background-position** list.

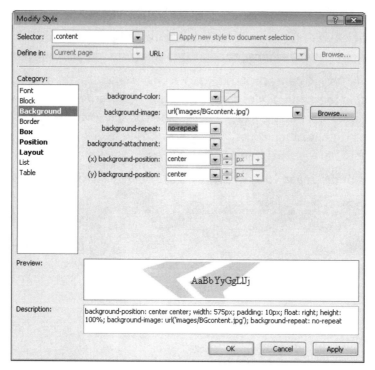

7. Click **OK** to save your changes and close the dialog box. Save your page and preview it in a browser.

   The background image shows only once.

8. Take this *watermark* background situation a little farther and make the following modifications to the style: In the **Apply Styles** task pane, right-click **.content**, and then click **Modify Style**. Specify the following settings:

Category	Option	Value
Position	height	300px
Layout	overflow	auto
Background	background-attachment	fixed

9. Click **OK** to close the dialog box and return to your page. Save the page and preview it in a browser.

The background image now stays static within the page and the text scrolls over it. It's looking more like a watermark background.

To use the CSS background image property for more than just showing an image, consider the previous exercise where you added text to an image by using Paint from within Expression Web 2. It showed text over a picture but that's about it, plus it wasn't something that a search engine would pick up or that a screen reading browser would be able to read.

10. In the Code pane, click just to the left of the <h1> tag in the content DIV element, type the following code, and then press Enter:

```
<div><p>Emergency Service</p></div>
```

11. In the Design pane, click this newly inserted DIV element, and then click **New Style** in the **Apply Styles** task pane.

12. In the **New Style** dialog box, change the **Selector** to **.emgsvc**, and then specify the following settings:

Category	Option	Value
	Define in	Current page
	Apply new style to document selection	Selected
Background	background-image	BGPagerCrop.jpg
	background-repeat	no-repeat
Position	width	129px
	height	156px
Layout	float	right

13. Click **OK** to save your changes and return to Design view in Expression Web 2.

> **Tip** In order to make designing easier, try this: create a new Web page, and save it in your images folder. Select all the images in the folder, and then drag them onto the page. The page now displays all the images, providing a visual cue as to which image is which. Expression Web 2 enters the dimensions of each image in its image tag.

14. Save the page, and preview it in a browser.

You've now got an image in your page via a styled background, and you've got text on top of it.

15. To make your text appear similar to the exercise in Paint, return to Expression Web 2, click the paragraph inside the *.emgsvc* DIV element that contains the words *Emergency Service*, and then click **New Style** in the **Apply Styles** task pane. Type **.emgtxt** in the **Selector** box, specify the following settings, and then click **OK** to close the dialog box:

Category	Option	Value
Font	font-size	13px
	font-weight	Bold
	color	#FF0000
Background	background-color	#FFFFFF
Box	margin top	143px (**Same for all** check box cleared)

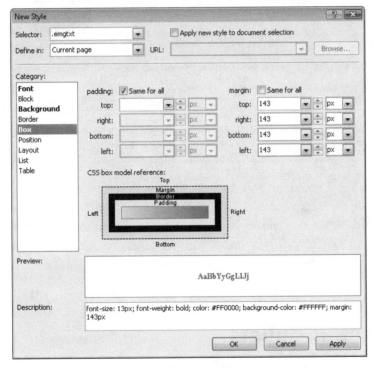

16. Save the page and preview it in a browser.

Notice that you've got a very close representation of the image you edited in an earlier exercise, but this time it's actual text within your page, not just an image of text superimposed on a picture.

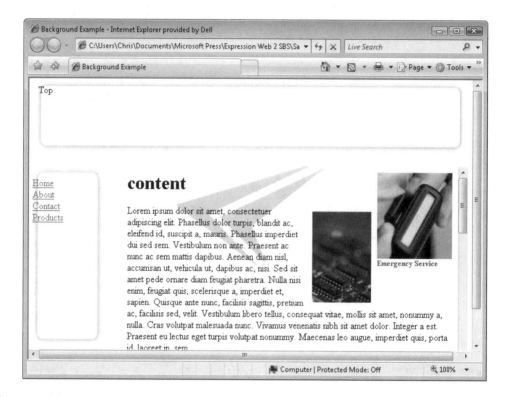

 BE SURE TO leave the *CH5* site open for use in the next exercise.

Although this exercise got you started with how to style background images and how to manipulate the background's property, it's not intended to be a treatise on CSS. You can do so much with CSS "styles" that entire books could be, and have been, written on the subject and even then they're forced to leave out some details. It's highly recommended that you take the time to learn about CSS and how you can really maximize its impact on how you design your pages.

Using Images as Bullets

Although there are a number of default bullet styles you can specify through CSS, sometimes you want to style a page in such a way as to take total control of the appearance of the bullets. Without CSS, you would have to resort to using paragraphs with positioned images, laying out a table to contain the images used for bullets, or both. In any case, you lose the semantic value of your list elements and load up your page with unnecessary markup. Using CSS, specifying images in an unordered list is a surprisingly simple matter.

In this exercise, you will substitute images for default bullets in a standards-compliant, semantically valid, easily maintainable way, and using very limited code.

USE the *CH5* sample site you modified in the previous exercise.

OPEN the *CH5* site, if it isn't already open, and display the *backgrounds.htm* page in Split view.

1. Select the unordered list in the content by clicking its representation on the quick tag selector bar.

2. In the **Apply Styles** task pane, click **New Style**.

3. Create a new style called **.notelist**, and select the **Apply new style to document selection** check box, but don't set any other properties. Then click **OK**.

4. In the **Apply Styles** task pane, right-click **.notelist**, and then click **New Style Copy**. Give this copy the selector **.notelist li**.

5. In the **Category** list, click **List**, click **Browse** next to the **list-style-image** box, navigate to the site's *images* folder, and double-click the *li* image. Then click **OK**.

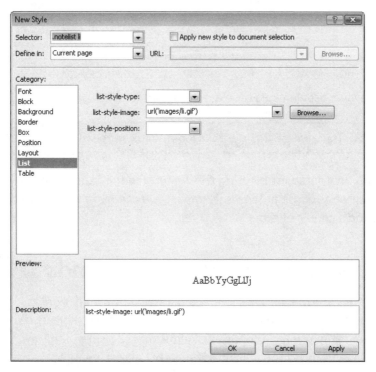

6. In the **Apply Styles** task pane, click **OK**.

A musical note appears for all the list item elements.

7. In the **Apply Styles** task pane, right-click **.notelist li**, and then click **New Style Copy**. Give this new copy the name **.notelist li li**.

8. In the **Category** list, click **List**, click **Browse** next to the **list-style-image** box, navigate to the site's *images* folder, and double-click the *lili* image. Then click **OK**.

9. Save the page and preview it in a browser.

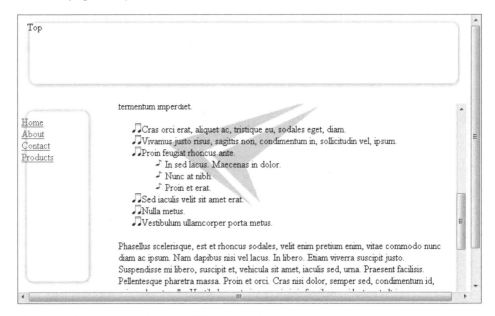

The inner list elements have a different list item image.

 BE SURE TO leave the *CH5* site open for use in the next exercise.

Styling an unordered list by using CSS features in the Expression Web 2 interface is remarkably easy. Consider the visual impact you can make with little more than a few images and a couple of clicks.

Using Images as Hyperlink Backgrounds

Using images as hyperlinks has long been a staple of Web design; the individual images serve as buttons, and combined within a page area, they serve as navigation bars. A designer might use JavaScript to make the images display a *roll-over* effect. The Interactive Buttons feature in Expression Web 2 makes it easy to create buttons like this by using images and JavaScript.

In this exercise, you will create an alternative to these buttons with nothing more than a regular text-based hyperlink, two images, and a little CSS, with *no JavaScript at all*.

USE the *CH5* sample site you modified in the previous exercise.

OPEN the *CH5* site if it isn't already open, and display the *backgrounds.htm* page in Split view.

1. In the Code pane, click just under the style block describing the **.left** style.

2. Paste or type the following code into your page.

```
.left a {
    width: 100px;
    height: 30px;
    display: block;
    background-image: url('images/BGlink.jpg');
    background-repeat: no-repeat;
    text-align: center;
    text-decoration: none;
    color: white;
    font-weight: bolder;
    font-size: 15px;
    padding-top: 5px;
    margin-left: 11px;
}
```

Tip Any code you need to enter in this exercise is available in a .css file that you imported into your site's *images* folder earlier in this chapter.

```
18    background repeat: no repeat;
19  }
20  .left a {
21      width: 100px;
22      height: 30px;
23      display: block;
24      background-image: url('images/BGlink.jpg');
25      background-repeat: no-repeat;
26      text-align: center;
27      text-decoration: none;
28      color: white;
29      font-weight: bolder;
30      font-size: 15px;
31      padding-top: 5px;
32      margin-left: 11px;
33  }
34
```

3. Save your page and preview it in a browser.

Notice that you've got a pretty nice arrangement that looks like a button. The only thing you don't have is the *image swap* feature common to graphic buttons.

4. Switch to Expression Web 2. In Code view, or in the Code pane of Split view, type the following code just below the block you entered in the previous step:

```
.left a:hover {
    background-image: url('images/BGlinkOver.jpg');
}
```

5. Save your page and preview it in a browser. Point to the links and notice the image swap effect they now have.

This is a very flexible technique, and, when compared to a JavaScript-based image button, is much better from the perspective of accessibility and ease of maintenance.

6. To wrap up this exercise and see how these style changes appear in the Expression Web 2 style builder, right-click **.left a** in the **Manage Styles** task pane, and then click **Modify Style** to open the **Modify Style** dialog box.

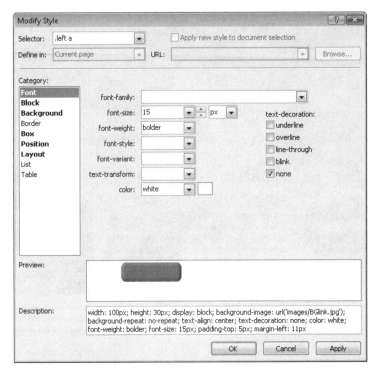

On the left of the dialog box, in the Category list, every category that has a modification made to it is in bold. You can click each of these modified category entries to see how these changes you entered directly into the page code are represented within the dialog box.

CLOSE the *CH5* sample site and any open browser windows. If you are not continuing directly to the next chapter, exit Expression Web 2.

Key Points

- Use images properly in your pages, being sure to avoid excessive page file size and download time without adding any descriptive value to the content.

- Expression Web 2 has tools to make rudimentary image editing possible from within its user interface.

- If you use CSS and a background image, you achieve the same results visually as you would by using an edited image, and you also gain additional semantic value, search-engine friendliness, and accessibility.

- By using the Expression Web 2 interface, you can easily replace default bullets with custom images.

- By using CSS, you can create image buttons that have a roll-over effect, minimizing page size and improving semantic value and accessibility.

- With the Import Adobe Photoshop feature in Expression Web 2, you can quickly import .psd files into your Web site in a format that's appropriate for Web display, and you can choose all layers or import layers selectively.

Chapter at a Glance

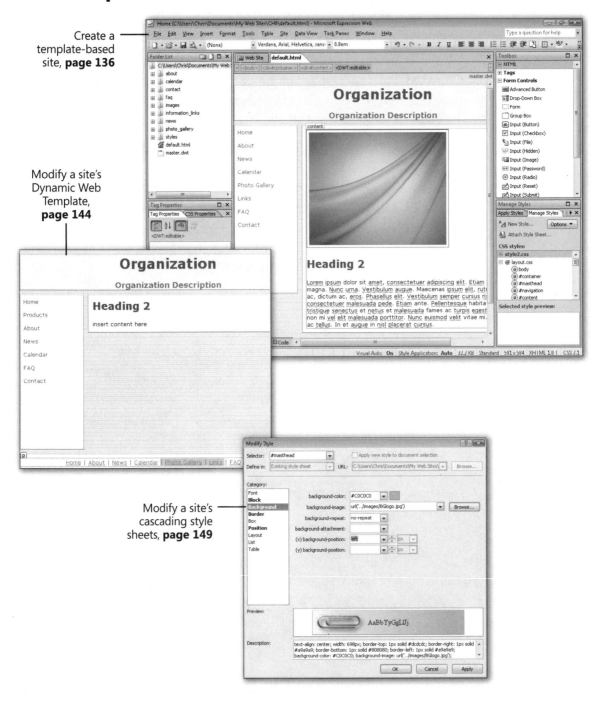

6 Creating a Web Site from a Template

In this chapter, you will learn to

✔ Create a template-based site.

✔ Organize Web site pages.

✔ Modify a site's Dynamic Web Template.

✔ Modify a site's cascading style sheets.

Creating a Web site from an empty folder is a daunting challenge for all but the smallest of sites. Fortunately, Microsoft Expression Web 2 comes with a collection of pre-installed *Web site templates* that you can use to get a head start on the process of creating a site. In these site templates, you'll find valid HTML code, and layouts that use cascading style sheets rather than tables for positioning. Each site relies on a Dynamic Web Template to control page layout and presentation. What you won't find are proprietary features, unattractive *clip art*, discouragingly deep table structure, or any of a multitude of issues that plagued predecessors of Expression Web 2.

The pre-installed templates are organized in three groups: Organization, Personal, and Small Business. This segregation is related more to the *architecture* of the templates (number of pages and page names) than to their actual purposes—so regardless of the purpose of the site you are building, consider all of the templates and find the one that best suits your aesthetic interests. It's easier to add or remove pages from a template-based site than it is to make major changes to the visual presentation of the site.

Templates such as those provided by Expression Web 2 aren't only a good way to get a quick start on your site project; they're also a good way to learn (by doing) about elements such as Dynamic Web Templates, cascading style sheet layouts, and general Expression Web 2 skills.

In this chapter, you will first learn about choosing a template that best suits the site you want to build. Then you'll learn how to modify a template-based site by organizing its pages, modifying its Dynamic Web Template, and modifying its cascading style sheet files.

Important Before you can use the practice files in this chapter, you need to install them from the book's companion CD to their default location. For more information about practice files, see "Using the Companion CD" at the beginning of this book.

Troubleshooting Graphics and operating system–related instructions in this book reflect the Windows Vista user interface. If your computer is running Windows XP and you experience trouble following the instructions as written, please refer to the "Information for Readers Running Windows XP" section at the beginning of this book.

To improve the readability of the graphics in this book, Expression Web 2 was set to use the Windows color scheme instead of the default Expression Studio 2 color scheme.

Creating a Template-Based Site

As you approach the task of creating a new Web site based on one of the templates that Expression Web 2 provides, you'll be wise to first have an idea of what you want the outcome to look like, and to then look at each of the templates with an eye toward finding the one that most closely represents the look you're seeking.

In this exercise, you will choose one of the supplied templates and create a new site from it.

BE SURE TO start Expression Web 2 before beginning this exercise. If Expression Web 2 opens a previous site, click Close Site on the File menu.

1. On the **File** menu, point to **New**, and then click **Web Site**.

   The New dialog box opens, displaying the Web Site tab.

2. On the left side of the **New** dialog box, click **Templates**.

   The installed templates appear in the center pane of the dialog box.

3. Click each template to see a description and *thumbnail* view of the site in the pane on the right side of the dialog box.

4. Examine each template, and then click the **Organization 5** template.

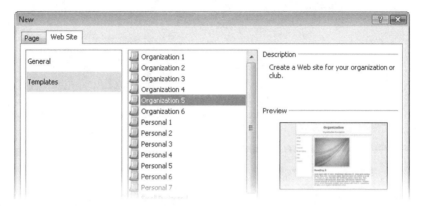

5. In the **New** dialog box, click **Browse**, and then navigate to the *Documents\My Web Sites* folder.

You will create the template-based site in this folder.

6. In the **New Web Site Location** dialog box displaying the contents of the *My Web Sites* folder, click the **New Folder** button, and then create a folder named **CH6**.

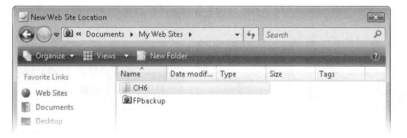

7. In the **New Web Site Location** dialog box, with the newly created *CH6* folder selected, click **Open**.

The New Web Site Location dialog box displays the selected location in the Specify The Location Of The New Web Site box.

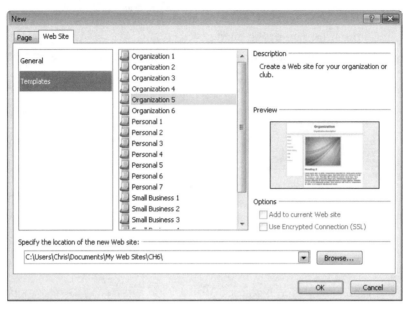

8. Click **OK**.

Expression Web 2 creates and opens a site based on the Organization 5 template.

9. In the **Folder List**, double-click the *default.html* page to have a closer look at what you've just created.

Because the Web site templates that come with Expression Web 2 rely on Dynamic Web Templates, an active cursor appears on only the content section of the page. Any changes you want to make to the template itself will be done by directly editing the Dynamic Web Template.

10. Preview this new page in a browser to see what it looks like as a visitor would encounter it, and be sure to click the links to the other pages within the site and examine them.

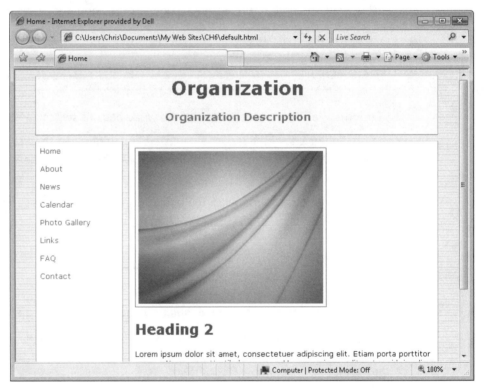

11. Close the browser window and return to Expression Web 2.

By this time, you should have a good idea of what pages are created with the template you selected, and which pages you want to keep, which pages you need to delete, and whether you need to add any pages that don't already exist.

 BE SURE TO leave the *CH6* site open for use in the next exercise.

Organizing Web Site Pages

After creating a site based on a template, as you did in the previous exercise, the first task you should undertake is organizing the pages. This task includes creating pages you need that don't yet exist, deleting pages you don't need, and organizing the folder locations and properties of existing pages.

In this exercise, you will delete the photo gallery and information links folders and the pages they contain, modify the properties of existing pages, and add a folder and a page.

> **USE** the *CH6* site you created in the previous exercise.
> **OPEN** the *CH6* site if it isn't already open.

1. Click the **Web Site** tab at the top of the workspace to switch to Web Site view.

2. In the **Folder List**, right-click the *photo_gallery* folder, and then click **Delete**. In the **Confirm Delete** message box, click **Yes**. Repeat this step for the *information_links* folder.

3. In the **Folder List**, double-click the *about* folder to expose the page within.

   The page is named *about.htm*.

4. Right-click *about.htm*, click **Rename**, and then rename the page **default.htm**. In the **Confirm Rename** message box asking whether you want to update all linked pages, click **Yes**.

5. Right-click the newly renamed *default.htm* page, and then click **Properties**.

6. In the **default.htm Properties** dialog box, change the original, and less than descriptive, *document title* from "About" to something like "About *site name*" or "About *business name*."

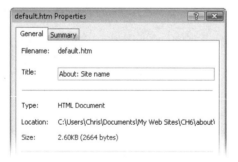

> **Tip** You can optimize search engine results by including the name of the business, person, or organization in the page title. To enhance search engine results for specific geographic regions, consider adding the business's or person's name, full address, and phone number at the bottom (footer area) of every page.

7. In the **default.htm Properties** dialog box, click **OK**.

8. Repeat steps 3 through 7 to rename the files listed in the following table to **default.htm**, and then change the page title to suit an actual Web site you're building or use the titles suggested in the table.

Folder	File	Title
calendar	calendar.htm	Calendar : Site Name
contact	contact.htm	Contact Us : Site Name
faq	faq.htm	Frequently Asked Questions : Site Name
news	news.htm	News : Site Name

Next, you will create another folder and page within the site.

New Document

9. In the **Folder List**, click the root folder. On the toolbar, click the **New Document** arrow, and then click **Folder**.

Expression Web 2 creates a folder named *New_Folder* and selects the folder name so you can change it.

10. Type **products**, and then press Enter.

To display content when a site visitor links to the *products* folder, you need to create a *default file* within it.

11. On the toolbar, click the **New Document** button.

Expression Web 2 creates a blank Web page named *Untitled_1.html*.

Save

12. On the toolbar, click **Save**.

13. In the **Save As** dialog box, navigate to the *products* folder. In the **File name** box, enter **default.htm**.

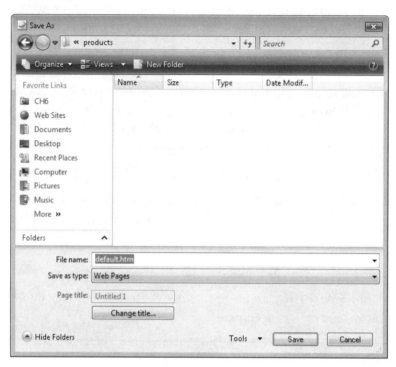

14. In the **Save As** dialog box, click **Change Title**, and give the page a title, such as **Products : Site Name**. Then click **Save**.

Notice that this page bears no resemblance to any of the other pages in this site. This is because this page is not attached to the Dynamic Web Template.

15. On the **Format** menu, point to **Dynamic Web Template**, and then click **Attach Dynamic Web Template**.

16. In the **Attach Dynamic Web Template** dialog box, browse to the site's *master.dwt* Dynamic Web Template, and select it.

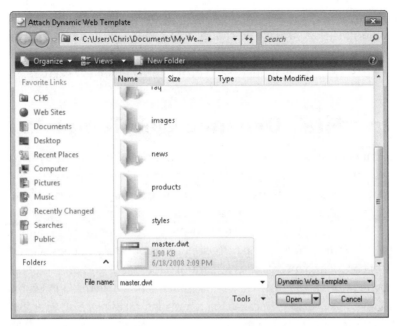

17. Click **OK** to close the dialog box and attach the template to your new page. Click **OK** in the **Update Confirmation** message box.

Your newly created page now has the correct template applied to it and is identical in style and layout to all the other pages in the site.

18. Click **Save** to save your changes.

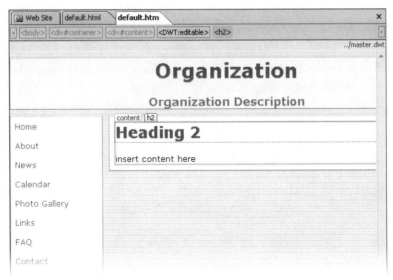

BE SURE TO leave the *CH6* site open for use in the next exercise.

You have just seen the big benefit of using Dynamic Web Templates to control layout of Web pages: There's virtually no chance that pages attached to a Dynamic Web Template can have an inconsistent appearance, not to mention the ease of maintaining *global elements* such as navigation, which you'll tackle in the next exercise.

Modifying a Site's Dynamic Web Template

All of the templates that are provided by Expression Web 2 use a Dynamic Web Template. There's a reason: it's virtually a necessity for today's Web site designer to use some sort of *templating system*, whether it's an ASP.NET *master page* arrangement, a Dynamic Web Template, or some other form of *server-side* template such as Smarty Template Engine (*http://smarty.net*) an open-source templating system for PHP files. Prior to the arrival of Expression Web 2, Web editing software used proprietary themes, shared borders, and all kinds of convoluted mechanisms to control page layout and presentation across a Web site. The Dynamic Web Template capabilities that are available through Expression Web 2 are still a "save time" feature, because the templating takes place on your local computer before your site is published to the server; so no proprietary server capabilities are required.

In this exercise, you will modify the Dynamic Web Template to reflect the navigational changes you made in the earlier exercises, you will add a link for the products page you created, and you will then add a logo to the top of the page.

> **USE** the *CH6* site you modified in the previous exercise.
> **OPEN** the *CH6* site if it isn't already open.

1. In the **Folder List**, double-click **master.dwt** in your site's root folder to open it for editing within Expression Web 2.

2. In Design view, in the left navigation section of the page, click **Photo Gallery**.

In the quick tag selector bar, notice that you're inside not only an <a> tag, but you're also inside an <li> list element because the navigation for this template is actually an unordered list.

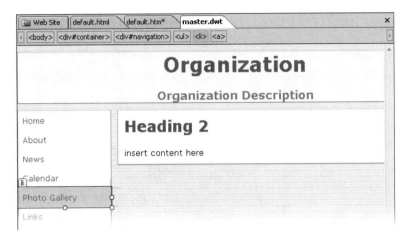

3. In the quick tag selector bar, click **<li>** to select the <a> tag and the <li> tag that contains it. Press Del to remove the link.

4. Repeat steps 2 and 3 for the list item and the link for the page titled *Links*.

   The two pages that you deleted are now removed from the navigation. Next, you will add a link for your new Products page.

5. In the Design pane, click just after the last letter in the word *Home* in the navigation section of the page, and then press Enter to break to a new line and create a new <li> tag. Type **Products**, select the word you just typed, right-click, and then click **Hyperlink**. In the **Insert Hyperlink** dialog box, browse to the *products* folder, and then click the *default.htm* file.

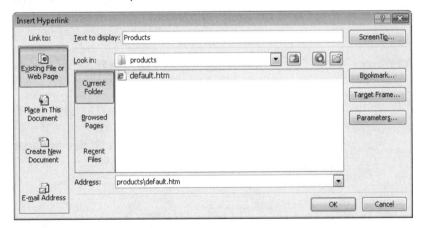

6. Click **OK** in the **Insert Hyperlink** dialog box to close it and set the link.

7. In the Design pane, click the bottom of the page just before the *pipe character* (|) that follows the entry for **Links**. Select back to and including the pipe character that follows the entry for **Calendar**, and then press Del to clear the removed pages from the lower link bar.

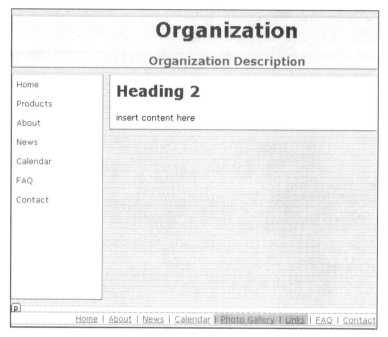

8. Click just after the pipe character that follows the entry for Home, press [Space], type **Products**, add another space, and then insert another pipe character (|) by pressing [Shift] + [\ ].

9. Select the word **Products**, being careful not to also include any empty spaces, right-click **Products**, and then click **Hyperlink**. In the **Insert Hyperlink** dialog box, browse to the *products* folder, and then click the **default.htm** file.

10. Click **OK** to close the dialog box and set the link.

11. In the **Folder List**, click the *images* folder. On the **File** menu, point to **Import**, and then click **File**.

12. In the **Import** dialog box, click **Add File**. In the **Add File to Import List** dialog box, navigate to the *Documents\Microsoft Press\Expression Web 2 SBS\Files* folder, select *logo.jpg* and *BGlogo.jpg*, and then click **Open** to add these images to the files list.

13. Click **OK** to import these images into your site's *images* folder.

14. In Design view, click the very beginning of the H1 element that contains *Organization*. On the **Insert** menu, point to **Picture**, and then click **From File**.

15. In the **Picture** dialog box, locate the *images* folder, click **logo.jpg**, and then click **Insert**. When you are prompted, give the image some descriptive alternate text, and then click **OK** to close the dialog box and insert the image.

Notice that your logo image is centered, along with the H1 element that contains it.

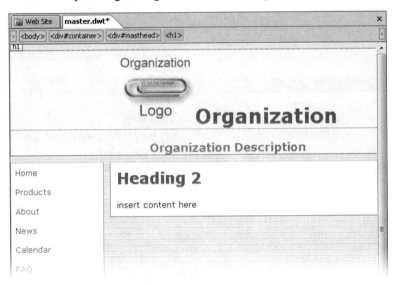

16. Right-click the image, and then click **Picture Properties**. On the **Appearance** tab, change the **Wrapping Style** to **Left**, and then click **OK** to close the dialog box.

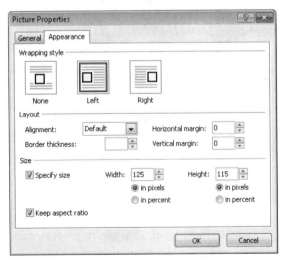

Your logo image now floats to the left of the text elements within the top banner of your page.

17. Save the page. In the message box that opens, asking if you want to update all the pages linked to the Dynamic Web Template, click **Yes**.

18. Open the *default.html* page from the root folder, and preview it in a browser. Check your links and layout to make sure that your changes to the Dynamic Web Template are present in the pages that the template is attached to.

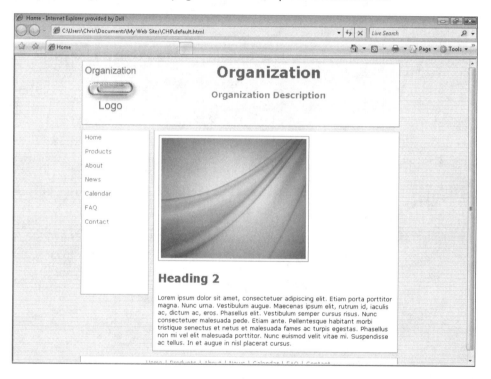

 BE SURE TO leave the *CH6* site open for use in the next exercise.

Obviously, if this exercise were the actual creation of a site, you would be working on other elements such as changing the text of the headings in the top banner, possibly adding graphics or other elements to the left navigation area, and other modifications that would be necessary for a real Web site. You should now be comfortable with working in a Dynamic Web Template to the extent that you will continue with the tasks that are needed to design a professional-looking Web site.

Modifying a Site's Cascading Style Sheets

As a wrap-up of the presentational work you started by modifying the Dynamic Web Template in the previous exercise, you will likely want to make some changes to colors, backgrounds, and other presentational elements of the template, which are controlled by the site's cascading style sheets.

In this exercise, you will modify the background of the top banner in order to provide a more visually appealing logo. You will change the behavior of the links in the lower navigation bar, and you'll experiment with the additional style sheets you will find within the site's *styles* folder that are provided by Expression Web 2.

> **USE** the *CH6* site you modified in the previous exercise.
> **OPEN** the *CH6* site if it isn't already open.

1. Open the *master.dwt* file located at the root of the site. On the **Format** menu, point to **CSS Styles**, and then click **Manage Style Sheet Links**.

    The Link Style Sheet dialog box opens.

    By default, this site's Dynamic Web Template is linked to *style2.css* in the *styles* subfolder.

2. Click **styles/style2.css**, and then click **Remove**. Next, click **Add**, navigate to the *styles* folder, and then click the *style1.css* file. Click **OK** to close the dialog box and switch to your page.

3. On the **File** menu, click **Save All**. Accept the updates to the Dynamic Web Template's attached pages, and then preview in a browser the *default.html* file from the root folder.

Notice the radical change that is present in the page visually.

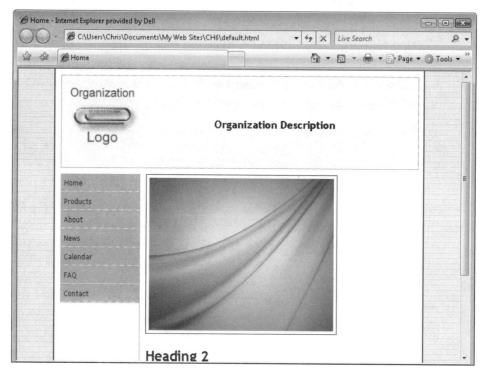

It's amazing that you can change the entire presentation of every page in a Web site without changing one single line of HTML code in the pages.

4. Close the browser window and switch to Expression Web 2 and the Dynamic Web Template. Repeat steps 2 and 3. However, this time, attach *style3.css*.

5. After you've examined the site when it has *style3.css* attached, close the browser, switch to Expression Web 2, and change the style sheet back to the *style2.css* file that was originally attached.

> **Tip** Every one of the templates that come with Expression Web 2 contains multiple style sheets. When you use one of these templates, make sure to check these alternate style sheets. They'll always be in the *styles* folder. If you're interested in seeing what other site developers can do with a style sheet, go to *www.csszengarden.com*. There, you'll find a single HTML file and dozens of user-submitted cascading style sheet files that style the HTML file. Some of the cascading style sheet files are incredible, but they all exhibit the variety of design effects style sheets can have on HTML files.

6. In Design view, click the logo image that you inserted in the previous exercise, and press ⌷Del. On the quick tag selector bar, click **<div#masthead>**.

7. In the **Manage Styles** task pane, right-click the second **<#masthead>** entry, and then click **Modify Style**.

The Modify Style dialog box opens.

> **Tip** The first <#masthead> entry is for the layout style sheet. Expression Web 2 uses indentation to show which style is on which style sheet. The Selected Style preview pane can be helpful in helping you decide which selector and on which style sheet you're working.
>
>

8. In the **Category** list, click **Background**, and then change the **background-color** value from *#fafaff* to **#C0C0C0**. Next to the **background-image** box, click **Browse**, locate the *images* folder, and then double-click the *BGlogo.jpg* image. In the **background-repeat** list, click **no-repeat**. In the **(x) background-position** list, click **left**.

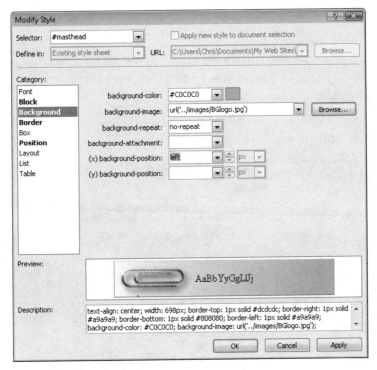

9. In the **Category** list, click **Position**. Type **115** into the **height** box, and then click **OK** to save your changes and close the dialog box.

10. Save the *master.dwt* file.

You will be prompted with the Save Embedded Files dialog box.

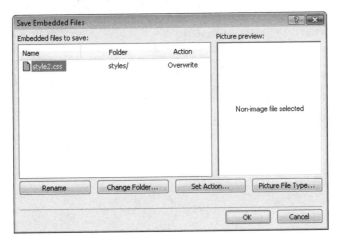

11. Accept the default **Overwrite** action, and click **OK** to save the file and close the dialog box.

12. When you are asked whether to save the changes to all the files in the site that this Dynamic Web Template is attached to, click **Yes**, and then click **Close** in the **Update Confirmation** message box.

13. Preview the *default.html* page from the root folder in a browser, and look at the presentation of the top banner.

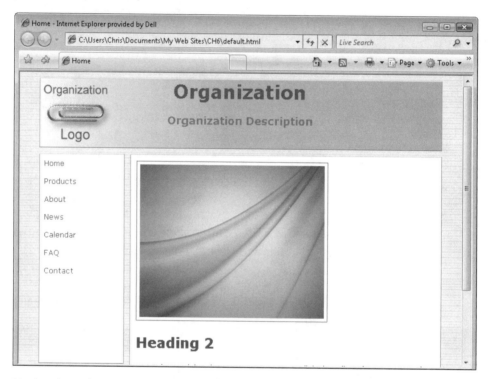

Notice that a logo has floated to the left and has a gradient that blends into the DIV element's background color on the right. Notice also that the header elements are not skewed to the right as they were in the example in the previous exercise.

14. Close the browser window and switch to Expression Web 2 and the Dynamic Web Template.

15. In Split view, double-click one of the links at the bottom of the site's Dynamic Web Template.

In the quick tag selector bar, notice that an <a> tag is inside a <div#footer> tag.

16. In the **Manage Styles** task pane on the lower right of the workspace, right-click the entry for **#footer a:hover**, and then click **Modify Style.**

17. In the **Modify Style** dialog box, click **Font** in the **Category** list.

Notice that the None check box is selected under text-decoration.

18. Select the **underline** and **overline** check boxes, which automatically clears the **none** check box.

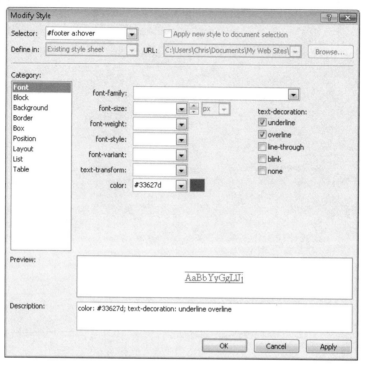

19. Click **OK** to change the style and close the dialog box.

20. Return to the Dynamic Web Template, and click one of the links in the footer again. In the **Manage Styles** task pane, right-click **#footer a**, and then click **Modify Style** to open the **Modify Style** dialog box.

The Underline check box is selected under text-decoration.

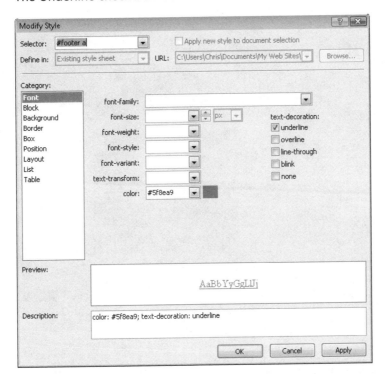

21. Select the **none** check box, click **OK** to save and close the dialog box, and then save the Dynamic Web Template. At the prompt in the **Save Embedded Files** dialog box, accept the default settings to save the file. Then accept the updates to attached pages, and click **OK** in the **Update Confirmation** message box.

22. Preview the *default.html* page from the root folder in a browser, and review your work.

Notice the rollover effect on the lower navigation bar.

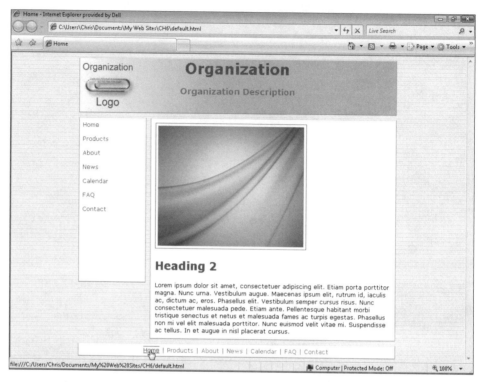

Now the links show no underline by default, and when you point to them, they show an underline and overline.

CLOSE the *CH6* site and any open browsers. If you are not continuing directly to the next chapter, exit Expression Web 2.

Key Points

- Expression Web 2 provides a number of Web site templates that you can use.
- Each template contains multiple style sheets, each giving the site a distinctively different appearance.
- Dynamic Web Templates are used in each of the Expression Web 2 site templates.
- Sweeping changes can be made on every page in a Web site by simply modifying the Dynamic Web Template.
- Changes to a Dynamic Web Template will be automatically applied to all pages the template is attached to.
- Modifying the cascading style sheets file for a site template causes all pages in the site to reflect those changes.

Chapter at a Glance

Import and use graphics and templates, **page 165**

Create a Dynamic Web Template, **page 170**

Organize your site, **page 179**

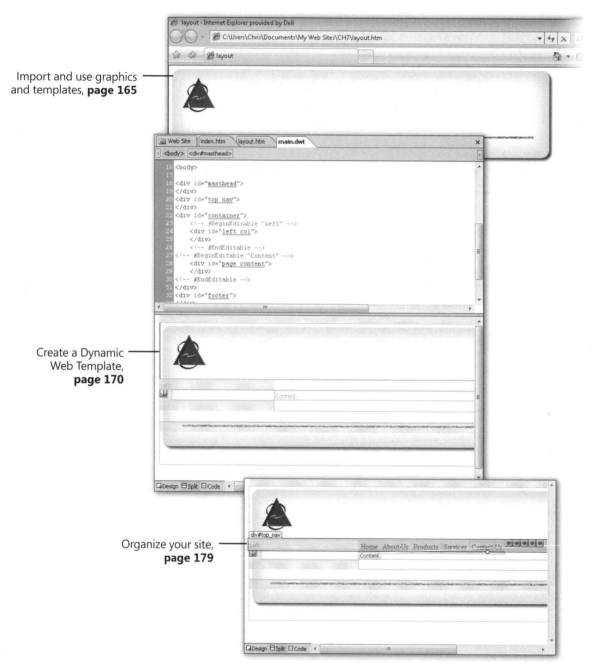

7 Creating a Web Site from Scratch

In this chapter, you will learn to

✔ Create an empty site.

✔ Import and use graphics and templates.

✔ Create a Dynamic Web Template.

✔ Create content pages.

✔ Organize your site.

Starting a site from scratch is usually done when a designer has designed the underlying graphics for the pages and is ready to translate the graphic elements into an HTML document. A designer sets up these graphics in a graphics editing application such as Microsoft Expression Design, Adobe Photoshop, Adobe Fireworks, or any other graphics application. In addition to designing the overall page graphics, the designer will *slice* the graphics, which results in multiple pieces of the original graphic that can be used in an HTML document as buttons, backgrounds, and various other graphic elements.

Another reason for starting a site from scratch might be that the designer purchased a template from an online outlet, such as Template Monster, Pixelmill, Classy Themes, or any of hundreds of other sites that sell Web site *template packages*.

Regardless of the reason for starting a Web site from scratch, the major work isn't in building the collection of pages that make up the site, but in developing that one single template page that all the other pages are based on.

Fortunately, Microsoft Expression Web 2 has all the tools that you need to start with an empty site and end up with a valid and accessible HTML template.

In this chapter, you will learn how to create an empty site, how to import and use graphics and templates, and how to create a Dynamic Web Template. You will learn to create content pages, and then you'll learn how to organize your site.

> **Important** Before you can use the practice files in this chapter, you need to install them from the book's companion CD to their default location. For more information about practice files, see "Using the Companion CD" at the beginning of this book.

> **Troubleshooting** Graphics and operating system–related instructions in this book reflect the Windows Vista user interface. If your computer is running Windows XP and you experience trouble following the instructions as written, please refer to the "Information for Readers Running Windows XP" section at the beginning of this book.
>
> To improve the readability of the graphics in this book, Expression Web 2 was set to use the Windows color scheme instead of the default Expression Studio 2 color scheme.

Creating an Empty Site

The first step in creating a site from scratch is to create a container for all the pages, folders, and images that will eventually reside within the site. Sometimes called a *root folder*, in Expression Web 2 this container is called a *site*, and it generally contains metadata that allows Expression Web 2 to keep track of various site details, including what pages the site contains, how the pages link to each other, when each file was last modified, and where the Web site has been published to. An empty site is much more than just an empty folder.

> **Tip** To change the Expression Web 2 default behavior of opening with the last site you worked on, on the Tools menu, click Application Options, and then on the General tab, clear the Open Last Web Site Automatically When Expression Web 2 Starts check box.

In this exercise, you will create an empty site and a page to serve as a template.

 BE SURE TO start Expression Web 2 before beginning this exercise. If Expression Web 2 opens a previous site, click Close Site on the File menu.

1. On the **File** menu, point to **New**, and then click **Web Site**. In the middle of the **New** dialog box, click **Empty Web Site**.

New Folder

2. Click the **Browse** button to the right of the **Location** box. Navigate to the *Documents\My Web Sites* folder. In the **New Web Site Location** dialog box displaying the contents of the *My Web Sites* folder, click the **New Folder** button, and create a folder named **CH7** for the new site. Then click **Open**.

You return to the New dialog box, and the location you just created appears in the Specify The Location Of The New Web Site box.

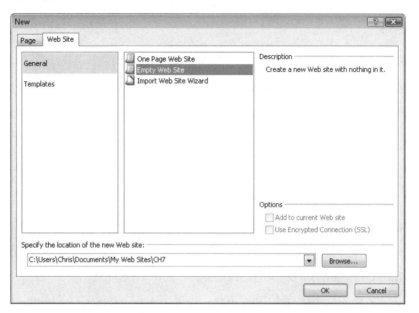

3. Click **OK** to create the site and close the dialog box.

A newly created, empty site opens in Expression Web 2. The first thing you need to do for your new site is create a folder to contain your graphics.

4. Right-click in the main workspace, point to **New**, and then click **Folder**. Name this newly created folder **images**.

This folder will serve as a container for all of the images you will use in your site.

The next thing you need is a page that you can use to start creating a template. You could start a Dynamic Web Template at this point, but it's easier to create a layout on a regular page, and then transfer that content over to a Dynamic Web Template later.

5. On the **File** menu, point to **New**, and then click **Page**. On the **Page** tab of the **New** dialog box, click **CSS layouts**, and then click **Header, nav, 2 columns, footer** (the fifth layout in the CSS layout list).

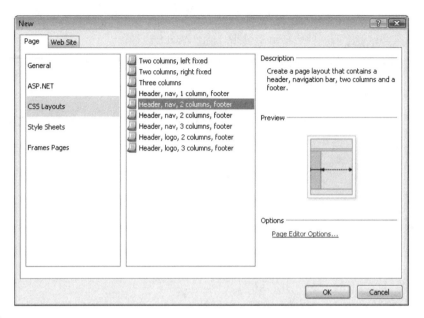

6. In the **New** dialog box, click **OK** to create the page.

Save

7. On the toolbar, click **Save**. In the **Save As** dialog box, click **Change title**. In the **Page title** field of the **Set Page Title** dialog box, type **layout**, and click **OK**. Then in the **File name** box, type **layout**.

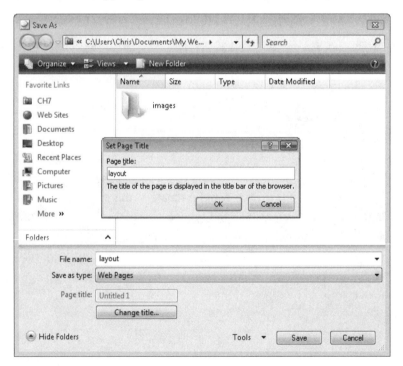

8. Click **Save** in the **Save As** dialog box.

You are prompted to save the CSS file that was created along with the new page.

9. Name the CSS file **main**, and then click **Save** to save it in the root folder of your site.

 BE SURE TO leave the *CH7* site open for use in the next exercise.

Visual Aids

When you create a page containing non-specific content such as DIV elements and styles, you will see visual representations of that content in Design view only if you display the visual aids.

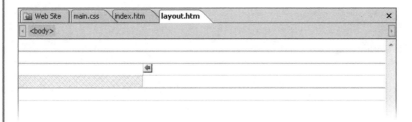

When the visual aids are hidden, you see only a blank page.

To display visual aids:

→ Point to **Visual Aids** on the **View** menu, click **Show**, and select all of the **Show** options.

That wraps up creating an empty site and adding a file to serve as your initial template layout page. It's a fairly simple process, but performing it as in the preceding steps ensures that Expression Web 2 will keep all of the files segregated from other folders and files on your hard disk. Expression Web 2 will also establish metadata, so that the application can keep track of some behind-the-scenes details and make sure that file associations within the site will be kept up to date and accurate.

Importing and Using Graphics and Templates

To start laying out graphics and progressing in the next exercise, you need to get all the graphics and associated files into your site structure. Although there are a number of ways to bring these files into your site structure, many of them can be problematic.

It's important to carefully follow the examples and instructions in the following exercise. The recommended method that is presented in the next exercise will ensure that Expression Web 2 recognizes what you're bringing in and can keep track of the locations of these files. Expression Web 2 will also recognize the files' physical size, file size, and date of last modification, among other things.

In this exercise, you will import graphics and use them in an HTML page.

> **Important**   For the following exercise, you need a graphics template. It can be from a commercial site such as one of those mentioned in the beginning of this chapter, or you can have one that you created yourself using your preferred graphics editor. Either way, graphics editors generally export your work under the same paradigm: they output an HTML file and sliced graphics to a folder.

> **USE**   the *CH7* site that you created in the preceding exercise.
>
> **OPEN**   the *CH7* site, if it isn't already open.

1. In the **Folder List**, click the root folder. On the **File** menu, point to **Import**, and then click **File**.

2. In the **Import** dialog box that opens, click **Add Folder**. In the **File Open** dialog box, navigate to the *Documents\Microsoft Press\Expression Web 2 SBS\Files\ CH7template* folder, and then click **Open**.

   The Import dialog box now displays all of the files inside the *CH7template* folder.

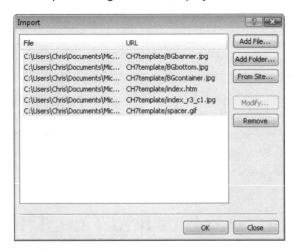

3. Click **OK** to import the folder and all of the files it contains.

4. In the **Folder List**, double-click the newly imported *CH7template* folder to expose the files it contains. Double-click the *index.htm* file within it and examine the layout.

Tip Although you cannot use this layout file for your template, it is valuable because you can use it to see what size the images are. You can also check the file size of the overall page in the lower-right corner of your design area. Split view is particularly helpful in this situation.

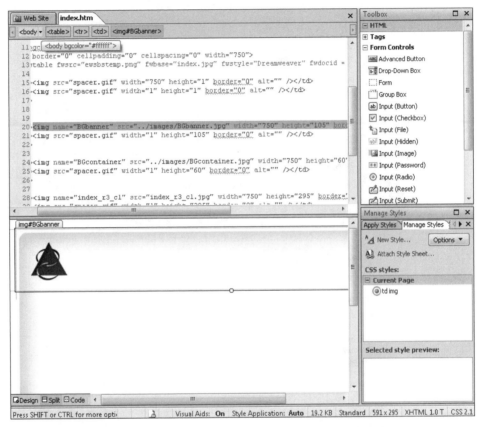

5. Open the *layout.htm* file that you created in the preceding exercise.

The first thing you need to do is appropriately style the *#container* DIV element.

6. In the *index.htm* file, locate *BGcontainer.jpg*. This graphic is 750 pixels wide and 60 pixels high. Switch to the *layout.htm* file, and on the quick tag selector bar, click **div#container**.

7. In the **CSS Properties** task pane, expand the **background** entry, click **background-image**, click the ellipsis button (...), and in the *CH7template* folder, click the *BGcontainer.jpg* file, and then click **Open**.

8. In the **CSS Properties** task pane, set the **background-repeat** value to **repeat-y**.

> **Tip** To make the following steps easier from a visual-aid perspective, on the View menu, turn on Visual Aids: Block Selection, Visible Borders, Empty Containers, Margins And Padding, and Template Region Labels. You may also find some visual assistance if you also turn on Formatting Marks: Positioned Absolute and Aligned Elements.

9. Change the **width** value to **750px**.

10. In the *layout.htm* file, select the top DIV element, which has the CSS ID **masthead**.

This DIV element uses the top image on the template page, *BGbanner.jpg*, which has a width of 750 pixels and a height of 105 pixels.

11. In the **CSS Properties** task pane, find the **background-image** entry, and then select *BGbanner.jpg*, and click **Open**. Set the **background-repeat** value to **no-repeat**, the **height** to **105px**, and the **width** to **750px**.

12. In the Code pane, click the bottom DIV element. In the **CSS Properties** task pane, click the ellipsis button (...) for the **background-image** value, and then, in the *CH7template* folder, double-click the *BGbottom.jpg* file.

13. Set the **background-repeat** value to **no-repeat**, the **height** to **60px**, and the **width** to **750px**. Save the page, and preview it in a browser.

The key page areas now have appropriate background images, and what was once an empty page is now beginning to have the appearance of a "real" Web page.

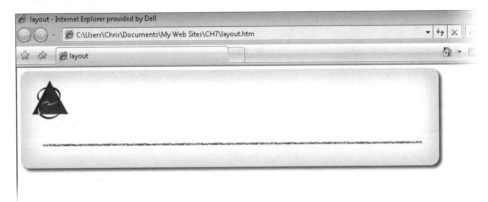

14. Return to Expression Web 2, and then click the DIV element with a CSS ID of **top_nav**. In the **CSS Properties** task pane, click the ellipsis button (...) for the **background-image** value, and then double-click *BGcontainer.jpg* in the *CH7template* folder.

15. Set the **background-repeat** value of this DIV element to **no-repeat**, the **width** to **750px**, and the **height** to **20px**.

16. In the Code pane, click the DIV element with a CSS ID of **left_col**. In the **CSS Properties** task pane, change the **left** value from 0px to **25px**.

The DIV element moves to the right 25 pixels so that navigation or content in the DIV element will be clear of the shadow area at the edge of the container.

17. In the Code pane, click the DIV element with a CSS ID of **page_content**. In the **CSS Properties** task pane, change the **margin-left** value from **200px** to **225px** to make up for the movement of the adjacent **left_col** DIV element that you modified in step 16.

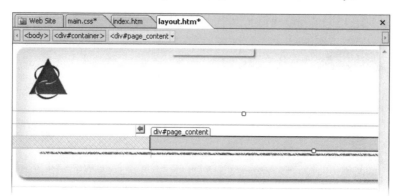

This concludes the process of inserting graphics into an HTML template as backgrounds for the DIV elements so that you can place content into them.

18. Save your page, and preview it in a browser for a final check.

BE SURE TO leave the *CH7* site open for use in the next exercise.

CLOSE any open Internet Explorer windows.

If you were actually creating a site, you'd still have work to do, such as styling the text that falls into the content area, designing and styling the links in the top navigation, and all kinds of other things. Taking you through each individual facet of CSS design is beyond the scope of this book, but you can easily use the lessons in previous chapters to enhance the design of this template. The preceding chapters contain examples of using cascading style sheets for navigation, content, lists, and other page elements.

Creating a Dynamic Web Template

When your general layout is done and your style sheet is able to present your layout and background as you want them, it's time to move the design to a Dynamic Web Template so that you can easily attach the design to any number of pages that you require. You'll also gain the benefit of updating the template in one single location, and of having those changes immediately affect all of the pages that are attached to the Dynamic Web Template.

In this exercise, you will create a Dynamic Web Template, move your layout design into it, and set up editable regions in both the visible Design view and the Code view (*HEAD* element).

USE the *CH7* site that you modified in the preceding exercise.

OPEN the *CH7* site if it isn't already open.

1. In the **Folder List**, click the root folder. In the **New Document** list, click **Page**.

The New dialog box opens.

2. In the **General** category on the **Page** tab, click **Dynamic Web Template**, and then click **OK** to create the Dynamic Web Template and close the dialog box.

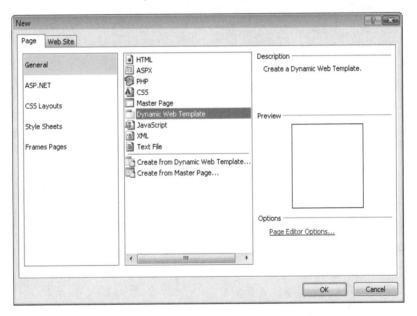

A file named *Untitled_1.dwt* is now open in Expression Web 2. Notice that this page has one <div> tag and one editable region named *body*. You need to move the layout from your previous page (*layout.htm*) into this page and set up editable regions where you want them.

3. Open the *layout.htm* file, and then, on the quick tag selector bar, click **<body>**.

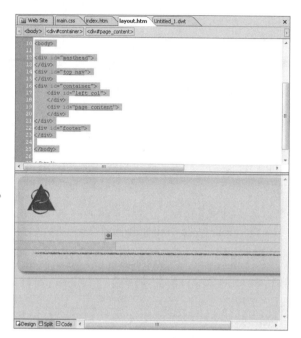

4. In the Code pane, right-click the highlighted code, and then click **Copy**.

5. Switch to the *Untitled_1.dwt* file, and then, on the quick tag selector bar, click **<body>**. In the Code pane, right-click the highlighted code, and then click **Paste**.

You've just transferred the layout of your original template page to this Dynamic Web Template. Notice that the Dynamic Web Template doesn't look at all like your original layout page. That's because it's not linked to the appropriate style sheet.

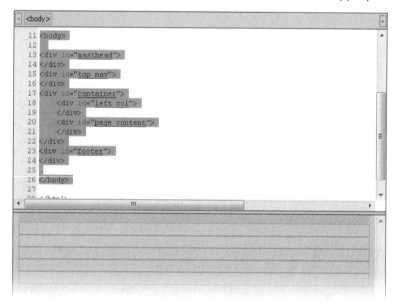

6. On the **Format** menu, point to **CSS Styles**, and then click **Attach Style Sheet**. In the **Attach Style Sheet** dialog box, click **Browse**, and double-click the *main.css* file, located in the root of your site.

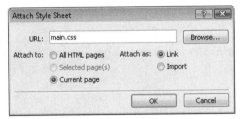

7. Click **OK** to attach the style sheet and close the dialog box.

Now your Dynamic Web Template looks identical to the layout page that you previously made.

Save

8. On the toolbar, click **Save** to save your changes to the Dynamic Web Template. In the **Save As** dialog box, give the template a file name of **main**. Click **Change title**, and change the title to **Template**.

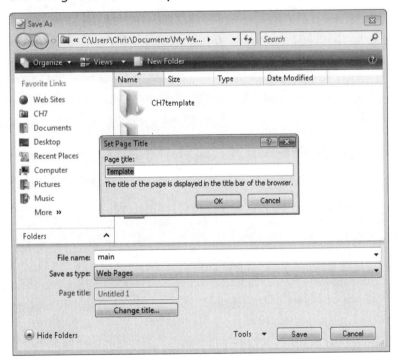

9. Click **OK**, and then click **Save** to save the file and close the **Save As** dialog box.

Now that your Dynamic Web Template is set up to look like the template you had at the beginning of this exercise, you need to add some editable regions to it. Rather than start in the obvious places (div#left_col and div#page_content), you're going to set up an editable region in the HEAD element.

10. Set your Dynamic Web Template in Split view, and scroll to the top of the file.

You'll see code that looks like this:

```
<head>
<meta content="text/html; charset=utf-8" http-equiv="Content-Type" /><!--
#BeginEditable "doctitle" -->
<title>Template</title>
<!-- #EndEditable -->
<link href="main.css" rel="stylesheet" type="text/css" />
</head>
```

As you can see, there's an editable region wrapped around the <title> element. This is in place so that each file you attach to the Dynamic Web Template can have its own unique title. It's a start, but it's not enough.

11. Right-click the Design pane, and click **Page Properties**. In the **Page Properties** dialog box, in the **Page description** box, type **This is the description of this particular page**. Type some keywords into the **Keywords** box. It doesn't matter what you put there for now, but you should use comma-separated words, such as **keyword, keywords, other keywords**. Click **OK** to close the dialog box.

In the Code pane, the beginning of the Dynamic Web Template now looks like this:

```
<head>
<meta content="text/html; charset=utf-8" http-equiv="Content-Type" />
<!-- #BeginEditable "doctitle" -->
<title>Template</title>
<!-- #EndEditable -->
<meta content="keyword, keywords, other keywords" name="keywords" />
<meta content="This is the description of this particular page"
name="description" />
<link href="main.css" rel="stylesheet" type="text/css" />
</head>
```

12. To include the keywords and description meta elements into the editable region, select the line *<!-- #EndEditable -->*, right-click the highlighted text, and then click **Cut**. Click just after the closing angle bracket at the end of the description <meta> element, and press Enter to advance one line. Right-click, and then click **Paste**.

The code now looks like this:

```
<head>
<meta content="text/html; charset=utf-8" http-equiv="Content-Type" /><!--
#BeginEditable "doctitle" -->
<title>Template</title>
<meta content="keyword, keywords, other keywords" name="keywords" />
<meta content="This is the description of this particular page"
name="description" />
<!-- #EndEditable -->
<link href="main.css" rel="stylesheet" type="text/css" />
</head>
```

You have moved the close of the editable region to below the keywords and description `<meta>` tags, ensuring that they can be changed in all of the pages that attach to the Dynamic Web Template.

13. On the toolbar, click **Save** to save the changes to the *main.dwt* file.

The next regions you set can be done through the graphical user interface (GUI).

14. In the Code pane, click the **page_content** DIV element. On the **Format** menu, point to **Dynamic Web Template**, and then click **Manage Editable Regions**.

The Editable Regions dialog box opens.

15. In the **Editable Regions** dialog box, type **Content**. Click **Add** to create a new editable region, and then click **Close**.

16. In the Code pane, click the **left_col** DIV element. On the **Format** menu, point to **Dynamic Web Template**, and then click **Manage Editable Regions**. In the **Editable Regions** dialog box, name the region **Left**, click **Add**, and then click **Close**.

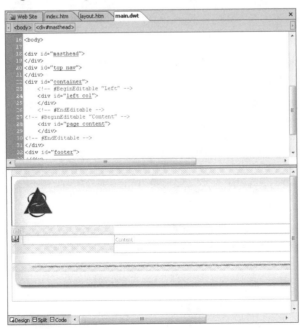

The editable regions are the only areas that a user can edit in a file that is attached to them, but you can enter any text into these areas. For example, you might want to enter some instructional text for your end user, such as a paragraph or two about what kind of text to enter, or how to perform certain operations. Although this text will show up in the content page when it's initially attached to the Dynamic Web Template, users can replace it with their own content.

17. For now, leave the editable regions as they are, and save the *main.dwt* file.

 BE SURE TO leave the *CH7* site open for use in the next exercise.

In the preceding exercise, you created a usable Dynamic Web Template at its most basic level. You would normally work on other things also, such as entering and styling a heading for the company name in the #masthead section, and maybe adding a slogan to be visible beside it. You would certainly enter and style a menu in the #top_nav DIV element, and you'd add links to certain key pages and a copyright notice in the #footer DIV element. All of these tasks should be obvious, and most of them would be done after the additional pages are created. You'll find examples and exercises to provide deeper detail on these tasks in other chapters in this book.

Creating Content Pages

Two important reasons for using Dynamic Web Templates are:

- The ability to create new pages that carry the same template as all other pages in a site or group of pages.

- To enable end users to edit, enter, and change content on the pages without the possibility of damaging the template.

In this exercise, you will create new pages that are based on a Dynamic Web Template, and you'll edit these pages and their page properties.

 USE the *CH7* site you modified in the previous exercise.
OPEN the *CH7* site if it isn't already open.

1. In the **New Document** list, click **Create from Dynamic Web Template**. In the **Attach Dynamic Web Template** dialog box, click **main.dwt**.

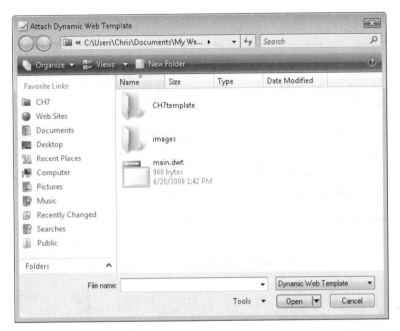

2. In the **Attach Dynamic Web Template** dialog box, click **Open**. Click **Close** on the **Update Confirmation** message box.

   Expression Web 2 creates a new page named *Untitled_1.html*.

Save

3. On the toolbar, click **Save** to save the new page. In the **File name** box of the **Save As** dialog box, type **default**, and then click **Change Title**. In the **Page title** box of the **Set Page Title** dialog box, type **Home Page**, and then click **OK**. In the **Save As** dialog box, click **Save** to save the page and close the dialog box.

   Notice that when you move the mouse pointer over the newly saved *default.html* file, it takes the form of an insertion point only in those editable regions.

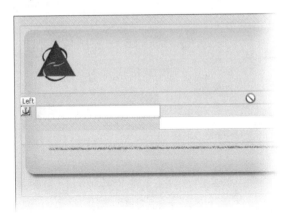

> **Tip** If you have a preference for the default file extension for HTM/HTML pages, you
> can easily set your preference by clicking Page Editor Options on the Tools menu, and
> on the Authoring tab of the Page Editor Options dialog box, select either .html or
> .htm for the Default HTML File Extension option.

4. Right-click the Design pane, and then click **Page Properties**.

    In the Page Properties dialog box, notice that you can see the same keywords and
    description that you set up in the Dynamic Web Template earlier in this exercise.

5. Change the content of the **Page description** and **Keywords** boxes to something that
    is appropriate for the page.

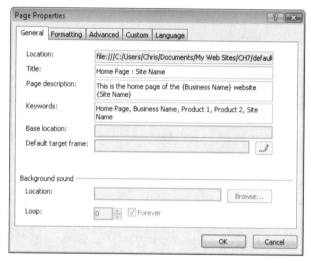

6. Click **OK** to close the **Page Properties** dialog box.

7. Repeat steps 1 through 6 to create some additional pages for your site. For this
    example, create the following pages: *about.html*, *products.html*, *services.html*,
    contact.html, and *legal.html*.

Tip You might find it faster to right-click the first page you created, click Copy, and then press Ctrl+V as many times as you need pages. Then, in Folders view, right-click the page, and click Rename. Open each page, right-click the Design pane, click Page Properties, and then change the content in the Title, Page Description, and Keywords boxes.

 BE SURE TO leave the *CH7* site open for use in the next exercise.

In the preceding exercise, you created enough pages to get your site project under way and to give you some pages to build menus for. This whole paradigm of a Dynamic Web Template to contain all of a site's common elements and content pages results in a powerful way to work. Not only can you keep end users from breaking your template, but you can also make it easy for users to work only in defined areas within pages.

You might have noticed that the Dynamic Web Template/Content Page arrangement is a very quick way to create a collection of pages. To go a step further, you could design a slightly different Dynamic Web Template for each section of a site, or multiple Dynamic Web Templates to provide different presentations. The Dynamic Web Template is also a great tool for a designer to use in order to show a client several different layouts, and when the client decides on a particular layout, it's a painless matter to build all of the necessary pages for the project based on the chosen template.

Organizing Your Site

Now that you have a collection of pages that are attached to a Dynamic Web Template, it's time to create some navigation to link them together and some basic text and links for the footer, and to clean up leftover pages and unnecessary files.

It's easier to keep unused files out of your site on an ongoing basis or at key milestones than it is to allow them to accumulate and then try to clean it all up at the end of the project.

In this exercise, you will create basic navigation, delete unnecessary pages, and organize your site.

 USE the *CH7* site that you modified in the previous exercise.
OPEN the *CH7* site, if it isn't already open, and close any open pages.

1. Open the *main.dwt* file in Split view.

To make a navigation bar for this site, you'll use an unordered list and place it in the top_nav DIV element of the *main.dwt* file.

2. Open the *CH7CSS* text file located in the *CH7template* folder you imported earlier, and copy its contents to the Clipboard. Then, switch to Expression Web 2 and the *main.dwt* file. In the Code pane, find the underlined style ID **top_nav**, hold down the ⌨Ctrl key, and click **top_nav**.

```html
<body>  <div#top_nav>

18
19 <body>
20
21 <div id="masthead">
22 </div>
23 <div id="top_nav">
24 <ul>
25     <li><a href="default.htm">Home</a></li>
26     <li><a href="about.htm">About Us</a></li>
27     <li><a href="products.htm">Products</a></li>
28     <li><a href="services.htm">Services</a></li>
29     <li><a href="contact.htm">Contact Us</a></li>
30 </ul>
31 </div>
32 <div id="container">
33     <div id="left_col">
```

This is called a code hyperlink and the effect is that it opens the style sheet it's linked to with that particular class or ID highlighted.

```css
Web Site   main.dwt*   main.css*                                    ×
1 /* CSS layout */
2 #masthead {
3     background-image: url('images/BGbanner.jpg');
4     background-repeat: no-repeat;
5     height: 105px;
6     width: 750px;
7 }
8
9 #top_nav {
10     background: url('images/BGcontainer.jpg') no-repeat;
11     height: 20px;
12     width: 750px;
13 }
14
15 #container {
16     position: relative;
17     width: 750px;
18     background-image: url('images/BGcontainer.jpg');
19     background-repeat: repeat-y;
20     height: 60px;
21 }
22
23 #left_col {
24     width: 200px;
25     position: absolute;
26     left: 25px;
27     top: 0px;
28 }
29
30 #page_content {
31     margin-left: 225px;
32 }
33
34 #footer {
35     background-image: url('images/BGbottom.jpg');
36     background-repeat: no-repeat;
37     height: 60px;
38     width: 750px;
39     font-size: x-small;
40     color: #810101;
41     text-align: center;
42     padding-top: 20px;
43 }
```

3. Right-click the highlighted code, click **Paste**, and then save the CSS file. Switch to *main.dwt*.

> **Tip** Rather than running through one more exercise on building cascading style sheets in Expression Web 2, you can simply copy and paste the code from the sample disk. If you're interested in seeing what happens in the Expression Web 2 interface, you can use the Manage Styles task pane to explore it within the Modify Styles dialog box.

Bullets

4. In the Design pane, click the **top_nav** DIV element. On the toolbar, click the **Bullets** button to set an unordered list, and then type: **Home**, **About Us**, **Products**, **Services**, and **Contact Us**, pressing `Enter` between each to make each of these entries a new list item.

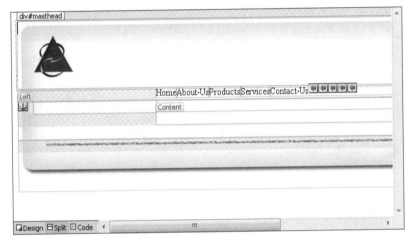

5. In the Design pane, for each of the list items you entered in the previous step, select the text, right-click the selected text, and click **Hyperlink**. Then in the **Insert Hyperlink** dialog box, click the appropriate page, and click **OK**.

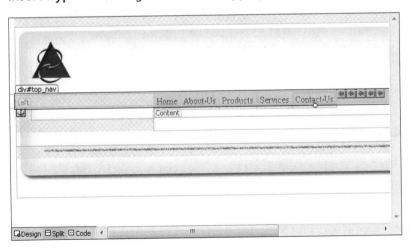

> **Tip** Double-clicking a word selects the entire word, and triple-clicking selects all of the words in a list item, or paragraph (such as About Us). In the Insert Hyperlink dialog box, double-clicking the page you want to link to selects that page and closes the dialog box.

6. Click the **footer** DIV element in the template. In the **Manage Styles** task pane, right-click **#footer**, and then click **Modify Style**. In the **Modify Style** dialog box, under the **Font** category, give the **font-size** a value of **x-small**, click the swatch next to **color**, pick up the eyedropper tool, select the burgundy color in the logo of your Dynamic Web Template, and then click **OK**.

7. In the **Category** list, click **Block**. Set the **text-align** value to **center**.

8. In the **Category** list, click **Box**. Clear the **Same for all** check box for the **padding**, and then set the padding's **top** value to **20 px**.

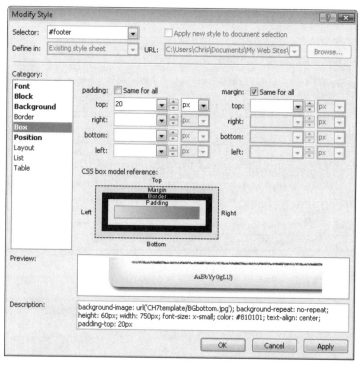

9. Click **OK** to close the dialog box and save your changes.

10. In the Design pane, type a copyright statement such as **Copyright 2008 SampleSite, 123 Any Street, Some Town, Some State. All rights reserved** into the **footer** DIV element in your *main.dwt* file.

11. Select the entire line that you typed in the previous step, right-click the highlighted text, click **Hyperlink**, click *legal.htm*, and then click **OK** to close the **Insert Hyperlink** dialog box.

Notice that when you set your hyperlink on that line of text, it loses its burgundy color and becomes the default blue of a normal hyperlink.

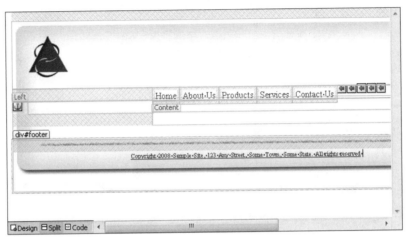

12. In the **Manage Styles** task pane, click **New Style**. In the **New Style** dialog box, give the **Selector** a value of **#footer a**. In the **Font** category, give the **color** entry a value of **#810101**, and then click **OK** to close the dialog box.

13. Save your page. When prompted, allow the CSS file to save, overwrite, and allow the Dynamic Web Template to update all the pages it's attached to.

14. Preview *default.html* in a browser and check your work. Click the navigation links and footer link to make sure they're all correct.

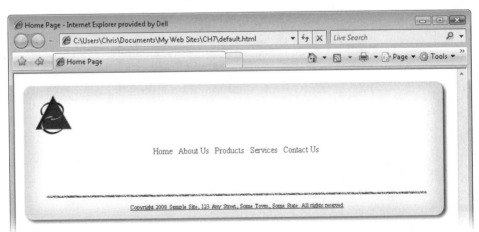

15. Switch to Expression Web 2, and expand the *CH7template* folder in the **Folder List** that you imported earlier in this set of exercises. Hold down the ⟨Ctrl⟩ key, and click the three files you used: *BGbanner.jpg*, *BGbottom.jpg*, and *BGcontainer.jpg*. Drag these files to the *images* folder in the **Folder List**.

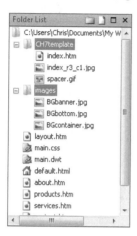

Expression Web 2 updates the references to those files throughout the site and in the CSS file.

16. On the **Site** menu, point to **Reports**, and then click **Site Summary**. Click **Unlinked Files**, and delete each of these unlinked and unnecessary files.

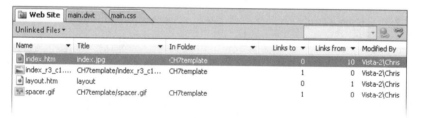

17. In the **Folder List**, delete the *CH7template* folder because it's now empty and also unnecessary.

That wraps up the organization of your site template.

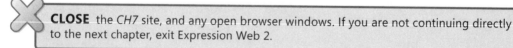

CLOSE the *CH7* site, and any open browser windows. If you are not continuing directly to the next chapter, exit Expression Web 2.

This chapter and its exercises provided you with a foundation for how to make a template in Expression Web 2. There are many fine points that you'll need to know, or need to learn, in order to produce professional-level work—that's not the purpose of this book. As you become comfortable with the general concepts that are outlined in this book, you should also learn the basics of cascading style sheets and many other techniques that, when combined, can be used to enable you to create top-level professional designs.

Key Points

- You can import any Web site template into an Expression Web 2 site and use it to create a Dynamic Web Template.

- Expression Web 2 contains a number of CSS page layouts that you can use to get a head start on creating a template.

- Editable regions can exist in both Design view and the code elements of a Dynamic Web Template.

- You can identify and remove unused files by using Reports view.

- Dragging and dropping files will update any instance of their use throughout your site.

Chapter at a Glance

Use layers
and behaviors,
page 204

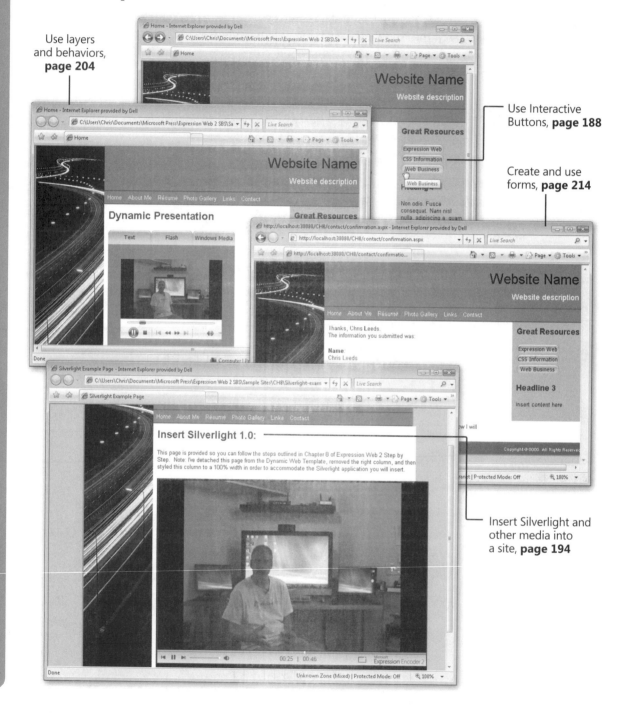

Use Interactive
Buttons, **page 188**

Create and use
forms, **page 214**

Insert Silverlight and
other media into
a site, **page 194**

8 Taking It to the Next Level

In this chapter, you will learn to

- ✔ Use Interactive Buttons.
- ✔ Insert Flash files, Windows Media Video files, and Silverlight applications into a site.
- ✔ Use layers and behaviors.
- ✔ Use Personal Web Packages.
- ✔ Create and use forms.

Beyond simply showing text, images, and other media on your pages, you can use the features in Microsoft Expression Web 2 to do more with *static pages* and provide your site visitors with a more interactive experience. By using these features, you'll be able to add both visual and functional elements to your pages.

In this chapter, you will learn to use the Interactive Buttons feature, layers, behaviors, Personal Web Packages, and forms to create interesting effects and functionality. You will also learn how to insert Adobe Flash files, Windows Media Video files, and Microsoft Silverlight applications.

Important Before you can use the practice files in this chapter, you need to install them from the book's companion CD to their default location. For more information about practice files, see "Using the Companion CD" at the beginning of this book.

Important In order for the Flash, Silverlight, and Windows Media Player examples to run in your browser, you will need to have their respective plug-ins installed on your computer.

> **Troubleshooting** Graphics and operating system–related instructions in this book reflect the Windows Vista user interface. If your computer is running Windows XP and you experience trouble following the instructions as written, please refer to the "Information for Readers Running Windows XP" section at the beginning of this book.
>
> To improve the readability of the graphics in this book, Expression Web 2 was set to use the Windows color scheme instead of the default Expression Studio 2 color scheme.

Using Interactive Buttons

Link bars, which are made up of a series of buttons, and even individual link buttons have long been a staple of Web site navigation. Previously, you would have to create the images to use for these buttons, often in multiple "*states*," and then create some JavaScript code to animate them and give them a "roll-over" effect. Even if you used the cascading style sheets–only method from Chapter 5, "Enhancing a Web Site with Images," you'd still need to create the images.

Expression Web 2 provides a nice feature for adding these buttons to a page without the need to create images, JavaScript, or even cascading style sheets (CSS). The feature is called *Interactive Buttons*. There are more than 220 different styles and colors available for you to insert into your pages.

Here's a scenario: in your site, you need to add an area that contains links to other "partner" sites that are similar in nature to the one you're working on. This link area needs to be on every page in your site. You don't want plain links; instead, you want buttons.

> **Tip** Because you need these link buttons on every page in this site, you can easily make use of the Dynamic Web Template to provide this functionality and to make maintaining these links very easy.

In this exercise, you will use the Interactive Buttons feature to create a group of links in all of the pages in your site.

> **USE** the *CH8* sample site. This sample site is located in the *Documents\Microsoft Press\Expression Web 2 SBS\Sample Sites* folder.
>
> **BE SURE TO** start Expression Web 2 before beginning this exercise.
>
> **OPEN** the *CH8* site by clicking Open Site on the File menu, and then display the *master.dwt* file in Split view.

1. On the **View** menu, click **Visual Aids**, and then enable **Block Selection**.

2. In the Design pane, click **Headline** 3.

   Notice the editable region.

3. Because you want this group of links to be present on all pages but not editable by other users working on those pages, click in the Code pane just before the line that reads <!-- #BeginEditable "sidebar" -->, and then type **Great Resources**.

```
        <!-- #EndEditable --></div>
    <!-- End Left Column -->
    <!-- Begin Right Column -->
    <div id="column right">
    Great Resources
        <!-- #BeginEditable "sidebar" -->
        <h3>Headline 3</h3>
        <p>insert content here</p>
        <!-- #EndEditable --></div>
    <!-- End Right Column -->
    <!-- Begin Footer -->
    <div id="footer">
        <div id="copyright">
            <p>Copyright © 0000. All Rights Reserved.</p>
        </div>
        <p><a href="default.htm">Home</a> | <a href="about me/about me.htm">Abou
```

(None) ▾
Style

4. In the Design pane, click the line you just typed. On the toolbar, click the **Style** arrow, and then click **Heading 3 <h3>**. Click at the end of the H3 element you just created (Great Resources), and then press [Enter] to insert a new paragraph.

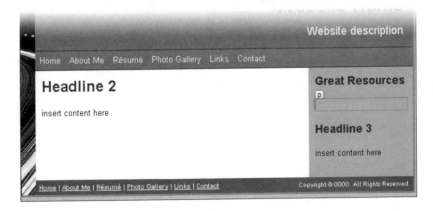

5. On the **Insert** menu, click **Interactive Button**.

The Interactive Buttons dialog box opens, with the Button tab displayed.

6. In the **Buttons** list, click **Embossed Capsule 6**. In the **Text** box, type **Expression Web**; in the **Link** box, type **http://ExpressionWebStepByStep.com**.

7. Click the **Font** tab, and notice the settings that you can change. For this example, leave the defaults in place, and click the **Image** tab.

> **Tip** The Image tab contains options to size the button, specify what image states are created, and whether they should be preloaded. Below these options are more, important options to create a *JPEG* image and specify a background color, or to create a *GIF* image that has a *transparent background*.

8. For the best-looking result, use a JPEG image, click the color list, and then click **More Colors** to open the **More Colors** dialog box. Click **Select**, and then click the Design pane of your page to pick up the background color of the area where you'll be placing the Interactive Button (*Hex={CC,BB,99}*).

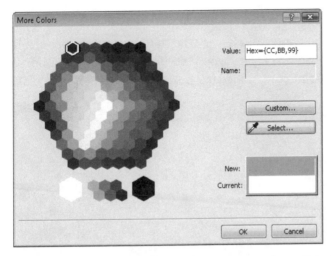

9. Click **OK** in the **More Colors** dialog box, and then click **OK** in the **Interactive Buttons** dialog box to insert the button on the page.

Although you could add more buttons by repeating the preceding steps, we will use the much faster method of copying the existing button and pasting it to the page in the Design pane.

10. Right-click the newly created button, and then click **Copy**. Click just after the button, press ⟨Shift⟩ + ⟨Enter⟩ to insert a line break, and then paste the copied button into the page. Click just after this second copy, and then press ⟨Shift⟩ + ⟨Enter⟩ again to create a new line. Paste another copy of the button in this third line.

> **Tip** Pressing Shift+Enter causes a line break to be inserted, while just pressing Enter either causes a new paragraph or a new list item to be inserted.

11. In the Design pane, double-click the second button to open the **Interactive Buttons** dialog box again, type **CSS Information** in the **Text** box, and then type **http://alistapart.com/** in the **Link** box.

12. Click **OK** to close the dialog box.

13. In the Design pane, double-click the third button to open the **Interactive Buttons** dialog box again, type **Web Business** in the **Text** box, and then type **http://sitepoint.com** in the **Link** box. Click **OK** to close the dialog box.

14. Save your page. In the **Save Embedded Files** dialog box, click **Change Folder**, click **images**, and then click **OK**.

The files in the Save Embedded Files dialog box are now saved in the *images* folder.

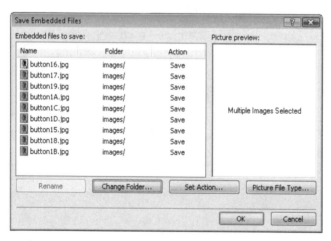

15. Click **OK** in the **Save Embedded Files** dialog box, open the *default.htm* page, and then preview it in a browser.

> **Tip** If you're using Windows Internet Explorer 7, its default behavior is to block the running of *scripts* and *ActiveX* controls. A yellow warning banner will appear above the page you're previewing. Click the warning, click Allow Blocked Content, and then click Yes in the warning confirmation.

Make sure that the interactive buttons behave as you expected, and browse through the pages of this site template to make sure that the buttons are present on all of the pages. Pay particular attention to the background color of the button and to what happens when the mouse pointer is over the button.

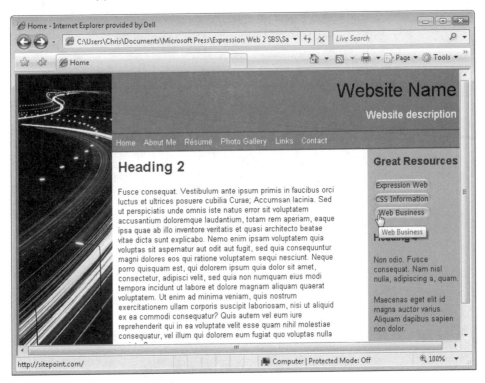

16. Close your browser, and switch to Expression Web 2.

 BE SURE TO leave the *CH8* site open for use in the next exercise.

Using the Interactive Buttons feature is very easy. If you take full advantage of it, you'll have a tremendous number of possible visual combinations, and these buttons are flexible enough to be used convincingly in any page area.

Because this sample site is attached to a Dynamic Web Template, inserting the interactive buttons into all of the pages at one time was also a snap. Maintaining all of the buttons on all of the pages—that is, adding, changing, or deleting buttons—can be done by editing one template file, and the update will cascade to all pages that are attached to it.

Inserting Flash Files, Windows Media Video Files, and Silverlight Applications into a Site

In the following exercises, you will insert an *Adobe Flash (.swf)* file, a movie in the *Windows Media Video (.wmv)* format, and a new *Silverlight 1.0* application technology into a site. You will also explore the properties dialog boxes available for these media types. The code that's generated in these exercises will be used later in this chapter, in the topic "Using Layers and Behaviors."

Inserting an Adobe Flash File

USE the *CH8* sample site you modified in the previous exercise.
OPEN the *CH8* site if it's not already open.

> **Tip** You can preview Flash .swf files in the Design view of a Web page in Microsoft Expression Web 2. To play or stop playing an .swf file, in Design view, right-click the .swf file, and then click Play Movie In Flash Format.

1. Double-click the file *Flash-example.htm* to open it for editing. Click in the sentence *Insert Your Flash File Here*, and on the quick tag selector bar, click the **<p>** tag that it's contained within to select the tag and its contents.

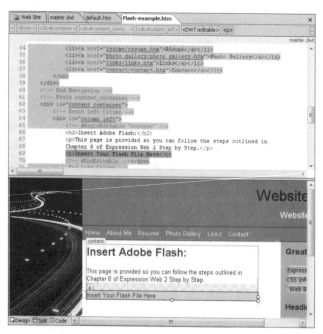

2. On the **Insert** menu, point to **Media**, and then click **Flash Movie**.

The Select Media File dialog box opens.

3. Browse to the *Documents\Microsoft Press\Expression Web 2 SBS\Files* folder, click the *Flash.swf* file, and then click **Insert**.

A Flash object is now visible in the page.

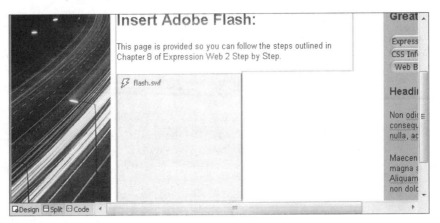

4. Save your page. In the **Save Embedded Files** dialog box, click **Change Folder**. In the **Change Folder** dialog box, double-click the *media* folder, and then click **OK**.

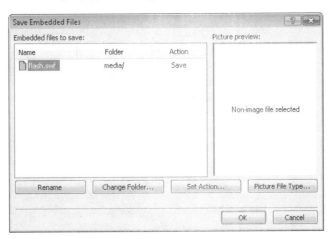

5. In the **Save Embedded Files** dialog box, click **OK**.

6. In the Design pane of Expression Web 2, right-click the Flash object, and then click **Play Movie in Flash Format**.

The Flash movie plays in the Design pane of Expression Web 2.

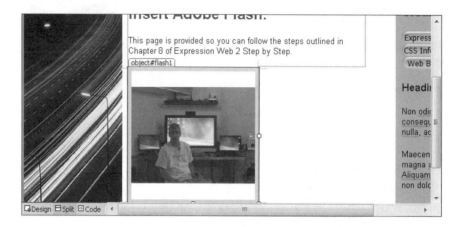

> **Tip** To stop a movie playing in the design surface, right-click the movie, and then clear the Play Movie In Flash Format check box.

7. In the design surface, right-click the Flash object, and then click **Flash SWF Properties**. The Flash SWF Properties dialog box opens.

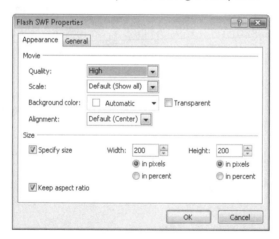

8. In the **Movie** area, leave the defaults in place. In the **Size** area, clear the **Keep aspect ratio** check box, and then change the width to **240** pixels and the height to **180** pixels.

9. On the **General** tab, change **Name** to **FlashExample**, and leave the other default settings in place. Then click **OK** to close the **Flash SWF Properties** dialog box.

10. Save your page and preview it in a browser.

Notice that the Flash object matches the movie size exactly in both Design view and in the browser.

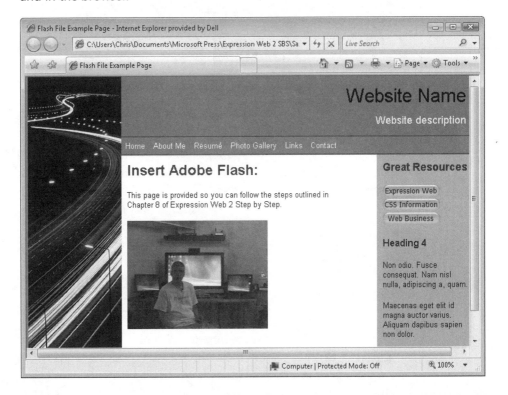

 BE SURE TO leave the *CH8* site open for use in the next exercise.

CLOSE the *Flash-example.htm* file, and any other open pages in the sample site.

Tip Although we've used the Flash SWF Properties dialog box to modify this page object, you can also select your Flash object in the design surface and then modify its properties by using the Tag Properties task pane.

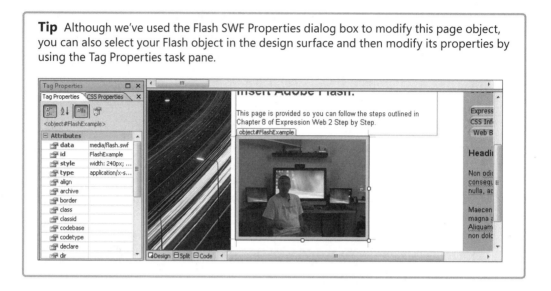

Although this exercise simply guided you through placing a video in .swf format into your page, this capability in Expression Web 2 isn't limited to video in a Flash file. In fact, any .swf file can be inserted and manipulated through the interface in Expression Web 2.

Inserting a Windows Media Video

USE the *CH8* sample site you modified in the previous exercise.
OPEN the *CH8* site if it's not already open.

1. Double click the *WindowsMedia-example.htm* file to open it for editing within Expression Web 2. Click in the sentence *Insert Your Windows Media File Here*, and on the quick tag selector bar, click the **<p>** tag that it's contained within to select the tag and its contents.

2. On the **Insert** menu point to **Media**, and then click **Windows Media Player** to open the **Select Media File** dialog box.

3. Browse to the *Documents\Microsoft Press\Expression Web 2 SBS\Files* folder, click the *WindowsMedia.wmv* file, and then click **Insert**.

A Windows Media Player object is now visible in the page.

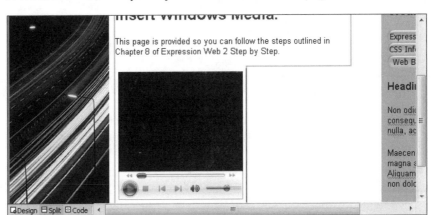

4. Save your page. In the **Save Embedded Files** dialog box, click **Change Folder**. In the **Change Folder** dialog box, double-click the **media** folder, and then click **OK**.

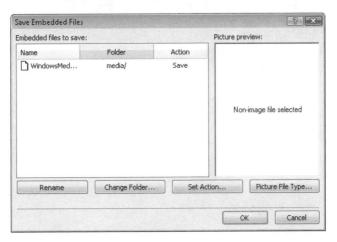

5. In the **Save Embedded Files** dialog box, click **OK**.

6. Right-click the Windows Media Player object in the Design pane of Expression Web 2, and then click **ActiveX Control Properties**. The **Windows Media Player Properties** dialog box opens.

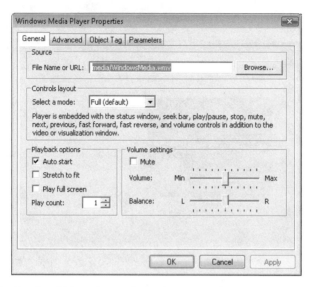

7. On the **Object Tag** tab, in the **Name** box, enter **ExpressionMediaExample**. Under **Size**, change the width to **240** and the height to **180**.

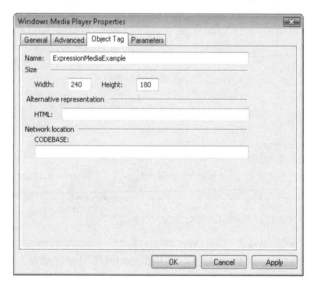

8. In the **Windows Media Player Properties** dialog box, click **OK**. Save your page and preview it in a browser.

Notice the player skin that Expression Web 2 added to your video. There are several skins (which give the player different appearances) that you can choose from in the Windows Media Player Properties dialog box.

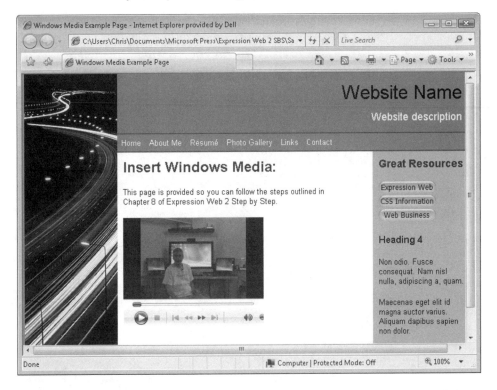

BE SURE TO leave the *CH8* site open for use in the next exercise.

CLOSE the *WindowsMedia-example.htm* file.

Although this exercise simply guided you through placing a video in .wmv format into your page, this capability in Expression Web 2 is controlled through a feature-rich Properties dialog box. Take this opportunity to view detailed help regarding the Windows Media Player Properties dialog box in the Expression Web 2 Help manual by pressing F1.

Inserting a Silverlight Application

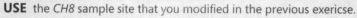

USE the *CH8* sample site that you modified in the previous exericse.

OPEN the *CH8* site if it isn't already open.

1. Double-click the *Silverlight-example.htm* file to open it for editing in Expression Web 2. Click in the sentence *Insert Your Silverlight Application Here*, and on the quick tag selector bar, click the **<p>** tag that it's contained within to select the tag and its contents.

2. On the **Insert** menu, point to **Media**, and then click **Silverlight**.

   The Insert Silverlight 1.0 dialog box opens.

3. Click **Select Folder** to open the **Select Silverlight Folder** dialog box. Browse to the *Documents\Microsoft Press\Expression Web 2 SBS\Files* folder, click the *silverlightsample* folder, and then click **Open**.

   The Select Silverlight Folder dialog box closes, and an <iframe> is inserted into your page.

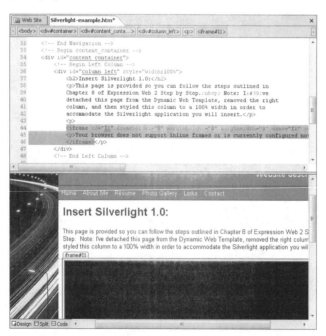

4. Save your page and preview it in a browser.

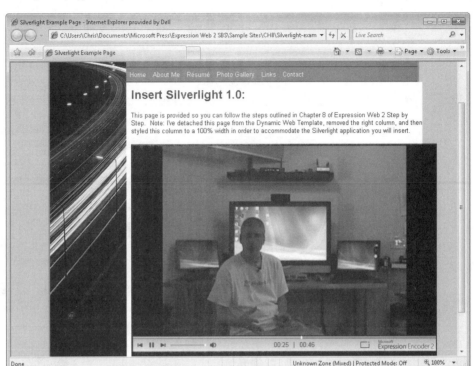

5. Explore the control set in the Silverlight player.

This video was made with and exported from Microsoft Expression Media Encoder 2.

> **Tip** The folder that Expression Web 2 adds to your Web site contains the imported assets for your Silverlight-based application. You can move and rename the imported folder, but you should not move or rename its contents; otherwise, the Silverlight-based application may not work.

 CLOSE any open pages, but leave the *CH8* sample site open if you plan to continue on to the next exercise.

Microsoft Silverlight is a relatively new technology and it's a big part of Microsoft Expression Studio. Interoperability between programs within the suite such as Expression Blend 2, Encoder 2, Media 2, and Web 2 offer a great opportunity to get into this technology quickly.

Using Layers and Behaviors

Expression Web 2 provides a visual interface for performing complicated *dynamic HTML* (*DHTML*) tasks. These tasks are accomplished by using the Expression Web 2 Layers and Behaviors task panes. In the next exercise, you will examine these capabilities and insert a DHTML-driven "viewer" into one of your pages. This viewer allows you to show information to a visitor in several ways without requiring navigation to different pages.

In this exercise, you will use the Interactive Buttons feature and the Layers and Behaviors panes to create a multimedia display area in your page.

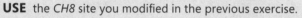

USE the *CH8* site you modified in the previous exercise.

BE SURE TO turn on Visual Aids, Block Selection, and Empty Containers if they're not on already.

OPEN the *CH8* site if it isn't already open, and display the *default.htm* page.

1. In the Design pane, delete **Headline 2**, and then type **Dynamic Presentation**. Click within the paragraph below, click **<p>** on the quick tag selector bar, and then press ⟨Del⟩. On the **Insert** menu, point to **HTML**, and then click **<div>**.

A new DIV element is placed in the page.

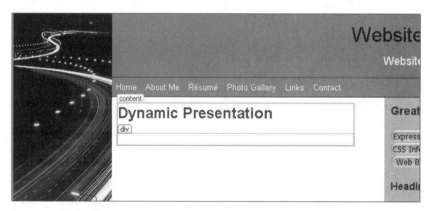

2. Save your page, and then click **<div>** on the quick tag selector bar for the DIV element that you just placed in the page. In the **Apply Styles** task pane, click **New Style**.

The New Style dialog box opens.

3. In the **New Style** dialog box, change the **Selector** box to **#controls**, select the **Apply new style to document selection** check box, click **Existing style sheet** in the **Define in** list, and then click **styles/style3.css** (the document's current style sheet) in the **URL** list.

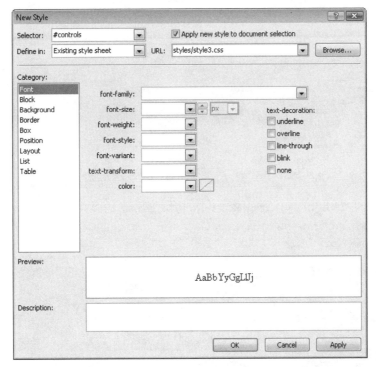

4. In the **Category** list, click **Background**. Click the **background-color** arrow, and then click **More Colors**.

5. In the **More Colors** dialog box that opens, click **Select**, use the eyedropper to select the background color of the main navigation bar (*Hex={99,88,66}*), and then click **OK**.

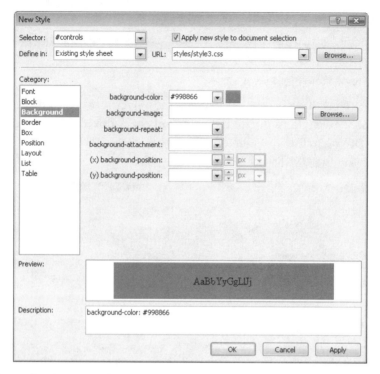

6. In the **Category** list, click **Position**, type **300px** in the **width** box, and then type **270px** in the **height** box. Click **OK** to set your changes and close the **New Style** dialog box.

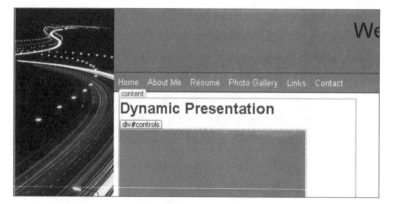

7. In the Design pane, click inside this newly styled DIV element. On the **Insert** menu, click **Interactive Button** to open the **Interactive Buttons** dialog box.

8. In the **Buttons** list of the **Interactive Buttons** dialog box, click **Embossed Tab 6**. In the **Text** box, type **Text**, and leave the **Link** box empty.

9. Click **OK** to insert the button into the page.

10. Repeat steps 8 and 9 twice more, using **Flash** and **Windows Media** for the button text and leaving the **Link** box empty.

A row of three buttons is created, with no spaces between the buttons.

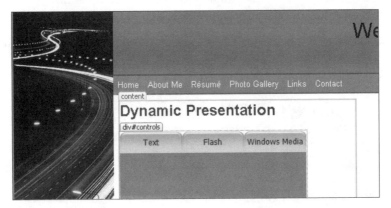

11. On the **Insert** menu, click **HTML**, and then click **<div>**.

A new DIV element is inserted into the page.

12. In the Design pane, set the mouse pointer inside this DIV element, and then, on the quick tag selector bar, click its representation to select the entire tag. In the **Manage Styles** pane, click **New Style** to open the **New Style** dialog box.

13. In the **Selector** box of the **New Style** dialog box, type **#presentation**, and select the **Apply new style to document selection** check box. In the **Define in** list, click **Existing style sheet**, and then click **style3.css** in the **URL** list. In the **Category** list, click **Box**, and then type **30px** in the **padding** box below **padding**. In the **Category** list, click **Position**, type **180px** in the **height** box, and then type **240px** in the **width** box. Click **OK** to close the dialog box.

Insert Layer

14. Click inside the new DIV element, and then, on the **Format** menu, click **Layers**. In the **Layers** task pane, click the **Insert Layer** button.

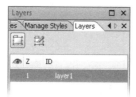

Expression Web 2 inserts a layer below your row of buttons.

15. In the **Layers** task pane, right-click **layer1**, and then click **Modify ID**. Change the ID to **player**. Right-click **player**, and then click **Borders and Shading**. On the **Shading** tab, change the **Background color** to **white**, and then click **OK**. Right-click **player** again, and then click **Positioning**. Type **240px** in the **width** box, type **180px** in the **height** box, and then click **OK**.

16. Click inside this newly styled DIV element, and type **Please select a viewing option by clicking one of the buttons above**. Save your page, and then click **OK** in the **Save Embedded Files** dialog box.

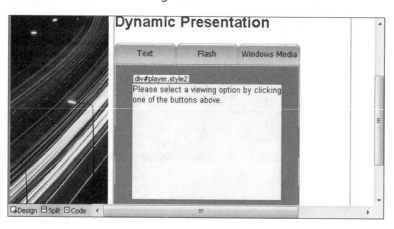

17. In the **Folder List**, open the *text-code.txt* file from the *media* folder. Select the code, and copy it to the Clipboard. Close the file, and switch to *default.htm*. In the Design pane, click the **Text** interactive button, and then, on the **Format** menu, click **Behaviors** to display the **Behaviors** task pane. In the **Behaviors** task pane, click **Insert,** point to **Set Text**, and then click **Set Text of Layer**.

18. In the **Set Text of Layer** dialog box that opens, paste the code from the Clipboard into the **New HTML** box.

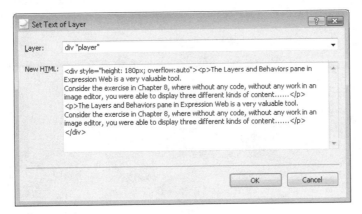

19. Click **OK** to set your changes.

20. In the **Folder List**, open the *Flash-example.htm* file. Click the Flash object in the Design pane of your page, and then right-click its highlighted code in the Code pane, and copy it to the clipboard. Close the file, and switch to *default.htm*. In the Design pane, click the **Flash** interactive button. In the **Behaviors** task pane, click **Insert**, point to **Set Text**, and then click **Set Text of Layer**. Paste the code from the Clipboard into the **New HTML** box, and then click **OK** to set your changes.

21. In the **Folder List**, open the *WindowsMedia-example.htm* file. Click the **Windows Media** object in the Design pane of your page, and then right click its highlighted code in the Code pane and copy it to the clipboard. Close the file, and switch to *default.htm*. In the Design pane, click the **Windows Media** interactive button. In the **Behaviors** task pane, click **Insert**, point to **Set Text**, and then click **Set Text of Layer**. Paste the code from the Clipboard into the **New HTML** box, and then click **OK** to set your changes.

22. Save your page and preview it in a browser. Explore your creation in the browser by clicking the buttons to check each delivery method.

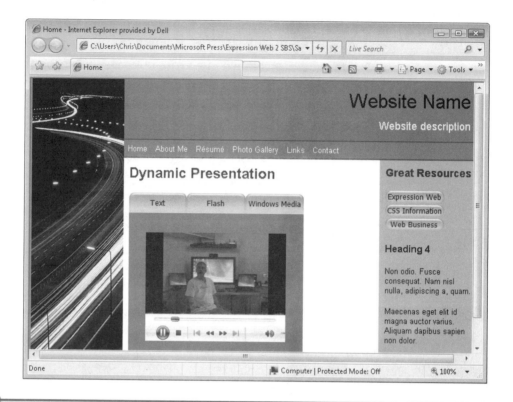

> **BE SURE TO** leave the *CH8* site open for use in the next exercise.
>
> **CLOSE** any open pages in Expression Web 2.

Although the video and audio files were provided for this exercise, consider the outcome: using only the user interface in Expression Web 2, you were able to set up a nice three-button rollover bar, and to set up the capability to deliver content to a visitor in three different ways. Consider also that by using the Set Text Of Layer function, no extra files will be downloaded unless the site visitor clicks one of the buttons. This way, the visitor can receive your page quickly, and can then click for "heavy" content such as video or audio. It's a much better user experience than if the running media content were placed on the surface of the page.

Using Personal Web Packages

If you're an experienced site designer, you've probably amassed a large collection of files and scripts such as shopping carts or database applications that you tend to use in all or most sites that you create. If you're very new to Web design, you will probably begin to develop this type of collection very soon.

With a Personal Web Package, you can export a collection of scripts or other assets from within a site; and you can save all of the data to a single file (an **FWP** file), which you can save on your local computer or distribute by any method you want, such as e-mail or a link on a Web site.

After a collection of files has been exported as an .fwp file, it can be imported very easily by any Expression Web 2 user.

Here's a scenario: The *media* folder in the sample site is a project that you want to save to reuse in another site. You can export the *media* folder as a Personal Web Package.

In this exercise, you will export and import a Personal Web Package.

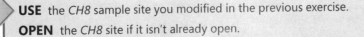

USE the *CH8* sample site you modified in the previous exercise.

OPEN the *CH8* site if it isn't already open.

1. On the **File** menu, point to **Export**, and then click **Personal Web Package** to open the **Export Web Package** dialog box.

2. The **Export Web Package** dialog box checks for file dependencies when you add a page to the export list. For instance, click **media** in the **Files in Web site** list, and then click **Add**. When Expression Web 2 asks if you would like to include the contents of the folder in your Web package, click **Yes**.

    The *media* folder is copied to the Files In Package list. It is copied because the files within the *media* folder don't depend on any files outside that folder.

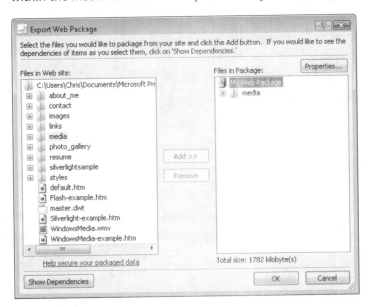

3. In the **Files in Web site** list, click **default.htm**, and then click **Add**.

All of the files in the site are now copied to the Files In Package list. That's because the default page is dependent on almost every file in the site: cascading style sheet files, images, the *master.dwt* file, even the pages that it links to.

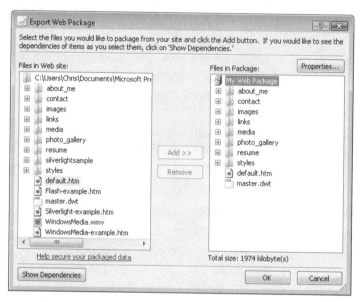

4. In the **Files in Package** list, select all of the files and folders, and then click **Remove** to clear the export project. In the **Files in Site** list, click **media**, and then click **Add**.

5. Click **Properties** to open the **Web Package Properties** dialog box. Change the name from **My Web Package** to **Media Files**. Add a description, author, and company name if you want.

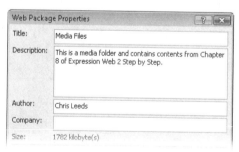

This information will be contained within the package. In the bottom of the dialog box, you can see a list of external dependencies, which are references to files outside the current site, such as pages that hyperlinks point to or absolute references to images or other files.

6. Click **OK** to close the dialog box.

7. In the **Export Web Package** dialog box, click **OK**.

   The File Save dialog box opens.

8. In the **File Save** dialog box, browse to a location where you want to save the exported Web package, and then click **Save**.

   Web package exports can really bolster your long-term asset and workflow strategy. Imagine setting up your favorite shopping cart, a package of utility-type scripts you use, and a few other items in logical arrangements as Web packages. You'd be able to easily bring them into any project that is open in Expression Web 2 with only a few clicks.

   > **Tip** You can use Web Package exports to cull files. If you've been working on a project for a while, the site probably has become loaded with revisions, old files, and all the other artifacts that a project tends to produce. If you want to pare the project down to the essential pieces—for instance, to send it to a customer or as a preparatory step before publishing to a server—you could select only the files you need to keep and let Expression Web 2 take care of adding the dependent files to your export list.
   >
   > You can simply export the Web Package and send it off to someone else, or you can create an empty site and import it. Regardless of how you use the Web Package, it's a fast way to isolate only the files you need and leave unnecessary files behind.

9. On the **File** menu, point to **Import**, and then click **Personal Web Package** to open the **File Open** dialog box. Browse to the *Documents\Microsoft Press\ Expression Web 2 SBS\Files* folder, click the *CH8.fwp* file, and then click **Open**.

   The Import Web Package dialog box opens. In this dialog box, you can select or deselect files and folders and view the properties of the Web Package.

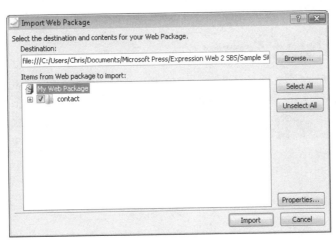

10. Click **Import** to import the *contact* folder and the files it contains to the root of your site.

11. In the security warning dialog box that opens, click **Run** to continue the process of importing the contents of this Web Package.

12. Click **OK** in the deployment complete message box to complete the process.

    A file named *confirmation.aspx* now exists in your site *contact* folder. This folder and its contents will be used in the next exercise, in which you will work with forms.

 BE SURE TO leave the *CH8* site open for use in the next exercise.

Personal Web Packages make certain functionality, graphics, and other assets portable. In addition to the portability benefit, the export process can be helpful in enabling you to package only files you want to keep and to discard unnecessary files.

Creating and Using Forms

Forms are a feature that enables you to provide varied levels of user interaction. Forms can be used for anything from the most complex database application to the simplest of e-mail–producing **contact forms**. Expression Web 2 provides several tools to assist in the creation of forms. All of the tools are available in the Toolbox task pane, under the Form Control group.

In this exercise, you will create a simple contact form and configure it to handle the user input.

> **USE** the *CH8* sample site you modified in the previous exercise.
>
> **OPEN** the *CH8* site if it isn't already open, and display the *contact.htm* page.

1. In the Design pane, click after the last numbered item under the heading **Driving Directions**, and then press ⟨Enter⟩ twice to break out of the ordered list and create a new paragraph.

Style

2. Type **Contact Form**, and press ⟨Enter⟩ again to start a new paragraph. Select the text you just typed, click the **Style** arrow on the toolbar, and then click **Heading 3 <h3>**.

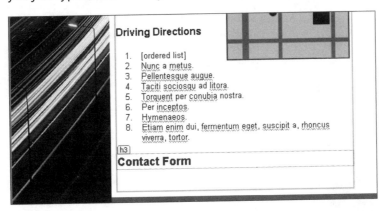

3. Click in the paragraph below the H3 element. If the **Toolbox** task pane isn't visible, on the **Task Panes** menu, click **Toolbox**. In the **Toolbox** task pane, expand **Form Controls**.

These form controls can be added to your page either by dragging them from the toolbox to where you want them or by setting the cursor in the design surface of the page where you want them and double-clicking their entry in the toolbox. You might also find it helpful to use Split view.

4. In the Design pane, click the **<p>** element below the heading you entered. On the quick tag selector bar, click **<p>** to select the entire element, and then, in the **Toolbox** task pane, double-click **Form**.

An empty form is inserted into your page in place of the paragraph.

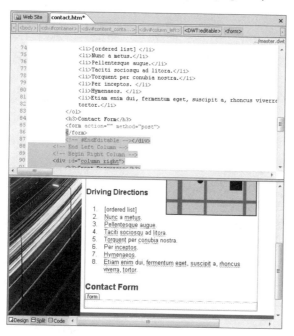

5. Type **Name**, and then press ⇧ Shift + Enter to insert a line break. In the **Toolbox** task pane, double-click **Input (Text)** to insert a text field.

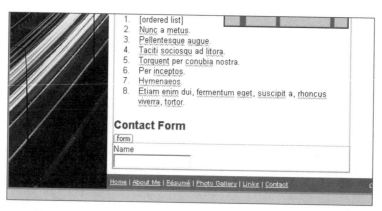

6. Right-click the text field, and then click **Form Field Properties** to open the **Text Box Properties** dialog box. Type **name** in the **Name** box, type **1** in the **Tab order** box, and then click **OK** to set the changes and close the dialog box.

7. Click just after the text field, and then press [Shift] + [Enter] to insert a line break.

8. Type **E-mail**, and then press [Shift] + [Enter] to insert a line break. In the **Toolbox** task pane, double-click **Input (Text)** to insert another text field.

9. Right-click the new text field, and then click **Form Field Properties**. Type **email** in the **Name** box, type **2** in the **Tab order** box, and then click **OK** to set the changes and close the dialog box. Click just after the text field, and then press [Shift] + [Enter] to insert a line break.

10. Type **Phone**, and then press [Shift] + [Enter] to insert a line break. In the **Toolbox** task pane, double-click **Input (Text)** to insert another text field.

11. Right-click the new text field, and then click **Form Field Properties**. Type **phone** in the **Name** box, type **3** in the **Tab order** box, and then click **OK** to set the changes and close the dialog box. Click just after the text field, and then press [Shift] + [Enter] to insert a line break.

12. Type **Your Message**, and then press [Shift] + [Enter] to insert a new line break. In the **Toolbox** task pane, double-click **Text Area** to insert a text area field into your form.

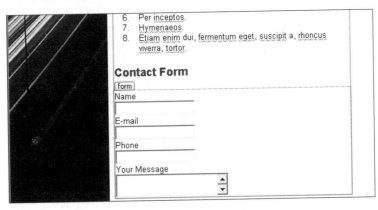

13. Right-click the text area field, and then click **Form Field Properties** to open the **TextArea Box Properties** dialog box. Type **message** in the **Name** box, type **40** in the **Width in characters** box, type **4** in the **Tab order** box, type **10** in the **Number of lines** box, and then click **OK** to set the changes and close the dialog box.

14. Click just after the text area field, and then press [Shift] + [Enter] to insert a line break. In the **Toolbox** task pane, double-click **Input (Reset)**, and then double-click **Input (Submit)**.

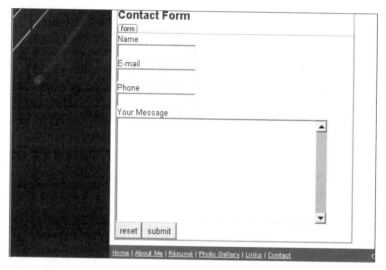

After setting the form field names and tab order, you can configure what happens when a site visitor uses the form by filling in the requested information and clicking the Submit button.

15. In the Design pane, right-click anywhere inside the form, and then click **Form Properties** to open the **Form Properties** dialog box.

> **Important** There are options on the Form Properties dialog box for features that require Microsoft Office FrontPage server extensions. These options require not only FrontPage server extensions but also require that e-mail transport be enabled in some cases and require FrontPage publishing. FTP publishing will cause them to fail. These FrontPage options are present only to enable an Expression Web 2 user to edit pages that were originally created in FrontPage and that use FrontPage extensions.

The Send To Other option is selected.

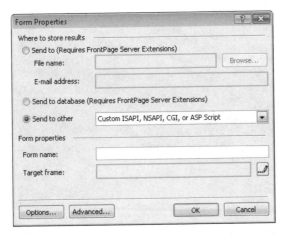

16. Type **Contact** in the **Form name** box, and then click **Options**. In the **Action** box of the **Options for Custom Form Handler** dialog box, type **confirmation.aspx**.

17. Click **OK** to set your changes in the **Options for Custom Form Handler** dialog box, click **OK** in the **Form Properties** dialog box, and then save the page.

18. Open the *confirmation.aspx* file from the *contact* folder. On the **Format** menu, point to **Dynamic Web Template**, and then click **Update Selected Page**.

> **Tip** If *confirmation.aspx* isn't in the *contact* folder, you must import the file. See step 9 of the exercise in "Using Personal Web Packages," earlier in this chapter, for instructions on importing files.

19. Save and preview *confirmation.aspx* in a browser. In the browser, click the **Contact** link, fill out the form, and then click **submit**.

The confirmation page shows the form input.

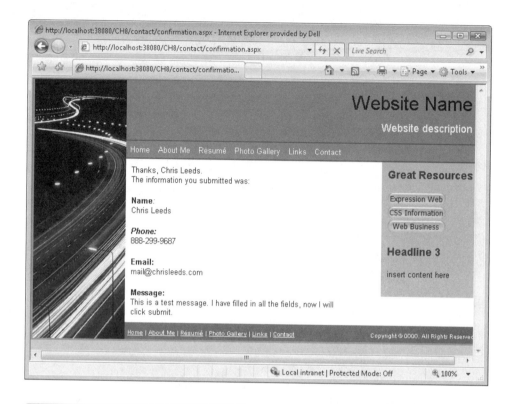

Tip The confirmation page is only intended to illustrate how to configure an HTML form in Expression Web 2. It is assumed that the site developer will have a script or form handler to submit an HTML form.

If you would like a free beta copy of a form handler designed specifically for Expression Web 2, see *http://ExpressionWebStepByStep.com/EFH*.

CLOSE the *CH8* site and any open Internet Explorer windows. If you are not continuing directly to the next chapter, exit Expression Web 2.

Key Points

- Expression Web 2 makes it easy to insert media files into your Web pages. Through the Expression Web 2 user interface, you can control various aspects of your media file's presentation.

- The Interactive Buttons feature provides a quick and easy way to provide attractive roll-over buttons without the need to use an image editor or write code to animate the buttons.

- You can use functionality from the Layers and Behaviors task panes to create interesting visual features and provide for user interaction without the need to write JavaScript code.

- Personal Web Packages provide a useful method for exporting files from or importing files to an Expression Web 2 site.

- Expression Web 2 provides tools to build and configure the actions of forms. In Expression Web 2, the Form Properties dialog box is also compatible with forms that were built by using FrontPage.

Chapter at a Glance

Publish by using FTP or HTTP,
pages 228 and 234

Publish to a disk location,
page 239

9 Publishing a Web Site

In this chapter, you will learn to

✔ Consider hosting requirements.

✔ Find and register a domain name.

✔ Use Microsoft Office Live Small Business.

✔ Publish by using FTP.

✔ Publish by using HTTP (FrontPage Server Extensions).

✔ Publish to a disk location.

After you've taken all the time and trouble to create a Web site and get everything set up the way you want, you are probably going to want people to be able to access it. Whether it's a site for only a select group of users (an *intranet site*), or a site for the general public (an *Internet site*), you will need the files and folders in your *local site* to reside on a *server*.

From a Microsoft Expression Web 2 standpoint, moving the local files and folders that comprise your site to a server is where *publishing* comes in. Although publishing might, on its surface, seem like simply copying files from your local site to a server, there's actually a lot more going on during this operation. In addition to the publishing operation copying the files and folders from one place to another, Expression Web 2 keeps tabs on what's been published, where it's been published to, and when each file was last published. Add to that the fact that, with Expression Web 2, you can publish not only from your local site to a server but also from a server back down to your local computer, or even from one server to another server without copying the files to your local computer at all, and the complexity and usefulness of the publishing functions of Expression Web 2 become quite apparent.

From within Expression Web 2, you have four choices for publishing:

- Microsoft Office FrontPage Server Extensions publishing
  - Requires FrontPage Server Extensions on the server. Check with your host to see if they are available.
  - Provides for encrypted transfer of user name and passwords by using the *HTTP* protocol to publish.
  - Allows for maximum exploitation of the Expression Web 2 features and greater security than File Transfer Protocol (*FTP*) publishing.
- *WebDAV* publishing
  - Requires Distributed Authoring and Versioning (DAV) to be set up on the server. Check with your host to see if this is an option for your site.
  - Is currently fairly rare but provides a feature set that is otherwise not available.

  See Also For more information about WebDAV, visit *www.webdav.org*.
- FTP publishing
  - Requires FTP to be set up on the server. Check with your host for FTP parameters for your site.
  - Is the most common and widely available form of publishing.
- File System publishing
  - Publishes a *disk-based site* from one folder structure to another.
  - Is generally used to "copy" a site from one location on your computer to another for administrative purposes.
  - Has no requirements, but also results in minimal capabilities at the publish location.

In this chapter, you will be introduced to the various types of publishing and to the publishing prerequisites, such as securing a domain name and *hosting* for your site.

Important Before you can use the practice files in this chapter, you need to install them from the book's companion CD to their default location. For more information about practice files, see "Using the Companion CD" at the beginning of this book.

> **Troubleshooting** Graphics and operating system–related instructions in this book reflect the Windows Vista user interface. If your computer is running Windows XP and you experience trouble following the instructions as written, please refer to the "Information for Readers Running Windows XP" section at the beginning of this book.
>
> To improve the readability of the graphics in this book, Expression Web 2 was set to use the Windows color scheme instead of the default Expression Studio 2 color scheme.

Considering Hosting Requirements

There are many server types on which you can host your domain and site. For the purposes of this discussion, we will divide them into two main categories: those that run a Windows operating system, and those that do not.

The decision about which server type to use depends solely on what kind of files and functionality you either have currently in your site or plan to include in the future. Use these guidelines:

- If your site has or will have Microsoft dynamic pages such as *ASP.NET*, or ASP files, or if the site requires a *Microsoft Office Access* or *Microsoft SQL Server database*, you should choose a Windows server with the appropriate Microsoft .NET Framework version and the appropriate *database* capabilities.

- If your site has or will have non-Windows dynamic pages such as PHP or a *MySQL* server, then you could use a non-Windows server, although PHP and MySQL run fine on a Windows server if the server administrator configures and allows it.

- If your site has only static pages (.htm/.html) and you don't intend to add server-side functionality, it really doesn't matter which server type you choose.

When choosing a server to host your site, it's important to make a good initial decision. It can be a tremendous hassle to move a site after it's been deployed to a server. The decision is complicated by the fact that there are literally tens of thousands of hosts you can choose from. A little due diligence is definitely required on this topic. A good place to start, by using the experience of others, is at *www.webhostingtalk.com*.

Some of the things you'll need after signing up for hosting space include:

- A user name and password for publishing. Whether you opt for HTTP, FTP, or WebDAV, you will be issued a unique user name and password.

- The URL or folder you are supposed to publish into. Some hosts have a specific folder in your Web space that you must publish into.

- The *DNS* settings your host requires you to use. To enable visitors to arrive at your site on your hosting space, you will need to use the appropriate DNS settings. These settings are changed within the account where you registered your domain name. At least two DNS entries are required—for example, NS1.EXAMPLE.COM and NS2.EXAMPLE.COM. When you change these settings at your *registrar*, it can take up to 72 hours for the settings to propagate throughout the Internet.

After you set up your hosting space, you'll be ready to move on to publishing your files and folders to the Internet. Resist the urge to find the cheapest host, or to make a quick decision. This is one of those points where taking some additional time in the beginning can save you much more time and trouble in the future.

Reseller Accounts

If you're a professional Web designer, or if you intend to get into the business, you should look into what's commonly known as a *reseller account*. Such an account will allow you to host your own site and all your customers' sites. You'll be able to access all the sites through a common control panel, and your clients will be able to access their own domain settings through their own unique *domain control panel*.

One provider of reseller accounts is High End Host (*www.highendhost.com*). Because a reseller account hosts not only your site but also your customers' sites that you're responsible for, even more weight must be placed on due diligence in the beginning. Reselling hosting to your customers can be very easy and profitable if you have the right host, or a recipe for disaster if you have the wrong host. You can also check *www.webhostingtalk.com* for reseller accounts.

Finding and Registering a Domain Name

In addition to having hosting space for your site, you'll also need a *domain name*. A domain name is the base of the alphanumeric address called the *URL* (Uniform Resource Locator), and it's the address visitors use to find a site. For example, the URL for Microsoft is *http://microsoft.com*, and their domain name is *microsoft.com*.

When you register your domain name, you will want to use your name, your company's name, or a word or phrase that's directly related to the products or services your company provides. It's important to give a great deal of thought to the domain name you choose, because it will have direct impact on search engine relevance of all the pages within your site. In addition, it's the name you'll tell people, and whether you tell them in print advertising, by phone, or in person, the name needs to be descriptive, easy to remember, and easy to spell.

> **Tip** Even if you need only one site, that doesn't necessarily mean you should have only one domain. You might want to register your company name with several extensions, such as *example.com*, *example.net*, and *example.org*. Another tactic is to register common misspellings of your "main" domain. That way, if visitors happen to type the domain name improperly, you can still get them to the correct site through various techniques.

Part of the choice in registering a domain name is the extension. Common *domain extensions* are: .com (intended for company and commercial sites), .net (intended for network sites), .org (intended for organizations), and .edu (intended for educational institutions). There are a great number of new domain extensions available today, but you should initially use the one that was designed for your site's purpose and profile.

For domain names to function as intended, it's absolutely necessary that each name be unique. Therefore, each domain name is registered. Registration of names is overseen by the Internet Corporation for Assigned Names and Numbers (*ICANN*).

Because there are a tremendous number of registrars where you can set up and register your domain name, you should do some research. ICANN's site, at *www.internic.com*, maintains a list of accredited registrars along with invaluable information on the topic. There's a lot of information, so this is another situation where learning from other people's experience pays off exponentially. Expect to pay between $7 and $30 per year for a registered domain.

> **Tip** People who are in business as Web site designers or developers might want to look into reselling domain name registration as well as reselling accounts for hosting. You make less money than you do with reselling hosting space, but the added level of convenience of having all your customers' domains registered through a common domain control panel might be worth it for you. Two of the most popular options are *www.wildwestdomains.com* and *www. enom.com*, although they each have different methodologies. A number of domain name reselling options are available, so this, as with all major decisions, also requires some research.

Using Microsoft Office Live Small Business

One possible solution for registering a domain name and setting up hosting in one step would be this new option from Microsoft: Office Live Small Business. Various levels of features are available at *smallbusiness.officelive.com*, which offers a free domain registration and Web site, but also provides you with the opportunity to add paid services such as extra storage space, an e-commerce set of features, and e-mail newsletter functionality. Office Live Small Business might be just what you're looking for, so you should spend some time checking it out.

> **Tip** In my research for this book, I found the Office Live servers to be the absolute fastest servers I'd ever published to. I found it convenient that the user name and password were the same as the Windows Live ID that I used when I signed up for them.

Publishing by Using FTP

Publishing by using FTP is a valuable capability, because virtually every server and every hosting space has FTP publishing available. It's definitely the most common method of transferring files to a server. Even if you prefer to use HTTP publishing, as many people do, a time will come when you need to use FTP. For example, you have a new customer with an existing Web site and you need to copy his online assets down to your local computer. If FrontPage Server Extensions do not exist on his hosting space, you won't have a choice, and you'll need to use FTP to transfer the files and folders from his Web space down to your computer. Knowing when and how to use FTP is a valuable skill, and it's one you will undoubtedly need sometime.

In this exercise, you will publish a site to a server by using FTP, and you will become familiar with the publishing settings that are available in Expression Web 2 for FTP publishing.

> **USE** the *CH9* sample site. This site is located in the *Documents\Microsoft Press\Expression Web 2 SBS\Sample Sites* folder.
>
> **BE SURE TO** start Expression Web 2 and have your FTP user name and password available before beginning this exercise.
>
> **OPEN** the *CH9* site by clicking Open Site on the File menu.

1. On the **File** menu, click **Publish Site**.

   The Remote Web Site Properties dialog box opens, displaying the most recent publishing destination and method used.

2. Click **FTP**. In the **Remote Web site location** box, type the FTP address of the location you will publish the site to.

You should have received this information from your host.

3. In the **FTP directory** box, type the name of the folder that your public files will reside in. Your host may require you to use a specific folder for your public files. If they don't require one, leave this field blank.

Expression Web 2 enables you to use either passive FTP or normal FTP. Note the Use Passive FTP check box, which is selected by default. Some network configurations work only with passive FTP mode turned on, while others work only with it turned off. Most network configurations support both modes. The passive FTP mode is considered more secure.

> **Tip** In the exercises in this chapter, you will see references in the graphics to *ExpressionWebStepbyStep.com*. It is assumed that readers will have their own site publishing parameters. This domain was set up specifically for the publishing operations demonstrated in this book, and then as a support site for its readers.

4. Click **OK**.

Expression Web 2 prompts you for your FTP site user name and password.

5. Enter your credentials in the logon dialog box. If you want Expression Web 2 to remember your user name and password, be sure to select the **Remember my password** check box, and then click **OK**.

Expression Web 2 displays the local and remote sites in Remote Web Site view.

> **Tip** When you log on to your site for the first time, you might see some folders in your site structure. This is generally normal; these folders are put there by your host. Often they're for *server logs*, Control Panel files, and so on.

6. At the top of the **Remote Web Site** view, click **Remote Web Site Properties**.

The Remote Web Site Properties dialog box opens.

7. You've already used the initial **Remote Web Site** tab, so click the **Optimize HTML** tab.

8. To enable the HTML optimization options, select the **When publishing, optimize HTML by removing the following elements** check box.

> **Important** These options are self-explanatory. In many cases, Expression Web 2 will rely on these comments and attributes being in the page code and that's why they're removed only when they're published to the server. One thing to keep in mind regarding the use of these optimization features is that if you strip out *comments* and attributes that Expression Web 2 needs and then publish from the server to your local computer, you will experience some usability issues when you edit the site in Expression Web 2.

9. Click the **Publishing** tab in the **Remote Web Site Properties** dialog box.

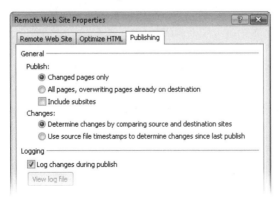

> **Tip** The options on this tab are also self-explanatory. You might change them from their defaults for issues relating to publishing speed or a publishing strategy. For example, if the application takes too long and *times out* while it is comparing files on the server to files in the local site, you can choose the option to use *timestamps* rather than comparison. If your local site contains *subsites*, you might choose the option to publish subsites on certain occasions. In general, the Publish tab default settings don't require change.

Take some time to familiarize yourself with the options on this tab. Another useful option enables you to choose whether you want the publishing operations to be logged and provides a link to view the *log file*.

10. Click **OK** to close the dialog box.

11. At the bottom of the **Remote Web Site** view, click **Publish Web site**.

During the publishing operation, the Status area in the lower-left corner of the workspace displays messages regarding the files being published.

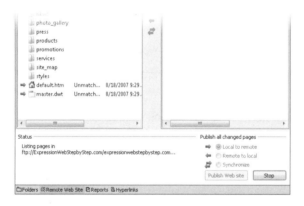

> **Tip** When you choose the Changed Pages Only option for publishing, if Expression Web 2 finds files or folders on the server that aren't present in the local site, you will be asked if you want to remove them. If you aren't absolutely sure you want the files or folders removed, click No.

12. If your site uses metadata, a warning dialog box opens. Because you're not using any FrontPage features and are purposely publishing by using FTP, click **OK**.

Publishing finishes and the Remote Web Site view shows a status message that indicates this status. There are also links below the status message to view the publish log file or open the remote Web site in Expression Web 2.

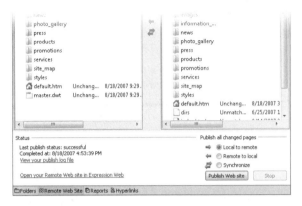

You have now published a local site to a remote server by using FTP in Expression Web 2. All of your local files are now on the server, and you can view them in a browser. Simply open a browser and type your site's domain in the address bar to check your work.

BE SURE TO leave the *CH9* site open for use in the next exercise.

CLOSE any open browser windows.

Troubleshooting Sometimes the hosting service places a *default file* in the root folder of your account. Index.htm, index.html, default.htm, and default.html are common default files for a Web server. If you publish your site and upon visiting the domain in a browser you don't see the home page that you published, you need to delete or rename the default file that the host created. Then your site's home page will take precedence and be passed to the browser as the default file of the domain. You can perform this action in Expression Web 2 in the Remote Web Site view by right-clicking the index file that your hosting company supplied in the Remote Web Site pane and clicking either Delete or Rename.

Important If you intend to publish your Expression Web 2 site by using FTP, it's recommended that you use the built-in FTP publishing rather than a *third-party FTP client*. The reason for this is that Expression Web 2 won't publish the *hidden folders* containing the site's metadata, but a third-party application won't make the distinction and will publish everything. This can often result in a longer than necessary publishing time and a larger than necessary cumulative folder size on the server.

Publishing by Using HTTP (FrontPage Server Extensions)

The most solid and secure publishing method from within Expression Web 2 is HTTP publishing. Although FrontPage Server Extensions are required on the *hosting account*, you don't need to rely on FrontPage features. The HTTP method provides the added benefit of *encoding* the user name and password that you use when publishing and can allow for publishing through a *Secure Sockets Layer* (SSL/HTTPS) if you have a *Secure Server Certificate* installed on your server space.

In this exercise, you will use HTTP publishing through Expression Web 2, and you will use the features that are available with this method.

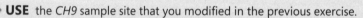

USE the *CH9* sample site that you modified in the previous exercise.
OPEN the *CH9* site if it is not already open.

1. On the **File** menu, click **Publish Site**.

The Remote Web Site Properties dialog box opens, displaying the most recent publishing destination and method used.

> **Troubleshooting** If a server logon dialog box opens, click Cancel.

2. Click **FrontPage Server Extensions**. In the **Remote Web site location** box, type the HTTP address you will publish to.

> **Tip** In the exercises in this chapter, you will see references in the graphics to *ExpressionWebStepbyStep.com*. This domain was set up specifically for the publishing operations demonstrated in this book, and then as a support site for its readers.

3. Click **OK**. You will be prompted for your FrontPage user name and password.

4. Type your credentials into the logon dialog box, and click **OK**. If you want Expression Web 2 to remember your user name and password, be sure to select the **Remember my password** check box.

The logon dialog box closes, and Expression Web 2 switches to Remote Web Site view.

Tip When you log on to your site for the first time, you may see some folders in your site structure. Generally, this is normal and these folders are put there by your host. Often they're for *server logs*, control panel files, and so on.

5. At the top of the **Remote Web Site** view, click **Remote Web Site Properties**.

The Remote Web Site Properties dialog box opens.

6. You've already used the initial **Remote Web Site** tab, so click the **Optimize HTML** tab.

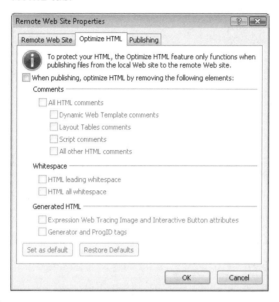

7. To enable the HTML optimization options, click the **When publishing, optimize HTML by removing the following elements** check box.

Important These options are self-explanatory. In many cases, Expression Web 2 will rely on these comments and attributes being in the page code and that's why they're only removed when they're published to the server. One thing to keep in mind regarding the use of these optimization features is that if you strip out comments and attributes that Expression Web 2 needs and then publish from the server to your local system, you will experience some usability issues when you edit the site in Expression Web 2.

---

8. In the **Remote Web Site Properties** dialog box, click the **Publishing** tab.

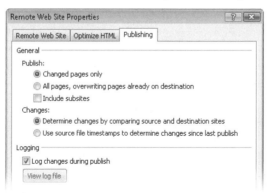

> **Tip** The options on this tab are also self-explanatory. Generally, a user will change them from their defaults for issues relating to publishing speed or a ***publishing strategy***. For example, if the application takes too long and times out while comparing files on the server to files in the local site, a user can choose the option to use timestamps rather than comparison. If the user's local site contains subsites, he or she might on certain occasions choose the option to publish subsites. The Publish tab default settings are usually appropriate.

9. Take some time to familiarize yourself with the options on this tab.

Another useful option enables you to choose whether you want the publishing operations to be logged and provides a link to view the log file.

10. Click **OK** to close the dialog box.

11. At the bottom of the **Remote Web Site** view, click **Publish Web site**.

During the publishing operation, the Status area in the lower-left corner of the workspace displays messages regarding the files being published.

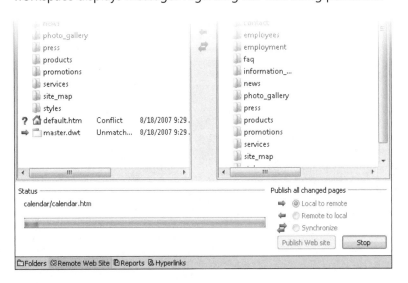

> **Tip** When you choose the Changed Pages Only option for publishing, if Expression Web 2 finds files or folders on the server that aren't present in the local site, you will be asked if you want to remove them. If you aren't absolutely sure you want the files or folders removed, click No.

Publishing finishes, and your Remote Web Site view shows a status message that indicates this status. There are also links below the status message to view the publish log file, view the remote Web site, or open the remote Web site in Expression Web 2.

12. Click **View your Remote Web site** beneath the status message to open your site in a browser.

You have now published a local site to a remote server by using HTTP in Expression Web 2. All of your local files are now on the server, and you have viewed them in a browser.

BE SURE TO leave the *CH9* site open for use in the next exercise.

CLOSE any open browser windows.

Publishing to a Disk Location

File system or disk location publishing is generally used to "copy" a site from one location on your computer or *local network* to another. You might find yourself needing to use this method in order to move a site from a folder location where you work on sites to another folder location where you archive finished work; or you might want to move a site from its existing folder location to a *network share* on your local network so that you can view it through a browser.

The method of publishing from disk location to disk location is superior to copying in Windows Explorer, because publishing ensures that all of your necessary files and none of the unnecessary files are moved. It's the best way to move a site and not run into problems with the metadata that Expression Web 2 uses to manage sites.

In this exercise, you will publish from one folder location to another by using Expression Web 2.

USE the *CH9* sample site you modified in the previous exercise.

OPEN the *CH9* site if it is not already open.

1. On the **File** menu, click **Publish Site**.

The Remote Web Site Properties dialog box opens.

> **Troubleshooting** This dialog box will remember the last publish destination and method you used. If you receive a server logon dialog box, click Cancel.

2. Click **File System**, click **Browse**, and then browse to the local folder in which you want to publish the site.

> **Tip** You can create a local folder location in the New Publish Location dialog box, or you can browse to *Documents\Microsoft Press\Expression Web 2 SBS\Sample Sites\ Publish\CH9.*

3. Create or select the folder you want, and then click **Open** to open the **Remote Web Site Properties** dialog box.

4. In the **Remote Web Site Properties** dialog box, click **OK**.

Expression Web 2 switches to Remote Web Site view.

5. At the top of the **Remote Web Site** view, click **Remote Web Site Properties**. Then in the **Remote Web Site Properties** dialog box, click the **Optimize HTML** tab.

6. To enable the HTML optimization options, select the **When publishing, optimize HTML by removing the following elements** check box.

> **Tip** These options are self-explanatory. In many cases, Expression Web 2 will rely on these comments and attributes being in the page code, and that's why they're only removed when they're published to the server. If you strip out comments and attributes that Expression Web 2 needs and then publish from the remote site to your local system, you will experience some usability issues when you edit the site in Expression Web 2.

7. In the **Remote Web Site Properties** dialog box, click the **Publishing tab**.

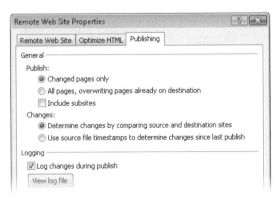

> **Tip** The options on this tab are also self-explanatory. Generally, a user will change them from their defaults for issues relating to publishing speed or a publishing strategy. For example, if the application takes too long and times out comparing files on the server to files in the local Web, a user can select the option to use timestamps rather than comparison. This will never be an issue in File System publishing. If the user's local site contains subsites, he or she may choose the option to publish subsites on certain occasions. In general, the Publish tab default settings don't require change.

8. Take some time to familiarize yourself with the options on this tab.

Another useful option that you can use is to choose whether you want the publishing operations to be logged and provides a link to view the log file.

9. Click **OK** to close the dialog box.

10. At the bottom of the **Remote Web Site** view, click **Publish Web site**.

During the publishing operation, the Status area in the lower-left corner of the workspace displays messages regarding the files being published.

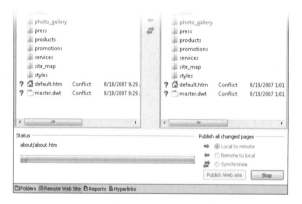

Because the publishing operation is from one local folder to another local folder, you will find this operation to be the fastest publishing method.

> **Tip** If you attempt to publish a local site to another local folder, as this exercise does, and the local site contains dynamic pages such as classic ASP or ASP.NET, you will be warned. The warning only alerts you to the fact that the dynamic pages won't function as they would on a server. There aren't any such pages in this sample site, but you should be aware of the possibility.

> **Tip** When you choose the Changed Pages Only option for publishing, if Expression Web 2 finds files or folders on the server that aren't present in the local site, you will be asked if you want to remove them. If you aren't absolutely sure you want the files or folders removed, click No.

Publishing finishes, and your Remote Web Site view shows a status message that indicates this status. There are also links below the status message to view the publish log file, view the remote Web site, or open the remote Web site in Expression Web 2.

11. Click **View your publish log file** beneath the status message.

    Your publish log opens in a browser. This log has an option box that enables you to filter the results for certain operations and makes deducing certain information easier.

> **Tip** Because this publish log file appears in a browser window, you have all the common browser file operations available, such as save and print. This functionality can be helpful if you need to save a record of publishing operations for a customer or to send information to the server administrator to report a problem.

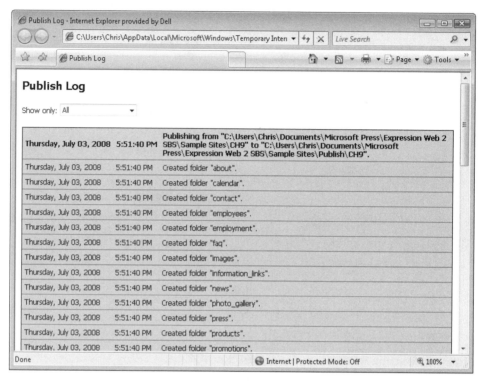

You have now published a local site to a file system location by using Expression Web 2. All of your local files were moved to a secondary local folder, and you have viewed the publish log file.

CLOSE the *CH9* site and any open browser windows. If you are not continuing directly to the next chapter, exit Expression Web 2.

Key Points

- Expression Web 2 provides four separate publishing methods: FTP, HTTP (FrontPage Server Extensions), WebDAV, and File System. Each serves a different purpose.

- Although FTP publishing is the most common publishing method, HTTP publishing provides several improved features and more functionality.

- Publishing by using File System is the most accurate and least error prone way to copy a site from one folder location to another.

- You can use WebDAV publishing in Expression Web 2 if you have it set up on your server.

- You can set various publishing options through the Remote Web Site Properties dialog box.

- You can optimize the HTML code of your pages by removing HTML comments, Interactive Button attributes, script comments, and other elements.

Chapter at a Glance

Edit server-based sites,
page 254

Publish selectively,
page 263

Use subsites,
page 266

10 Managing a Web Site

In this chapter, you will learn to

✔ Back up server-based sites.

✔ Edit server-based sites.

✔ Use site settings.

✔ Publish selectively.

✔ Use subsites.

Whether you're the owner of a single site or a professional webmaster who is responsible for a great number of sites, one of the requirements you will have is site management. This task takes many forms and comes into play at many points in the process.

In addition to being a good editing and publishing tool, Microsoft Expression Web 2 contains a number of features that offer the user a management system that's truly second to none. Possibly the most useful of these features is the ability to open and manipulate a site "live" on the server.

In this chapter, you will learn to back up and edit server-based sites, use site settings, publish pages selectively, and use subsites.

Important Before you can use the practice files in this chapter, you need to install them from the book's companion CD to their default location. For more information about practice files, see "Using the Companion CD" at the beginning of this book.

Troubleshooting Graphics and operating system–related instructions in this book reflect the Windows Vista user interface. If your computer is running Windows XP and you experience trouble following the instructions as written, please refer to the "Information for Readers Running Windows XP" section at the beginning of this book.

To improve the readability of the graphics in this book, Expression Web 2 was set to use the Windows color scheme instead of the default Expression Studio 2 color scheme.

Backing Up Server-Based Sites

Occasionally, the files on a *server-based site* can actually be newer than the files in the local copy of the same site. For example, if the server-based site contains *form data*, is a *shopping cart*, or is a type of *dynamic site* that takes user input, the server-based site will have more or newer information than the local copy. In this case, a backup copy of the server-based site is essential.

Another reason to back up a server-based site is that the local copy might become lost or corrupt, or be compromised in some way. Still another reason to back up a server-based site is that you might acquire a new customer and need all of their online assets to be brought down to your local computer so that you can work on them.

In all of these scenarios and others, Expression Web 2 takes care of everything. To fully exploit its capabilities, all you need is an understanding of how the features function.

In this exercise, you will back up to your local computer a site that exists on a server. No practice files are required for this exercise.

USE your own published site and server parameters for this exercise.
BE SURE TO start Expression Web 2 and have an active Internet connection before beginning this exercise.

1. On the **File** menu, click **Open Site** to open the **Open Site** dialog box.
2. In the **Open Site** dialog box, type the HTTP address of your server into the **Site name** box, and then click **Open**.

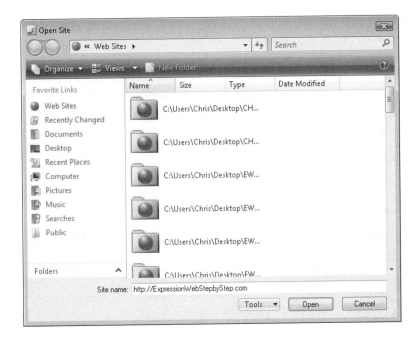

> **Important** This step assumes that your site has FrontPage Server Extensions applied. If it does not, skip to step 8 to follow the FTP method for backing up a server-based site to your local computer.

3. In the server logon dialog box, type your user name and password.

Your server-based site opens in Expression Web 2.

> **Tip** For this exercise, the server-based site that appears in the graphics is the one that was published in Chapter 9, "Publishing a Web Site."

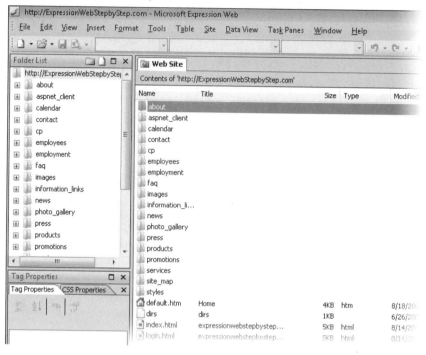

4. On the **File** menu, click **Publish Site**.

   The Remote Web Site Properties dialog box opens.

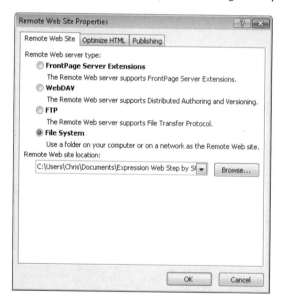

5. Click **File System**, browse to the local folder where you want this backup to reside, and then click **OK**.

> **Tip** If you want to create a new location, click New Folder at the top of the New Publish Location dialog box, name the folder, and then click Open.

Expression Web 2 switches to Remote Site view, with the local and remote sites in the workspace.

6. Click **Publish Site**.

Expression Web 2 publishes the site. The status message in the lower-left corner indicates where the publishing operation is in the process and when it finishes.

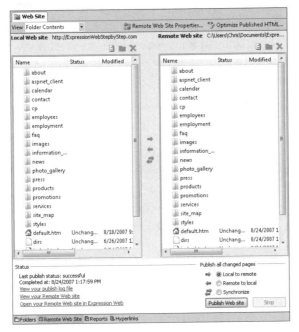

7. On the **File** menu, click **Close Site**.

Expression Web 2 switches to an empty user interface, with no site open.

8. On the **File** menu, click **Open Site**, type the FTP location of your server-based site into the **Site name** box, and then click **Open**.

The server logon dialog box opens.

9. Log on with your FTP credentials. If you want to have Expression Web 2 remember your credentials, select the **Remember my password** check box.

The Remote Web Site Editing Options dialog box opens. This dialog box enables you to open and edit an FTP site live on the server, or to edit a local copy and publish it at a later time.

10. In the **Remote Web Site Editing Options** dialog box, click **Edit local copy now, and publish changes to the server later**.

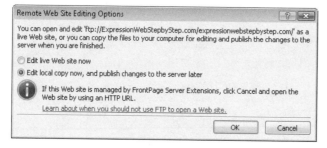

The function of this option is identical to performing a backup by publishing a server-based site to a local computer.

11. Click **OK** in the **Remote Web Site Editing Options** dialog box.

The Web Site Setup dialog box opens.

12. In the **Web Site Setup** dialog box, type the site's root directory into the **Root Directory** box.

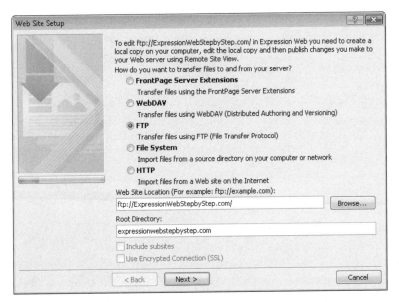

13. Click **Next** to start the **Import Web Site Wizard**. On the wizard's first page, click **Browse**.

The New Publish Location dialog box opens.

14. Browse to a location on your local computer to which you want to copy the site. Either click an existing folder, or create a new one by clicking the **New Folder** button at the top of the dialog box. After selecting the appropriate location, click **Open**.

You are returned to the Import Web Site Wizard, with the name of the folder that you clicked in the previous step now in the Local Copy Location box.

15. Click **Next**. Then on the final page of the wizard, click **Finish**.

The wizard closes, and Expression Web 2 switches to Remote Web Site view.

16. Click **Publish Web site**.

Publishing from the FTP site to the file system location begins. As publishing continues, the status message indicates where the publishing operation is in the process.

Publishing finishes when activity in the status message at the bottom of the workspace stops and the Publish Web Site button becomes active again.

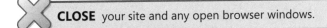

CLOSE your site and any open browser windows.

You've just published a server-based site to your local computer to create a backup. Expression Web 2 enables you to publish such a site by using either the HTTP or the FTP method.

The more frequently you back up a site, the more secured the data will be. These backup methods are also necessary for working on a site that has never been stored on your local computer, such as when you need a copy of a new customer's site to work on, or when you need a copy of a site for archival purposes.

> **Tip** One little-known feature of HTTP publishing is that you can open the server-based site and publish it to another server-based location. This feature can be useful in a number of situations; your local computer and local Internet connection are bypassed, and local connection speed is negated.

Editing Server-Based Sites

Occasionally, you will want to make a change directly to a server-based site. Rather than changing a local file and publishing it, you can make the changes directly to the files that reside on the server.

One reason for editing directly on the server is that you might not have access to a computer that contains a local copy of the site.

Another common reason to work on a server-based site is that you might be trying to fine-tune some server-side scripting and want to bypass the process of changing a local file, publishing it, and then checking the server-based file with a browser. By working directly on the server, you can make your change and test it, all from within the Expression Web 2 user interface.

In this exercise, you will make changes directly to a server-based site. No practice files are required for this exercise.

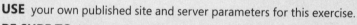

USE your own published site and server parameters for this exercise.
BE SURE TO have an active Internet connection before beginning this exercise.

1. On the **File** menu, click **Open Site**. In the **Open Site** dialog box, type the HTTP address of the server-based site that you want to open, and then click **Open**.

> **Troubleshooting** This step assumes that your site has FrontPage Server Extensions applied. If it does not, skip to step 10 to follow the FTP method for editing a site directly on the server.

The server logon dialog box opens.

2. Type your user name and password in this dialog box, and then click **OK**.

   The server-based site opens in Expression Web 2.

Save

3. Open any page in the site and make a change. It doesn't matter what you change, as long as you can recognize it when you view the file in a browser. Then on the toolbar, click the **Save** button.

Preview

4. Click the **Preview** button.

   The server-based Web page opens in a browser, and the change that you made is visible.

5. Close your browser, and switch to Expression Web 2.

6. On the **File** menu, point to **New**, and then click **Create From Dynamic Web Template**.

The Attach Dynamic Web Template dialog box opens.

7. Click **master.dwt**, and then click **Open**.

Expression Web 2 creates a new page based on the selected Dynamic Web Template.

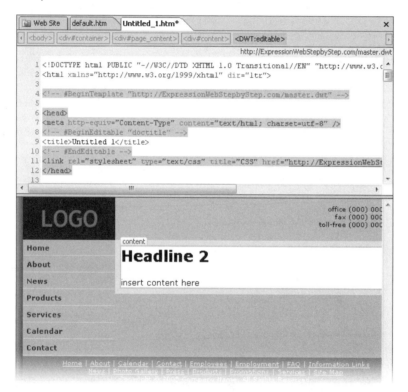

8. Click the **Save** button. In the **File name** box of the **Save As** dialog box, type **livepage.htm**, and then click **Save**. Click the **Preview** button to preview the newly created page in a browser.

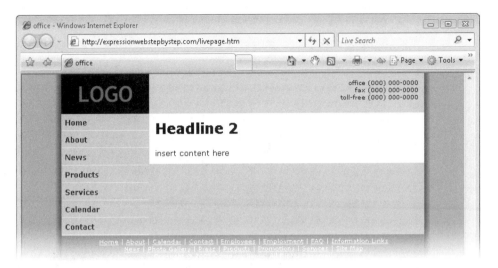

9. Close the open browser window, and switch to Expression Web 2. On the **File** menu, click **Close Site**.

   The site closes, and Expression Web 2 switches to an empty user interface, with no site open.

   > **Important** It's important that you either open a server-based site by using http:// (FrontPage Server Extensions) *or* FTP. Using FTP on a site with server extensions can cause them to become corrupted.

10. On the **File** menu, click **Open Site**. In the **Open Site** dialog box, type the FTP address of your server-based site, and then click **Open**.

11. In the server logon dialog box that opens, log on with your FTP credentials. If you want to have Expression Web 2 remember your credentials, select the **Remember my password** check box. Then click **OK**.

    The Remote Web Site Editing Options dialog box opens.

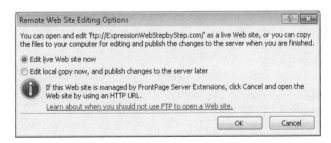

12. Accept the default selection, which is **Edit live Web site now**, and then click **OK**.

The site opens in Expression Web 2.

13. If there is a default folder for your public files, click it to reveal its contents. Open a page that you want to edit, and then make a change to the open file.

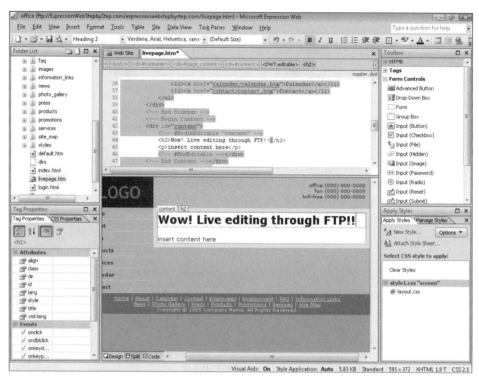

14. Save your page and preview it in a browser.

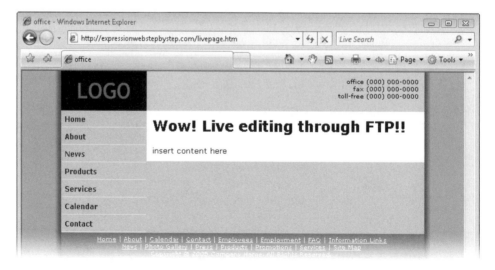

> **Troubleshooting** The first time you attempt to preview an FTP-based site, you have the option of setting up a custom URL to replace the ftp:// with http:// and append a domain name. If you select that option, you can set up the custom URL on the Preview tab of the Site Settings dialog box that opens. The main obstacle to overcome with setting up a custom preview URL in the Site Settings dialog box is the default folder. If your host configures your account to publish into ftp://{domain}, it will function properly; if you have to publish into ftp://{domain}/{root FTP folder}, it won't.
>
> If you can't open your FTP-based site through the Expression Web 2 user interface by using the custom URL, then open a browser window and type in the http:// address of the page you want to view.

 CLOSE your site and any open browser windows.

Microsoft Office FrontPage users have had the ability to edit a live site through HTTP for a long time, but the ability in Expression Web 2 to open and modify a live site through FTP is truly revolutionary. It's a capability you will not find in any other HTML editor.The capabilities of live editing and manipulation are much more robust through the HTTP protocol, but having these capabilities through FTP is also very useful.

Using Site Settings

Whether you have a local site from backing up a server-based site, or a site that you're developing from the start on your local computer, there are some management features available in a less than obvious location: the Site Settings dialog box. By using the Site Settings dialog box, you can customize the workflow and certain default settings for a site, on a global basis. You can also do a few things within the dialog box to troubleshoot a site that isn't functioning properly.

In this exercise, you will use the Site Settings dialog box to make global changes in a site, and you will troubleshoot some functionality problems of the type that might occur as you work on a site.

 USE the *CH10* sample site. This sample site is located in the *Documents\Microsoft Press\ Expression Web 2 SBS\Sample Sites* folder.
OPEN the *CH10* site by clicking Open Site on the File menu.

1. On the **Site** menu, click **Site Settings**.

The Site Settings dialog box opens. The Web Name box on the General tab is where you can change the site name.

> **Important** Using the Web Name box is the only way that you should change an Expression Web 2 site name. If you change the name in Windows Explorer, issues might arise with the site's metadata.

The Manage The Web Site Using Hidden Metadata Files check box enables you to selectively use or not use the Expression Web 2 metadata.

> **Important** This is a feature that you will generally leave enabled. The metadata aids Expression Web 2 in such functions as keeping links maintained, keeping the correct Dynamic Web Template attached to the correct pages, and remembering where the site has been published. If you clear the check box, Expression Web 2 will not only stop using metadata, it will also strip it from the site. Stripping the metadata might be purposely done if you were going to compress the site and send it to another developer or designer who publishes with a third-party FTP client, for example. The best practice for stripping metadata is to publish to another file-based location; in the publishing options, optimize HTML by selecting all options on the Optimize HTML tab, and then open the published site and clear the Manage The Web Site Using Hidden Metadata Files check box on the General tab of the Site Settings dialog box to strip the metadata from the published site.

2. In the **Site Settings** dialog box, click the **Preview** tab.

On the Preview tab, the Preview Using Web Site URL option enables the preview to reflect the URL that the site is opened from. The Use Microsoft Expression Development Server check box is selected by default, and so is its suboption, For Only PHP And ASP.NET Web Pages. The For All Web Pages option causes any page to be previewed by using the *ASP.NET Development Server* that comes with Expression Web 2.

The ASP.NET Development Server passes any page to the browser during preview, but it runs server-side scripting only in the PHP or the ASP.NET languages. It will not execute *Classic ASP*, or any other *server-side scripting*.

Here's one example that illustrates why you might want to pass all pages through the Development Server: you're designing a static HTML site, but you're setting your links to the folder that contains the page rather than the page itself. Your links will be to, for example, */about/* rather than */about/default.htm*. If you're not using a server when you click a link such as this in browser preview, you will be presented with a Windows Explorer view of the folder, and the browser will not display the default file within that folder. Enabling the ASP.NET Development Server will remedy this situation and pass the default file in a folder to the browser.

3. In the **Site Settings** dialog box, click the **Advanced** tab.

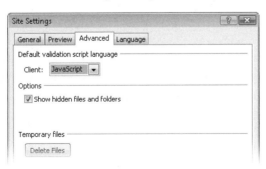

The Default Validation Script Language option enables you to select a default language for *form validation*. Generally, JavaScript should always be selected for this option, because not all browsers can handle *VBScript*.

The Show Hidden Files And Folders check box changes the default behavior of whether Expression Web 2 shows folders beginning with an underscore. For example, if you name a folder *_DontShowMe*, and this check box is not selected, the folder will not be visible in any of the Expression Web 2 views, such as the Folder List or the Folders view.

> **Tip** The Show Hidden Files And Folders check box can be used for greater functionality and better management. Here's a scenario: you've built a site, and other users are going to update page content. You've used a Dynamic Web Template to ensure that the other users don't edit outside the editable regions you've set up. If you put the Dynamic Web Template in a hidden folder and clear the Show Hidden Files And Folders check box, the users will be much less likely to find the Dynamic Web Template and to make unwanted changes to it.

Finally, on the Advanced tab, under Temporary Files, is the Delete Files button. This button does just that: it deletes temporary files that Expression Web 2 creates behind the scenes while you're working on a site.

> **Troubleshooting** The Delete Files button should be remembered. If Expression Web 2 begins to run into problems while publishing a site, or updating Dynamic Web Template–attached pages, the remedy is to use the Delete Files button to delete the temporary files, and then click Recalculate Hyperlinks on the Site menu. This operation almost always resolves the problem.

4. In the **Site Settings** dialog box, click the **Language** tab.

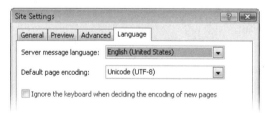

With the Server Message Language option, you can set the language for the messages a server passes to the browser. You can change this language only when you have a server-based site open in Expression Web 2 and the server it's on is a Windows server with FrontPage Server Extensions.

Default Page Encoding enables you to set the default encoding method of new pages. If you change it, you should also select the Ignore The Keyboard When Deciding The Encoding Of New Pages check box.

You've explored all the tabs and functionality that are available in the Site Settings dialog box. This dialog box can be used on a local site and it can also be used on a server-based site that is opened through Expression Web 2.

 BE SURE TO leave the *CH10* site open for use in the next exercise.

Publishing Selectively

From the standpoint of speed during publishing, you might not want to rely on letting Expression Web 2 deduce which pages have changed. For example, if you changed only one file in a site, and you want only that file to be published to the server, you don't have to go through a full publishing operation.

Expression Web 2 provides an easy method for publishing specific files, and provides a method for ensuring that certain files are never published. One reason that you might not want specific files to be published is that if you keep original artwork inside of a local site for management, you don't want the large original files to be published to the server. Another reason is that you might have a *configuration file* in your local site that is different on the server-based site.

In this exercise, you will publish selected files by using File System publishing, and you will also prevent files from being published.

Tip You can also use these steps to publish to a server-based Expression Web 2 site.

 USE the *CH10* sample site that you modified in the previous exercise.
OPEN the *CH10* site if it is not already open.

1. On the **File** menu, click **Publish Site**.

   The Remote Web Site Properties dialog box opens.

2. Click **File System**, and then click **Browse**. In the **New Site Location** dialog box, navigate to the *Documents\Microsoft Press\Expression Web 2 SBS\Sample Sites\ Publish\CH10SelectivePublish* folder, and then click **Open**.

The Remote Web Site Properties dialog box reopens. The Remote Web Site Location box displays the selected folder.

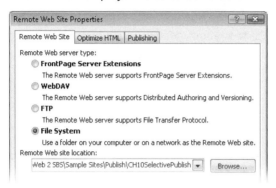

3. Click **OK**.

   Expression Web 2 switches to Remote Web Site view.

4. At the bottom of the workspace, click **Folders**.

   Expression Web 2 switches to Folders view.

5. Right-click **default.htm**, and then select the **Don't Publish** check box.

   A Don't Publish icon is added to the *default.htm* file's representation in Folders view.

6. At the bottom of the workspace, click **Remote Web Site**.

   Expression Web 2 switches back to Remote Web Site view. The Don't Publish icon appears next to *default.htm*.

7. Click **Publish Web site**. When publishing finishes, click **View your Remote Web site**.

Notice that the default page does not open in a browser, as is the customary behavior, but the site opens in Windows Explorer. The reason for this behavior is that the site lacks a default file (home page) because you set the default file to Don't Publish.

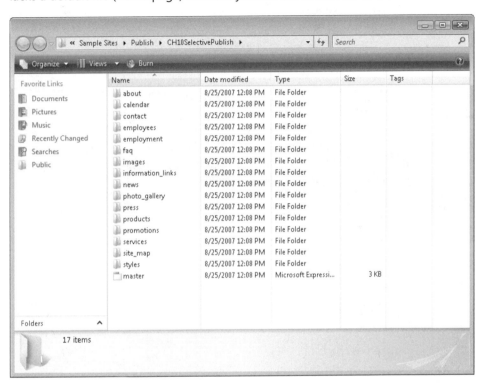

8. Close Windows Explorer, and switch to Expression Web 2. Right-click **default.htm**, and then clear the **Don't Publish** check box.

After you clear the check box, the page icon returns to normal.

9. Right-click **default.htm**, and then click **Publish Selected Files**.

Expression Web 2 publishes the *default.htm* page to the remote site.

10. Click **View your Remote Web site**.

The site's default file opens in a browser.

11. Close the browser, and switch to Expression Web 2.

To make the most of the Don't Publish and Publish Selected Files options, you should be aware that you can select multiple files and then select either of those options. This capability is particularly useful when you have a group of files that you want to selectively publish or set to not be published. For example, you might have a folder in your site that contains files you want only on your local computer. The files might be original artwork, notes you keep about the site, or files that must be different on the local and remote site, such as a configuration file for a shopping cart or other database application.

BE SURE TO leave the *CH10* site open for use in the next exercise.
CLOSE any open Windows Explorer or Internet Explorer windows.

You've now explored methods for publishing specific files, and also for setting files to never publish. These are very useful methods to use when you're working locally on a site that also exists on a server, and you want to publish only a single file that you've changed, or when you want to make sure that a local file never overwrites a server-based site file, such as a Microsoft Office Access database file (.mdb or .accdb), which often contains more or newer information.

Using Subsites

Subsites are an important concept for site management. Expression Web 2 treats subsites as though they were completely independent sites.

One reason that you might want to segregate certain folders in a site as subsites is that you might have a large number of files within those folders, and the files don't change as often as the other files in the root of the site. There's no reason to wait out a long file-comparison cycle during an Expression Web 2 publishing session when you know that the files haven't changed. Also, you may want to publish a segment of your site via the secure sockets layer (https://) if it contains sensitive files such as e-commerce site configuration or database files.

Another good reason to use subsites is that you might be developing a replacement site. You can create a subsite on your server-based site, such as *ExpressionWebStepbyStep.com/ new-design/*, and then publish your new design directly into the subsite. That way, you can show it to people by giving them the direct address to it, but the general public wouldn't know it was there and therefore wouldn't see it.

Subsites are a good way to segregate files for architectural reasons and also to provide for greater publishing efficiency.

In this exercise, you will convert a folder to a subsite, publish a subsite, and convert a subsite to a folder.

USE the *CH10* sample site that you modified in the last exercise.

OPEN the *CH10* site if it is not already open.

1. In the **Folder List**, click **SecondSite** to display its contents in the workspace.

   It contains all of the files necessary for a stand-alone site. Imagine that the *SecondSite* folder is a new template or replacement site that you are working on within the *CH10* root site.

2. In the **Folder List**, right-click **SecondSite**, and then click **Convert to Web**.

3. In the warning box Expression Web 2 displays, click **Yes**.

   > **Tip** This warning box is to inform you of the fact that Expression Web 2 will consider the folder as a completely separate site.

   Expression Web 2 converts the folder to a subsite. It now has a different icon, and the workspace displays a notice that Expression Web 2 cannot display the contents of a subsite.

4. In the **Folder List**, double-click **SecondSite** to open it in a new instance of Expression Web 2.

With the subsite open in Expression Web 2, you can perform any operation that you could perform on any other Expression Web 2 site, with the added benefit of being able to publish it independently of the parent site that contains it.

There are two ways to publish a subsite. One method is to open a subsite within Expression Web 2 and publish it as you would any other site. The second method is to perform the following actions: with the parent site open, click Publish on the File menu. On the Publishing tab of the Remote Web Site Properties dialog box, select the Include Subsites check box.

> **Troubleshooting** When you publish a subsite by opening it directly in Expression Web 2, be sure to append the publish location with the name of the subsite. For example, if you publish the parent site to *http://example.com*, but you want to publish a subsite to the server, just append *http://example.com* with /{name of the subsite}, resulting in a URL such as *http://example.com/subsite*. If you don't append the subsite name, all of the subsite's files will be placed in the root of the parent site. When it publishes a subsite for the first time, Expression Web 2 prompts you that a site does not exist at the location you're trying to publish to and offers to create a site in that location. Click Yes.

5. Close the Expression Web 2 window that contains the subsite, and switch to the Expression Web 2 window that contains the *CH10* sample site.

6. In the **Folder List**, right-click **SecondSite**, and then click **Convert to Folder**.

7. Click **Yes** in the warning box.

The subsite is returned to a conventional folder, and its contents are now displayed in the workspace.

 CLOSE the *CH10* site. If you are not continuing directly to the next chapter, exit Expression Web 2.

You've now converted a folder to a subsite and a subsite back to a folder within Expression Web 2. Because Expression Web 2 treats subsites as though they were completely independent sites, subsites can be an advantage for organizing and publishing efficiency. Keep in mind, however, that because they're treated as completely independent sites, you can't use an asset such as a Dynamic Web Template across the subsite boundaries.

Key Points

- With Expression Web 2, publishing is the preferred method of creating a backup. Whether you publish from one file system location to another, or from a server-based site to a file system location, the Expression Web 2 publishing operation is the key to success.

- With Expression Web 2, you can open a site live on the server and edit it as if it were a local site. New features in Expression Web 2 enable you to edit a server-based site by using HTTP or FTP protocols.

- Features in the Expression Web 2 Site Settings dialog box lay the groundwork for setting up an efficient workflow and for managing a site.

- In addition to the Publish Site operation in Expression Web 2, you can selectively publish individual files or groups of files individually, and you can also set pages to not be published at all.

- Using subsites can greatly aid in overall site management and publishing efficiency. Subsites can segregate files in a logical way and enhance the basic parent/child folder architecture of a site.

Chapter at a Glance

Use ASP.NET
master pages,
page 272

Use site
navigation controls,
page 282

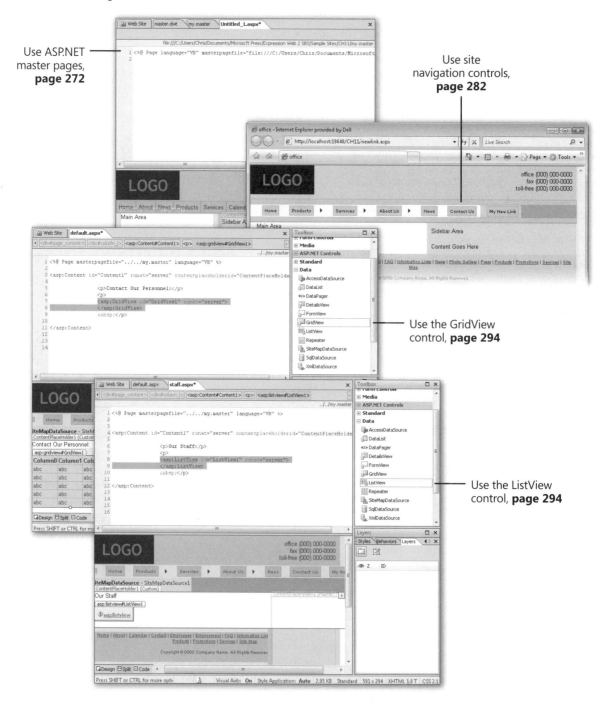

Use the GridView
control, **page 294**

Use the ListView
control, **page 294**

11 Using ASP.NET Features

In this chapter, you will learn to

✔ Use ASP.NET master pages.

✔ Use site-navigation controls.

✔ Use the AdRotator control.

✔ Link to data sources and use data controls.

Although Microsoft ASP.NET might be new to some users, the first beta release was in late 2000. It's a platform that was developed by Microsoft, and it's a huge source of capability. What can you do with ASP.NET? Literally, anything that can be done!

Microsoft Expression Web 2 and ASP.NET make a great combination that enables you to insert some rather advanced controls into your pages without writing any code.

To facilitate using ASP.NET within Expression Web 2, there is a group in the Toolbox task pane that has most of the commonly used ASP.NET controls that are used in Web pages.

One great feature that you can install along with Expression Web 2 is the ASP.NET Development Server. This development server is of particular value, because you can build a site in any folder-based location, and Expression Web 2 will preview that page for you through the built-in server. It's so much more convenient and straight-forward than having to set up a server on your local computer and previewing your pages by browsing them through that server, and it definitely beats having to publish your pages to an external Web server just to preview them.

In addition to providing the Toolbox task pane and the ASP.NET Development Server, Expression Web 2 enables you to modify the properties of ASP.NET controls by using the Tag Properties task pane in much the same way that you can modify cascading style sheet (CSS) or HTML elements.

For a designer, some of the most attractive controls that Expression Web 2 provides are master pages, *site-navigation controls*, *data access components*, *AJAX controls*, and *DataView controls*.

Expression Web 2 is intended to help you to work with ASP.NET controls and features; but if you're interested in full-scale ASP.NET programming, you're going to need more than this book and a copy of Expression Web 2. You'll need Microsoft *Visual Web Developer*, *Microsoft Visual Studio .NET*, or another code editor, and you'll need to learn a whole set of programming skills. You can use books or online resources such as *MSDN* or one of the many sites dedicated to teaching people ASP.NET. You'll find information about these resources at the end of this chapter.

In this chapter, you will learn about some of the ASP.NET capabilities, which of those capabilities are available from within Expression Web 2, and how to use the most design-related features to assist you in creating Web pages and sites that make use of those features.

Important Before you can use the practice files in this chapter, you need to install them from the book's companion CD to their default location. For more information about practice files, see "Using the Companion CD" at the beginning of this book.

Troubleshooting Graphics and operating system–related instructions in this book reflect the Windows Vista user interface. If your computer is running Windows XP and you experience trouble following the instructions as written, please refer to the "Information for Readers Running Windows XP" section at the beginning of this book.

To improve the readability of the graphics in this book, Expression Web 2 was set to use the Windows color scheme instead of the default Expression Studio 2 color scheme.

Using ASP.NET Master Pages

One of the most useful features in ASP.NET 2.0 for designers is master pages. They're similar to the Dynamic Web Templates that you've learned about in previous chapters; but, unlike Dynamic Web Templates, the master page content is not actually saved to the pages that it's attached to. Instead, the master page content is combined with the pages that it's attached to by the server just before the combined page is passed off to the browser. Therefore, master pages can save a considerable amount of space on your server and allow programmatic access to the template that you just don't have with a Dynamic Web Template. However, when you're ready to publish your site to a public server, you must publish it to a server that has ASP.NET 2.0 at a minimum.

The ASP.NET segment of the Toolbox task pane is divided into the following seven groups, each containing controls that you can use in your pages:

- **Standard.** Standard ASP.NET controls such as radio buttons, image controls, content placeholders, and other standard controls that are commonly added to Web pages.

- **Data.** Controls that allow you to easily connect to data sources and to insert data that the controls gather from the data source into a Web page.

- **Validation.** Controls that are designed to enable you to perform validation on your ASP.NET forms.

- **Navigation.** Controls that are designed to enable you to create navigation systems without having to write any programming code.

- **Login.** Controls that are designed to enable you to implement the user interface for membership systems in an ASP.NET site.

- **WebParts.** Controls for creating Web sites that enable end users to modify the content, appearance, and behavior of Web pages directly from a browser.

- **AJAX.** Controls for creating rich client behavior with little or no client script, such as partial-page updating (refreshing selected parts of the page instead of refreshing the whole page with a postback). Asynchronous partial-page updates avoid the appearance in the browser that the entire page has reloaded.

> **Tip** When you're adding ASP.NET controls to your page, it will be much easier if you can see a visual representation of them. To do so, point to Visual Aids on the View menu, and then enable Block Selection, Visible Borders, Empty Containers, ASP.NET Non-visual Controls, and Template Region Labels.

In this exercise, you will create a master page and then create new pages from the master page.

> **USE** the *CH11* sample site. This sample site is located in the *Documents\Microsoft Press\ Expression Web 2 SBS\Sample Sites* folder.
> **BE SURE TO** start Expression Web 2 before beginning this exercise.
> **OPEN** the *CH11* site by clicking Open Site on the File menu.

> **Tip** The Web site for Chapter 11 is based on the Small Business 3 template. The *DotNetVersion* folder at the root of the site contains ASP.NET example pages and other files that are necessary for the exercises.

1. Open the *master.dwt* file in Split view.

This is the default Dynamic Web Template for this site.

2. Click the **<body>** arrow on the quick tag selector bar, and then click **Select Tag Contents**. Right-click the highlighted <body> tag contents in the Code pane, and then click **Copy**.

This Dynamic Web Template will be used as a basis for the ASP.NET master page that you will create in the following steps.

3. On the **File** menu, point to **New**, and then click **Page**.

4. In the **New** dialog box, click **ASP.NET** in the left pane, click **Master Page** in the center pane, and ensure that the **Programming Language** is set to **VB**.

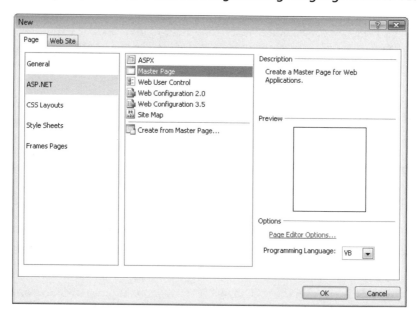

> **Tip** Expression Web 2 provides you with two choices for a programming language in the New dialog box: VB and C#. There is very little difference among these languages from a capability perspective. Select the one that you feel most comfortable with. If the master page is to be part of an existing ASP.NET site or application, you should obviously select the programming language that's already being used.

5. In the **New** dialog box, click **OK**.

Expression Web 2 creates a new file named *Untitled_1.master*.

6. Examine *Untitled_1.master*.

Notice that it's set up with all of the required elements for an ASP.NET master page. It has the VB language declaration above the <head> element of the page, and there's an ASP.NET FORM element and content placeholder in the <body> element.

> **Tip** Because this is an ASP.NET Web page, it requires a FORM element within the BODY element. In fact, if you delete the FORM element, Expression Web 2 replaces it automatically. Notice also that the <form> start tag has the same runat="server" attribute that the <head> tag has, which enables the ASP.NET runtime to have access to the form and its contents before the server passes the file to the browser.

> **Tip** You can design the ASP.NET master page by using the same method that you used to design your own Dynamic Web Template earlier in this book. Instead of inserting editable regions, you would insert content placeholders, which are available from the Toolbox task pane under the ASP.NET Controls/Standard headings.

7. In the Design pane, click **ContentPlaceHolder1**, and then on the quick tag selector bar, click **<asp:contentplaceh...#ContentPlaceH...>**.

8. Right-click the highlighted content in the Code pane, click **Paste**, and then click anywhere in the Design pane to show the changes in that pane.

9. On the **Format** menu, point to **CSS Styles**, and then click **Manage Style Sheet Links**. In the **Link Style Sheet** dialog box, click **Add**.

   In order to differentiate the page you're creating, choose a different style sheet than the *styles/style3.css* that the original Dynamic Web Template was linked to.

10. In the **Select Style Sheet** dialog box, click **style2.css**, and click **OK**. Then click **OK** in the **Link Style Sheet** dialog box.

    Notice that the logo image at the top of your template isn't appearing.

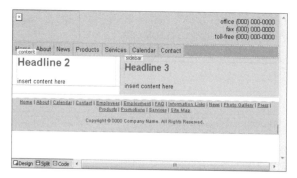

> **Troubleshooting** When you use an image in the HTML code of an ASP.NET master page, you should use the ASP.NET Image control, which is available in the Toolbox task pane. If you use this control, ASP.NET is able to correctly maintain the path to the image regardless of the folder level of the content page that the master page is attached to.

11. In the Design pane, click the image to select it.

12. In the **Toolbox** task pane, expand **ASP.NET Controls**, and then expand **Standard**. Double-click **Image** to replace the original image with the ASP.NET Image control.

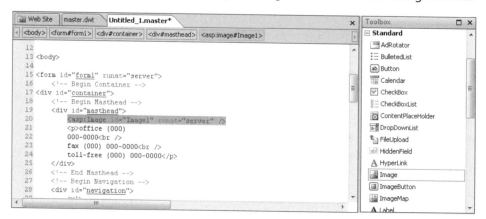

Your original image is now replaced with an *ASP.NET Image control*.

Save

13. On the toolbar, click **Save** to open the **Save As** dialog box. Save the page at the root folder of the site, with the name **my.master**.

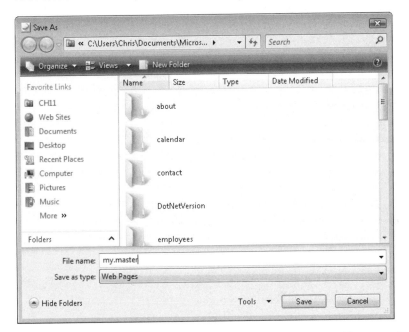

Be sure to save the page in the root folder of this site, and be sure that it has the file extension of .master, which is required for an ASP.NET master page.

14. With the newly inserted ASP.NET Image control selected, in the **Appearance** group of the **Tag Properties** task pane, click **ImageUrl**, and then click the ellipsis (...) button that appears to the right. In the **Select Image** dialog box, browse to the site's *images* folder, click **logo.gif**, and then click **Open**.

The broken image link is now corrected.

> **Tip** If you have trouble finding a particular task pane, clicking a specific pane on the Task Pane menu will bring it to the top of the Task Pane group.

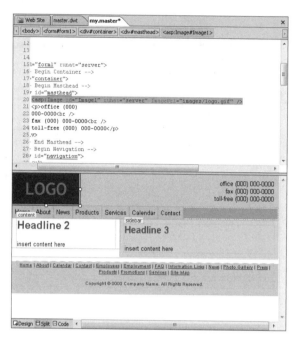

15. In the **Tag Properties** task pane, in the **Appearance** group, type **Company Logo** into the **AlternateText** box.

16. In the Design pane, click the editable region that contains **Headline 2**, and then click <DWT:editable> on the quick tag selector bar. In the **Toolbox** task pane, double-click **ContentPlaceHolder** to replace the Dynamic Web Template's editable region with an ASP.NET content placeholder.

17. Repeat this process on the editable region on the right.

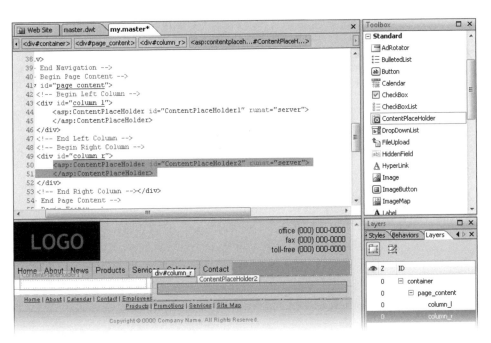

18. In the Design pane, click within **ContentPlaceHolder1** on the left, type **Main Content Area**, press ⎵Enter⎵ to insert a new paragraph, and then type **Content Goes Here**.

19. Click within **ContentPlaceHolder2** on the right, type **Sidebar Area**, press ⎵Enter⎵ to insert a new paragraph, and then type **Content Goes Here**.

20. Click **Save** to save the changes you've made so far.

> **Tip** These content placeholders work similarly to the Dynamic Web Template that you used in the previous chapters. The content that is within the placeholders in the master page will be written into the pages they're attached to. The content can be replaced within the content page. In a production setting, you could put meaningful text in these content placeholders so that users wouldn't necessarily have to replace the content; but if they chose to do so, the option would be there. For example, if you had a sidebar area that contained a content placeholder, you could insert meaningful text that would be appropriate for any page on the site, such as customer statements, special price deals, or announcements. Then, the default text could be replaced on a page-by-page basis or left as is.

21. On the **File** menu, point to **New**, and then click **Create from Master Page** to open the **Select a Master Page** dialog box. Click **Browse**, locate and click **my.master**, click **Open**, and then click **OK** to create a new page named *Untitled_1.aspx*.

22. In the Design pane, click **ContentPlaceHolder1 (Master)** on the left to select it. Click the small arrow that appears to its right, and then click **Create Custom Content**.

The content placeholder becomes editable.

23. Replace the text *Content Goes Here.* with **Custom content has been inserted**. Then click the small arrow to the right of the content placeholder.

Notice that the Create Custom Content option has been replaced with Default To Master's Content. This option resets any custom content that's been entered into a content placeholder to whatever content is in the master page.

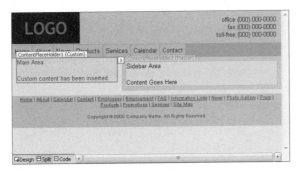

24. Click **Save**. In the **Save As** dialog box, name the page **text.aspx**, and then click **Save**.

Preview

25. On the toolbar, click the **Preview** button to preview the page. The ASP.NET Development Server starts and your page appears in a browser.

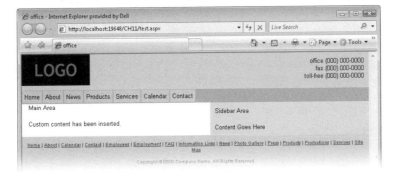

The ASP.NET Development Server makes possible a local preview of your page. Notice how it changes the URL of the page from the disk-based location to *http://localhost*, and then appends it with a ***port number***. By passing the page to the browser by means of the Development Server, you are able to preview the combination of the master page and the content page in real time. It's a very helpful feature for developing ASP.NET pages.

> **Troubleshooting** If you have problems previewing pages through the ASP.NET Development Server, you need to diagnose why it's not working and then take steps to correct the issue. Because it's a development server, it shows you detailed error reports if something goes wrong. Generally, there won't be a problem and common issues can usually be solved by downloading ASP.NET 2.0 redistributable from Microsoft and by running the package on your local computer.

> **Tip** If you switch to *text.aspx* and look at the Status bar at the bottom of the work area in Expression Web 2, you will see that the file is approximately 3 KB in size. Look at *my.master*, and you will see that it is approximately 5.5 KB. If these two pages were combined locally, such as with a Dynamic Web Template, you would have a page of approximately 8.5 KB.
>
> The file size of the template is always combined with the file size of the content page. Not so with a master page—the content page is not combined with the master page until the server prepares it to pass to the browser. In the case of a site with hundreds or even thousands of pages, the savings in file size would be significant.

BE SURE TO leave the *CH11* site open for use in the next exercise.

CLOSE any open Internet Explorer windows, and any pages in Expression Web 2.

By now, you should be aware of how easily you can keep all the pages in a site uniform by using the master page/content page arrangement, and also aware of how you can save file space on your server by using this ASP.NET 2.0 feature and create your own master page in Expression Web 2.

Using Site-Navigation Controls

ASP.NET 2.0 comes with three types of site-navigation controls: *Menu control*, *SiteMapPath control*, and *TreeView control*. They can all draw the navigational information from an XML file named *Web.sitemap*, which is saved in the root of your site. The Menu control is the *Dynamic HTML* type of menu that you might be familiar with. When you point to a link that has *child pages* below it, a secondary menu appears. The TreeView control is similar to what you will find at a site such as *msdn.microsoft.com* and is appropriate for organizing very large sites that have lots of *hierarchical information*. The SiteMapPath control provides what you might be familiar with as *breadcrumb* navigation, where it will indicate the page the browser is currently showing and pages in the navigation structure that come before and after it.

Each of these types of site-navigation controls can be inserted into your page from the ASP.NET Controls/Navigation group in the Toolbox task pane.

In this exercise, you will replace the original navigation in the master page that you created in the previous exercise with an ASP.NET navigation control, and you will also add a *node* to the sitemap file so that you can get a feel for editing a sitemap's XML structure.

USE the *CH11* sample site you modified in the previous exercise.

OPEN the *CH11* site if it isn't already open, and display the *my.master* page.

> **Troubleshooting** In order to follow the steps in this exercise, you will need to have completed the preceding exercise, specifically creating the files *my.master* and *test.aspx*.

1. In the Design pane, click **Home** in the navigation area at the top of the page. Click the **<div#navigation>** arrow on the quick tag selector bar, and then click **Select Tag Contents** to select all of the contents of this <div> tag.

2. In the **Toolbox** task pane, expand **ASP.NET Controls**, and then expand **Navigation**. Double-click **Menu** to insert an ASP.NET Menu control into the page and to replace the code you selected in step 1.

3. In the **Menu Tasks** pop-up window, click **AutoFormat**.

   The Auto Format dialog box opens.

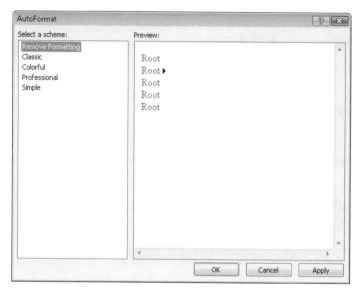

4. Click **Colorful**, and then click **OK**.

5. In the **Menu Tasks** pop-up window, in the **Choose Data Source** box, click **New data source**. In the **Data Source Configuration Wizard**, click **Site Map**.

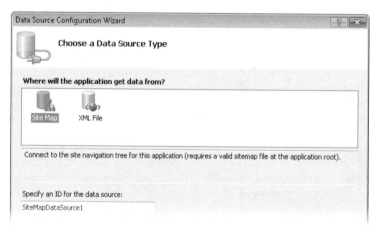

6. Click **OK** in the **Data Source Configuration Wizard** to set your changes and close the wizard. In the **Tag Properties** task pane, scroll down to the **Behavior** group, and type **2** into the **StaticDisplayLevels** box.

7. Scroll down to the **Layout** group, and in the **Orientation** list, click **Horizontal**.

8. Click **Save** to save the changes you made to the master page.

Preview

9. In the **Folder List**, click the *text.aspx* page that you made in the previous exercise. On the toolbar, click the **Preview** button to start the ASP.NET Development Server and preview your page in a browser. Although it's not attractive, pay attention to the functionality of the site-navigation control.

The page that is displayed in the browser has a link on the navigation bar that's formatted differently, and when you point to pages that have child pages below them, a *fly-out menu* appears. All of the visual aspects of this site-navigation control can be modified very easily by using the Tag Properties task pane, and you can change the colors and appearance to match the page template if you want to.

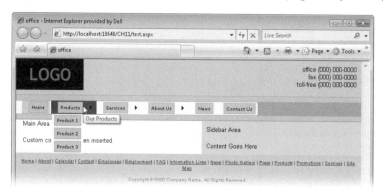

> **Tip** The other site-navigation controls can be inserted into a page and modified by using the same workflow. Take some time to experiment with them after you complete this exercise.

10. Close the browser window, and switch to Expression Web 2.

Because the site map file was already provided for you, the next steps will show you how to create a new page and add it to the site map file.

11. On the **File** menu, point to **New**, and then click **Create from Master Page**. In the **Select a Master Page** dialog box, click **Browse**, click **my.master**, click **Open**, and then click **OK** to create a new page.

Save

12. On the toolbar, click **Save**. In the **Save As** dialog box, name the page **newlink.aspx**, and then click **Save**.

Now you've created a new page, and you're ready to add it to the navigation of your site.

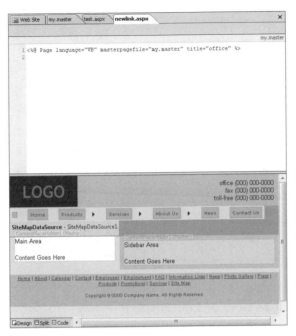

13. In the **Folder List**, double-click the file **Web.sitemap** to open it.

14. Type the following code just above the closing </siteMapNode> tag at the bottom of the page:

```
<siteMapNode url="newlink.aspx" title="My New Link" description="Just Added" />
```

15. Click **Save** to save your change to the site map file. Switch back to the file you created in steps 11 and 12 (*newlink.aspx*), and click the **Preview** button.

Your new page is now represented on the site-navigation control. Consider that the only file you saved was the *Web.sitemap* file. The addition of this link in the navigation control was done automatically by ASP.NET 2.0 and the ASP.NET Development Server.

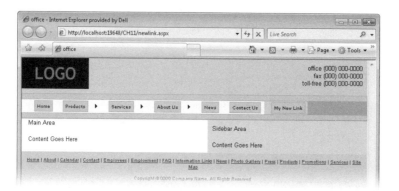

 BE SURE TO leave the *CH11* site open for use in the next exercise.
CLOSE any open Internet Explorer windows and any pages in Expression Web 2.

Consider this exercise: with nothing but an easily updated XML site map file, a few clicks of the mouse, and a couple of adjustments in the Tag Properties task pane, you've generated an easily styled and very usable menu for every page in your site.

Creating this type of menu by other means would have required substantial hand coding of JavaScript or the use of a third-party application to build the menu.

As you use these ASP.NET site-navigation controls, you should experiment with modifying the properties by using the Tag Properties task pane. There are literally limitless combinations of color, action, placement, and orientation that you can achieve by editing the properties of the entire menu or specific levels by using the Tag Properties task pane.

Adding, removing, or modifying pages within the sitemap is done in one XML file. No other pages need to be edited, but the change shows on every page that's attached to the master page that contains the control. These site-navigation controls can open a whole new world to you in your site design workflow.

Using the AdRotator Control

Now that you have had a chance to explore master pages and site-navigation controls, you will learn about another control from the Standard group in the Toolbox task pane: the *AdRotator* control. This control uses the information in an XML file to display advertising banners in a page.

In this case, you will add the banner to the master page in order to ensure that the banner is displayed in all the pages in your site that are attached to it. You will put the banner inside of the ContentPlaceHolder control of the master page so that a user can change it on a page-by-page basis.

In this exercise, you will insert an ASP.NET AdRotator control and modify the XML file that provides the information to display the ads.

> **USE** the *CH11* sample site you modified in the previous exercise.
>
> **OPEN** the *CH11* site if it isn't already open.

1. Double-click the file *my.master* in the **Folder List** pane to open it for editing in Expression Web 2. In the Design pane, click **ContentPlaceHolder2** on the right side of the page, click the **<asp:ContentPlaceH…#ContentPlaceH…>** arrow on the quick tag selector bar, and then click **Select Tag Contents**.

2. In the **Toolbox** task pane, expand **ASP.NET Controls**, expand **Standard**, and then double-click **AdRotator** to insert it where your ContentPlaceHolder control's content was.

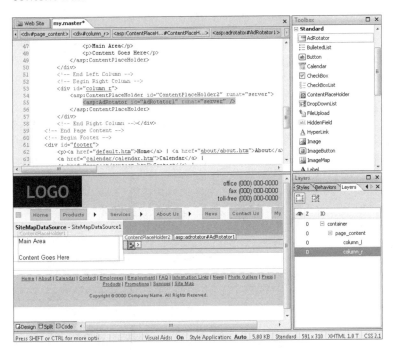

3. In the **AdRotator Tasks** pop-up window, click **New data source** in the **Choose Data Source** box. In the **Data Source Configuration Wizard**, click **XML File**, and then click **OK**. In the **Configure Data Source** dialog box, click **Browse** next to the **Data file** box, click **banners.xml**, and then click **Open**.

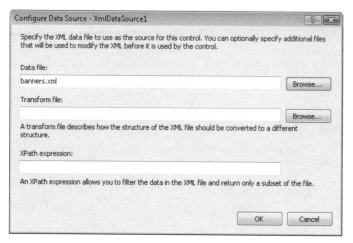

Save

Preview

4. In the **Configure Data Source** dialog box, click **OK**. On the toolbar, click **Save** to save the change you made to the master page, click **text.aspx** in the **Folder List**, and then click the **Preview** button to start the ASP.NET Development Server and preview *text.aspx* in a browser.

5. Click some links on the site-navigation control in your browser view.

Notice that the banner image changes randomly with each page load. Also notice that the area containing the AdRotator control doesn't look exactly as it should. You'll address that issue in the next few steps.

6. Close your browser window, and switch to Expression Web 2 and the master page. In order to fix the presentation of the template, click the **AdRotator** control in the Design pane. In the **Layout** group of the **Tag Properties** task pane, set the **height** to **300px** and the **width** to **150px**.

7. Click **<div#column_r>** on the quick tag selector bar to select the right column. On the **CSS Properties** tab, in the **Position** group of the **Tag Properties** task pane, set the **height** to **300px** and the **width** to **150px**.

8. In the Design pane, click **ContentPlaceHolder1**, and then click **<div#column_l>** on the quick tag selector bar. In the **CSS Properties** task pane, in the **Position** group, type **100%** in the **width** box, and remove the values from the **margin** box.

9. On the quick tag selector bar, click **<div#page_content>**. In the **CSS Properties** task pane, in the **Position** group, type **500px** in the **min-height** box.

10. Click **Save** to save your changes to the master page. When prompted, save the changes to the style sheet, accepting the default action of **Overwrite**.

11. In the **Folder List** task pane, open **text.aspx**, and then click the **Preview** button to preview your changes in a browser.

12. Close your browser window, and switch to Expression Web 2. In the **Folder List**, double-click **banners.xml** to open it.

You will add another node to the file in order to display the final unused banner image.

13. Insert the following code just before the closing </Advertisements> tag.

> **Tip** You don't actually have to type the code. Just copy the last node in the file from the start <Ad> tag to the end </Ad> tag (Expression Web 2), paste it above the closing </Advertisements> tag, and then replace the instances of "Web" with "Studio". If the nodes become out of alignment from working on the XML file, just right-click the page and click Reformat XML.

```
<Ad>
    <ImageUrl>~/images/studio-banner.jpg</ImageUrl>
    <NavigateUrl>http://www.microsoft.com/expression/products/
        overview.aspx?key=studio</NavigateUrl>
    <AlternateText>Visit Microsoft's Expression Studio Site</AlternateText>
    <Height>300</Height>
    <Width>150</Width>
    <Keywords>
    </Keywords>
    <Impressions>
    </Impressions>
</Ad>
```

14. On the toolbar, click **Save** to save the changes to the XML file.

15. In the **Folder List**, click **test.aspx**, and then click the **Preview** button to view the file in a browser. Click **Refresh** on the browser several times to make sure that you see the Expression Studio image.

 BE SURE TO leave the *CH11* site open for use in the next exercise.

CLOSE any open Internet Explorer windows and any pages in Expression Web 2.

In the preceding exercise, you were able to insert a dynamic banner rotator into your master page that gets its content data from an XML file. You formatted the control and added a new banner to the XML file by directly editing its contents. The impressive thing is that you were able to insert a control such as this without writing one single line of programming code.

> **Tip** Just because it's called an AdRotator control doesn't mean that's all you can use it for. For instance, you could use this control to show graphical links to pages within your own site that you want to draw attention to.

Linking to Data Sources and Using Data Controls

The ability to draw information from a database and display it on a Web page has previously been a fairly complicated task. Not so with ASP.NET. Because ASP.NET uses *providers* and has the ability to deal with data natively, you don't need to write any programming code to display data from a database on your Web pages.

ASP.NET can work with Microsoft Office Access databases, *Microsoft SQL Server databases*, XML files, *Microsoft Office Excel files*, and even *Oracle*, *IBM DB2*, and MySQL databases.

In this exercise, you will display information from a Microsoft Office Access database in your Web page.

USE the *CH11* sample site you modified in the previous exercise.
OPEN the *CH11* site if it isn't already open.

1. In the **Folder List** task pane, expand the *DotNetVersion* folder, expand the *contact* folder, and then double-click **default.aspx** to open it for editing. In the Design pane, click **ContentPlaceHolder1**, and then click the small arrow button in its upper-right corner. Click **Create Custom Content**.

2. Click inside the **ContentPlaceHolder**, delete any existing text from the area, and type **Contact Our Personnel:**. Then press [Enter] to create a new paragraph.

3. In the **Toolbox** task pane, expand **ASP.NET Controls**, expand **Data**, and then double-click **GridView** to insert an ASP.NET GridView control.

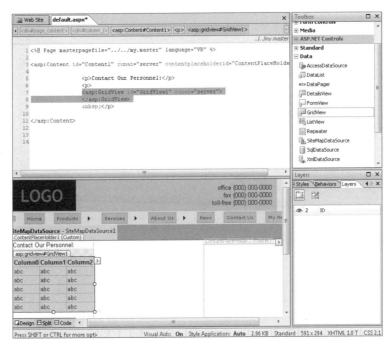

4. In the **GridView Tasks** pop-up window, in the **Choose Data Source** box, click **New data source**. In the **Data Source Configuration Wizard**, click **Access Database**.

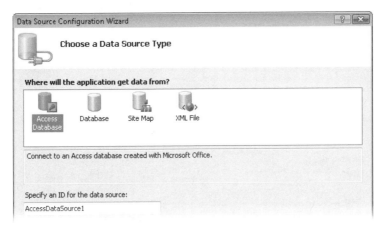

5. Click **OK** in the wizard. In the **Configure Data Source** dialog box, click **Browse**, click the **CH11** database in the root of the site, and then click **Open**.

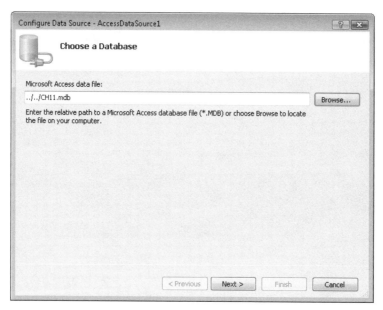

6. Click **Next**. This part of the wizard helps you select the data you want to display. In the **Name** list, click **Employees**. Under **Columns**, select the **FirstName**, **LastName**, **E-mail Address**, **Business Phone**, and **Job Title** check boxes.

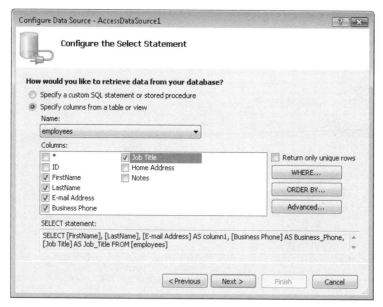

7. Click **Next**. On the **Test Query** page, click **Test Query** to ensure that you are connecting to the database.

If the query functions properly, you will see a table of the data that you selected in step 6.

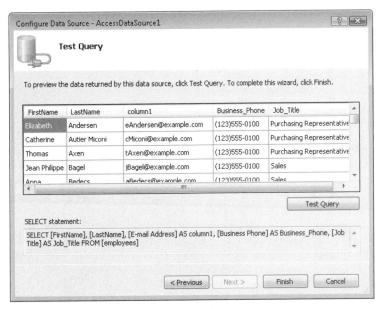

8. Click **Finish** to close the **Configure Data Source Wizard**.

You now have a GridView control in your page.

Save

9. On the toolbar, click **Save**, and then click the **Preview** button to view the page and its grid view in a browser.

Preview

10. Close the browser window, and switch to Expression Web 2. Examine the grid view that you inserted into the page.

Notice that there are now more options on the GridView Tasks pop-up window.

11. Click **Edit Columns** to open the **Fields** dialog box.

12. In the **Selected Fields** list, click **Business_Phone**, and then under **BoundField properties**, in the **HeaderText** box, replace *Business_Phone* with **Phone**. Repeat the process to replace *Job_Title* with **Title**, *FirstName* with **First Name**, *LastName* with **Last Name**, and *column1*, with **E-mail**.

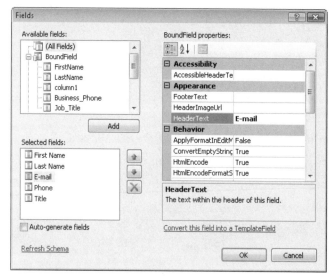

13. Click **OK** in the **Fields** dialog box. In the **GridView Tasks** pop-up window, select the **Enable Paging** and the **Enable Sorting** check boxes.

14. With the GridView control still selected, in the **Tag Properties** task pane **Layout** group, type **400px** in the **width** box.

15. On the toolbar, click **Save**, and then click **Preview** to preview the page in a browser.

The column headers are now hyperlinks that sort the rows below them, in addition to having different text. If you scroll to the bottom of the page, you'll see that numerical paging is also set up on the employee list.

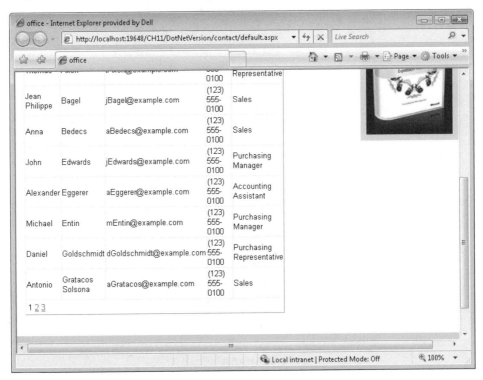

16. Close your browser and return to Expression Web 2. Expand the *About* folder within the *DotNetVersion* folder. Double-click **staff.aspx** to open it for editing.

17. In the **Design** pane, click **ContentPlaceHolder1**, and click the small arrow in its upper-right corner. Then click **Create Custom Content**.

18. Click inside the **ContentPlaceHolder**, delete any existing text from the area, and type **Our Staff:**. Then press ⌷Enter⌷ to create a new paragraph.

19. In the **ASP.NET Controls** group of the **Toolbox** task pane, double-click **ListView** to insert an ASP.NET ListView control.

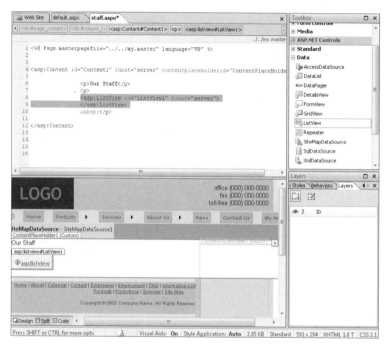

20. Click the red warning (**asp:listview**) link in the design pane.

The Confirm message box opens.

The message informs you that the ListView control requires the .NET Framework version 3.5, and asks whether you'd like to add a web.config file to your site in order to support that framework.

21. Click **Yes** in the message box. Then on the toolbar, click the **Save** button.

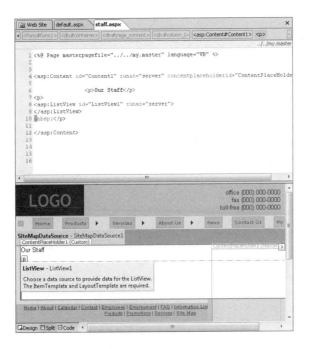

> **Troubleshooting** If you don't have a visual representation of the ListView control at this point, close and reopen the page you're working on.

22. Click the **ListView control** arrow to reveal the **ListView Tasks** pop-up window, click the **Choose Data Source** arrow, and then click **New Data Source**.

The Data Source Configuration Wizard opens.

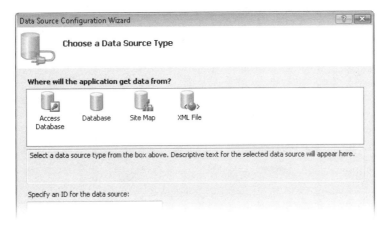

23. Click **Access Database**, and then click **OK** to open the **Choose a Database** dialog box. Browse to the *CH11* Access database file in the root of this site.

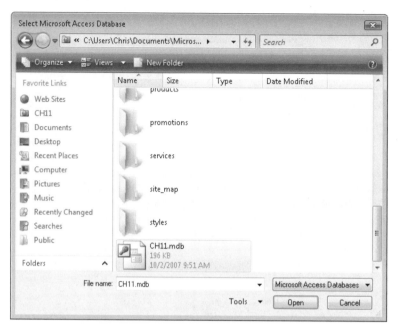

24. Click **CH11.mdb**, and then click **Open**. In the **Choose a Database** dialog box, click **Next** to open the **Configure the Select Statement** dialog box. Select the **FirstName**, **LastName**, **Job Title**, and **Notes** check boxes.

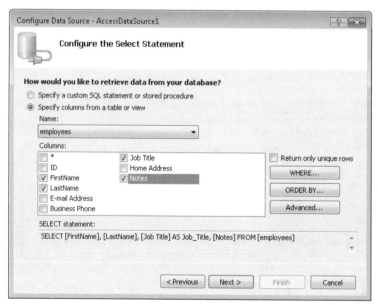

25. Click **Next**, and then **Finish**. In the **ListView Tasks** pop-up window, click **Configure ListView**.

The Configure ListView dialog box opens.

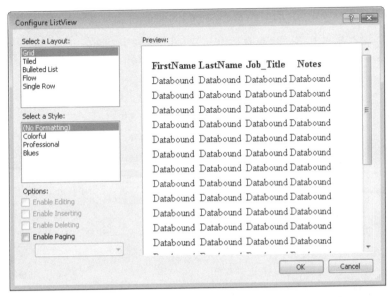

26. Under **Select a Layout**, click **Bulleted List**. Select the **Enable Paging** check box and ensure that Next/Previous Pages is in the list below it. Then click **OK**.

27. On the toolbar, click the **Save** button, and then click the **Preview** button.

Staff.aspx opens in a browser.

28. Examine your bulleted list. Notice the paging buttons at the bottom of the list.

29. Close your browser, and return to Expression Web 2. In the **ListView Tasks** pop-up window, change **Current View** to **ItemTemplate**.

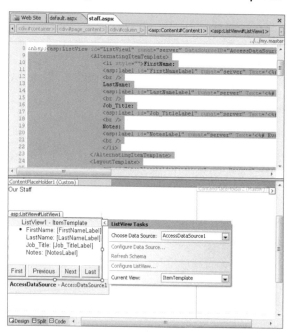

30. Set your cursor inside the list in the template, and delete the text **FirstName:** and **LastName:**. Then set your cursor just in front of **[LastNameLabel]** and press `Backspace` so that **[FirstNameLabel]** and **[LastNameLabel]** are on one line, with a space between them, and then delete the text **Job_Title:** and **Notes:**, leaving each of those labels on separate lines.

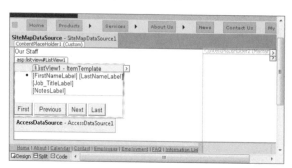

31. In the **ListView Tasks** pop-up window, change **Current View:** to **AlternatingItemTemplate**, and modify it exactly as you did in step 30. On the toolbar, click **Save** and **Preview** to check your list in a browser.

 CLOSE the *CH11* site and any open browser windows. If you are not continuing directly to the next chapter, exit Expression Web 2.

Creating a connection to a database, and then selecting the data you want and writing it into a page was a fairly technical and difficult task in the past. With Expression Web 2 and ASP.NET, you can do all that, and more, without writing a single line of code. Consider also that when ASP.NET renders this data to the page, it's just (X)HTML code, so you can style it by using CSS to limitless different appearances.

It's more impressive as you dig deeper into the capabilities provided by these data source controls and data views. If you've ever had to write code by hand, you will undoubtedly appreciate the added, advanced features that are available, such as Enable Sorting, and even editing the data in a browser.

Additional Resources

As this chapter draws to a close, the important point to take away is that there's so much available to you as a designer by using ASP.NET and Expression Web 2 that it isn't possible to show it all in this book. The ASP.NET features alone in Expression Web 2 could literally fill a book twice as long as this.

If you like what you've seen and done in this chapter with ASP.NET, you should continue to explore the features and capabilities by experimenting within the Expression Web 2 interface, participating in newsgroups, reading other books, visiting informational sites, and exploring ASP.NET applications that you can download from the Internet and examine within Expression Web 2.

This topic provides some information to get started in your endeavor to learn all that's possible with ASP.NET and Expression Web 2.

Dedicated programmers have spent countless hours putting together great tutorials just to help users who are new to ASP.NET to get a start with the platform. Some of the best tutorials can be found at the following locations:

- *msdn.microsoft.com.* A Microsoft site dedicated to developers.
- *asp.net.* The official ASP.NET Web site.
- *www.microsoft.com/expression/.* The official Expression product studio Web site.
- *asp101.com.* A great informational site with plenty of ASP.NET samples and tutorials.
- *dotnetspider.com.* Provides beginner-oriented tutorials for users who are interested in ASP.NET.

Some people learn best by downloading an application, opening it within Expression Web 2, and experimenting with it. If you'd like to try that method, the following are good applications to get started with:

- *www.microsoft.com/expression/kc/resources.aspx.* The Design Portfolio Starter Kit and Partner Portal Starter Kit from Microsoft. The Design Portfolio Starter Kit forms the basis of a portfolio application. The Partner Portal Starter Kit is more complex; it forms the basis of a partner portal and uses ASP.NET Login and Calendar controls.
- *comersus.net.* Comersus .NET Cart is an open source shopping cart application written in ASP.NET 2.0. It runs against an Access database, and if you open it with Expression Web 2, it runs in the ASP.NET Development Server just as it would on a public Web server.
- *quickstarts.asp.net.* Provides a good selection of applications that you can download and explore.

Key Points

- Master pages are a good alternative to Dynamic Web Templates.
- ASP.NET site-navigation controls are easy to deploy in Expression Web 2 and are very flexible.
- By using ASP.NET in Expression Web 2, you can insert a banner rotator without writing any programming code.
- You can easily use Expression Web 2 and ASP.NET 2.0 to write database content into a Web page without writing a single line of programming code.
- The appearance of ASP.NET controls can be easily modified by using the Tag Properties task pane.

Chapter at a Glance

Set up PHP,
page 310

Use PHP includes,
page 321

Use PHP functions
and variables,
page 325

12 Using PHP Features

In this chapter, you will learn to

- ✔ Set up PHP.
- ✔ Create a PHP page.
- ✔ Convert an HTML page to PHP.
- ✔ Use PHP includes in Expression Web 2.
- ✔ Use PHP functions and variables.

PHP is a powerful scripting language that is platform independent. As long as your host has PHP installed on your server, you can use it regardless of server type. When a browser requests a PHP page, the PHP script is executed on the server and the resulting HTML is sent to the browser. PHP pages may contain text, HTML, and *script blocks*, and offer similar functionality to *Legacy ASP* pages.

Microsoft Expression Web 2 provides several tools to make working with PHP easier and also assists the user in creating and previewing PHP files. Programming in PHP is a very broad topic and is outside the scope of this book.

In this chapter, you will become familiar with the tools that come with Expression Web 2 and how to use them. You will learn how to create a PHP page and convert an HTML page to PHP. You will also learn how to work with PHP functions, variables, and includes in Expression Web 2. At the end of the chapter, you will find references to more information about programming in PHP.

Important Before you can use the practice files in this chapter, you need to install them from the book's companion CD to their default location. For more information about practice files, see "Using the Companion CD" at the beginning of this book.

> **Troubleshooting** Graphics and operating system–related instructions in this book reflect the Windows Vista user interface. If your computer is running Windows XP and you experience trouble following the instructions as written, please refer to the "Information for Readers Running Windows XP" section at the beginning of this book.
>
> To improve the readability of the graphics in this book, Expression Web 2 was set to use the Windows color scheme instead of the default Expression Studio 2 color scheme.

Setting Up PHP

In order to preview PHP files and execute the PHP code on your local computer, you must install PHP.

In this exercise, you will install PHP on your local computer and set it as an option in the Expression Web 2 Development Server.

> **USE** the *CH12* sample site. This sample site is located in the *Documents\Microsoft Press\ Expression Web 2 SBS\Sample Sites* folder.
>
> **BE SURE TO** start Expression Web 2 before beginning this exercise.
>
> **OPEN** the *CH12* site by clicking Open Site on the File menu.

1. Go to *php.net/downloads.php*, and under the Windows Binaries heading, download the latest PHP.zip file. In the **Download File** dialog box, click **Save**. Then, in the **Save As** dialog box, browse to the location of your choice.

2. Right-click the downloaded folder, and then click **Extract All**.

3. In the **Extract Compressed (Zipped) Folders** dialog box, click **Browse**. In the **Select a destination** dialog box that opens, select the drive C location, and click **Make New Folder**. Then create a folder named **PHP**.

4. Click **OK** in the **Select a Destination** dialog box. Then in the **Extract Compressed Folders** dialog box, click **Extract**.

   All of the PHP files are extracted to the folder location that you set up in the previous steps.

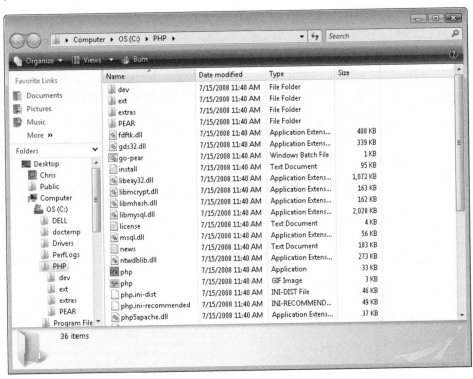

5. In the folder where you extracted the PHP files, locate the **php.ini-recommended** file. Right-click it, and click **Copy**. Then right-click whitespace in the folder, and click **Paste**.

6. Right-click the copied file, and then click **Rename**. Rename the file to **php.ini**.

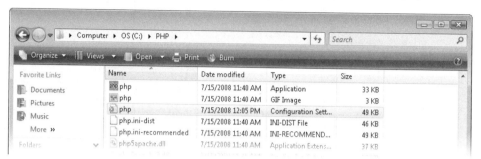

7. Close any open Windows Explorer and browser windows and return to Expression Web 2.

8. On the **Site** menu, click **Site Settings**. In the **Site Settings** dialog box that opens, click the **Preview** tab. Ensure that the **Use Microsoft Expression Development Server** check box is selected, and choose either **For only PHP and ASP.NET web pages** or **For all web pages**.

9. By default, Expression Web 2 looks for the php-cgi.exe file in the *C:\PHP* folder or the *C:\Program Files\PHP* folder. If you installed the PHP distribution in a different location or want to specify a different location for a specific Web site (perhaps to test against an older PHP version), click **Use a PHP executable only for this website**, and then click **Browse**. When the **Select the PHP Executable to use** dialog box opens, browse to your installation folder.

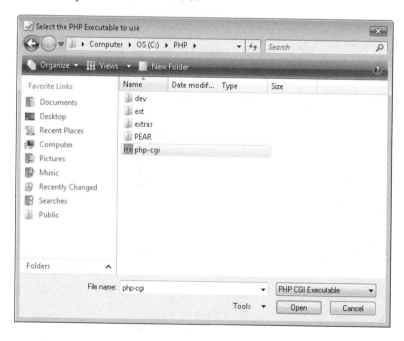

10. Click the **php-cgi** file, and then click **Open** to open the **Site Settings** dialog box.

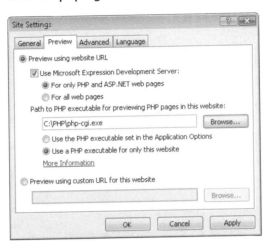

11. In the **Site Settings** dialog box, set the path to the PHP executable, and then click **OK**.

12. Return to Expression Web 2. In the **Folder List**, double-click the **default.php** file to open it for editing in Expression Web 2.

Only one snippet of PHP code is contained in the page.

13. To enable a visible representation of your PHP code blocks, on the **View** menu, point to **Formatting Marks**, and then click **Script Blocks**.

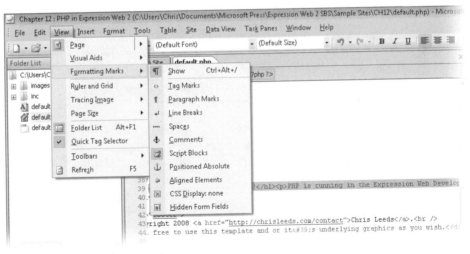

Preview

14. To test your path to the PHP executable, on the toolbar, click the **Preview** button.

The Expression Web Development Server opens and displays the file in a browser. The PHP *echo* statement executes and shows HTML content where the script block tag was in the preview pane.

 BE SURE TO leave the *CH12* site open for use in the next exercise.

CLOSE your browser and return to Expression Web 2.

Tip If the file fails to execute and you don't see the HTML content in the previous image, look on the Preview tab in the Site Settings dialog box for the correct path to your PHP executable and Development Server options.

The first time you preview a page through the Development Server, you may see an alert dialog box stating "The php.ini file is not configured correctly. Would you like Expression Web to configure this file?"

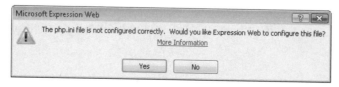

Click Yes so that Expression Web 2 corrects the .ini file for you.

Now that you have PHP installed on your computer and configured for your site, you are ready to move on to using some of the features available in Expression Web 2.

Creating a PHP Page

Although just about any HTM or HTML file can be renamed to have a .php extension, you may run into trouble with Byte Order Marks (BOMs). A BOM is a Unicode character used to denote the beginning of a string of Unicode characters and to serve as a marker that indicates the text is encoded in UTF-8, UTF-16, or UTF-32. In most cases, it will never be visible in a browser but it can cause problems in PHP files.

To avoid a BOM, it's best to create a new PHP file directly from the New Document menu in Expression Web 2. However, converting an existing HTM/HTML file to PHP is a solution you may need when working within an existing file that you want to run PHP scripting on. You'll learn how to do this in the next topic.

In this exercise, you will create a PHP page in Expression Web 2.

USE the *CH12* sample site you modified in the previous exercise.

OPEN the *CH12* site if it isn't already open.

> **Troubleshooting** In order to follow the steps in this exercise, you will need to have completed the preceding exercise—specifically, installing and configuring PHP on your computer and ensuring that the Expression Web 2 Development Server is set to the correct path leading to the PHP executable.

1. In the **Folder List**, double-click the **default.php** file to open it for editing. Right-click the script block in the Design pane, and then click **Copy**.

New Document

2. Click the **New Document** arrow, and then click **PHP**.

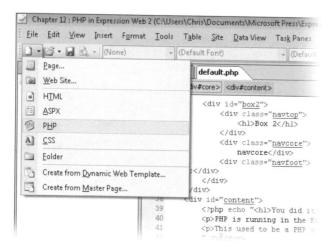

Expression Web 2 creates a new PHP file named *Untitled_1.php*.

3. Right-click in the Design pane of your new page, and then click **Paste** to paste the code block you copied in step 1.

4. Save your page to the root folder of your site as **MyPHP.php**, and preview it in a browser to ensure that the PHP code executes.

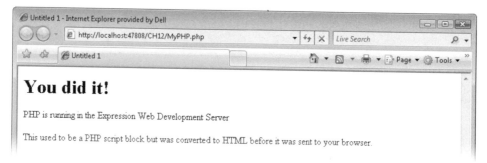

5. Close your browser and return to Expression Web 2. On the **Format** menu, point to **Dynamic Web Template**, and then click **Attach Dynamic Web Template**.

The Attach Dynamic Web Template dialog box opens.

6. In the **Attach Dynamic Web Template** dialog box, click the **default.dwt** file, and then click **Open**.

The Match Editable Regions dialog box opens.

7. In the **Match Editable Regions** dialog box, keep the default selection, and click **OK**. Then click **Close** in the updated pages dialog box that opens.

You now have a PHP page with an Expression Web Dynamic Web Template attached to it.

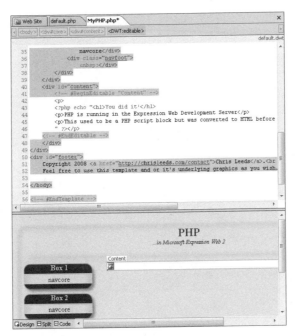

Depending on your workflow and the type of Web site you're working on, the ability to attach a Dynamic Web Template to a PHP file can be very useful.

8. Save your page and preview it in a browser to ensure that it works and displays the content contained in the PHP *echo* statement.

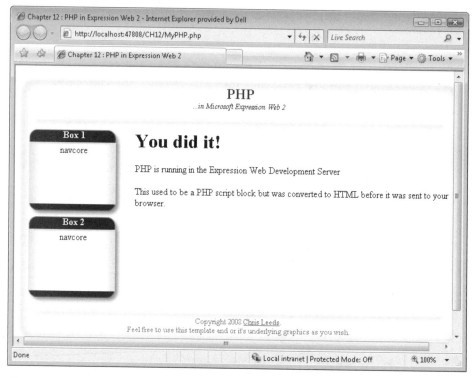

9. Close your browser and return to Expression Web 2.

 BE SURE TO leave the *CH12* site open for use in the next exercise.

Converting an HTML Page to PHP

Another way to create a PHP page is to rename an .htm or .html page to have a .php file extension. Caution should be taken if this is the desired method. A BOM, which is desirable in some HTML files, can be detrimental to reliably executing PHP in some cases.

In this exercise, you will convert an HTML file to PHP in Expression Web 2 and ensure that there's no BOM.

USE the *CH12* sample site you modified in the previous exercise.
OPEN the *CH12* site if it isn't already open.

1. In the **Folder List**, expand the *inc* folder, and double-click the **convertme.html** file to open it for editing. Right-click the Code pane, and then click **Encoding**.

The Page Properties dialog box opens.

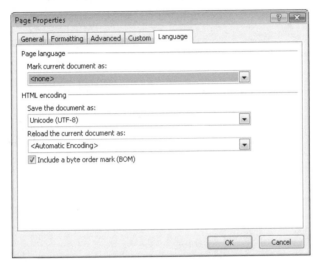

2. Clear the **Include a byte order mark (BOM)** check box, and then click **OK**.

Notice that *convertme.html* is now marked as a changed file. That's because the existing BOM was removed from the file.

Marked as a changed file

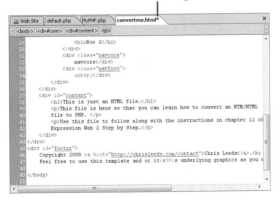

3. Save and close your page. Then in the **Folder List**, right-click the **convertme.html** file, and click **Rename**. Replace the *.html* with **.php**, and then press ⌷Enter⌷ to save the name change.

4. Double-click the newly named file to open it for editing. In the Design pane, set your cursor after the period in the last sentence of the content, and then press ⌷Enter⌷ to create a new paragraph.

5. On the **Insert** menu, point to **PHP**, and then click **Echo**.

A PHP echo statement is added to the Code pane of your page, with your insertion point set inside it.

6. Type "**PHP Runs**".

7. Save your page and preview it in a browser.

You have used the PHP *echo* to test whether the page will execute.

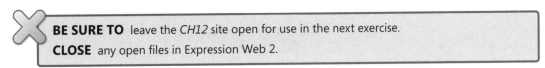

BE SURE TO leave the *CH12* site open for use in the next exercise.

CLOSE any open files in Expression Web 2.

Now that you are familiar with how to create new PHP files by two different methods in Expression Web 2, we can start to delve more deeply into some other Expression Web 2 features.

Using PHP Includes in Expression Web 2

Expression Web 2 makes working with PHP code in both Design and Code view easy. One of the features that aids in this is the ability to view include files in the design surface of Expression Web 2. The PHP Include feature yields results similar to a Dynamic Web Template.

In this exercise, you will move elements from within a page to a separate file, and then include the content of that file back into the page dynamically by using the PHP Include feature.

> **USE** the *CH12* sample site you modified in the previous exercise.
>
> **OPEN** the *CH12* site if it isn't already open.

1. In the **Folder List**, double-click the **MyPHP.php** file that you created earlier in this chapter.

Because we're experimenting with PHP exclusively in the coming steps, you will need to detach your page from the Dynamic Web Template

2. On the **Format** menu, point to **Dynamic Web Template**, click **Detach From Dynamic Web Template**, and then click **Close** on the updated files dialog box that opens.

3. Right-click in the Code pane of your page, and then click **Reformat HTML**. Save your page.

In the following steps, you will move the boxes from the left side of your page to a separate file, which you will include through PHP into your page.

4. In the Design pane, set your cursor in the **Box1** heading. On the quick tag selector bar, click the **<div#leftstuff>** arrow, and then click **Select Tag Contents**.

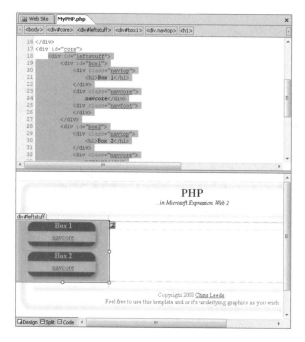

5. In the Code pane, right click the highlighted code, and then click **Cut**.

New Document

6. Click the **New Document** arrow, and then click **PHP**.

Expression Web 2 creates a file named *Untitled_1.php*.

7. Set your cursor in the Code pane, right-click, and click **Select All**. Then right-click again, and select **Paste**.

Because you will be including this page within another, you don't want the head, body, and Doctype tags.

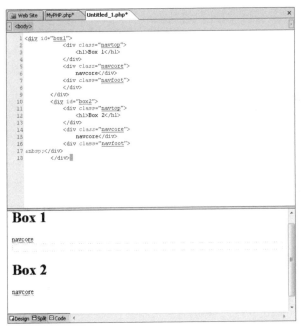

Save

8. On the toolbar, click the **Save** button. In the **Save As** dialog box, save your page to the */inc* folder as **leftstuff.php**.

9. Return to *MyPHP.php*, and set your cursor inside **<div#leftstuff>**. On the **Insert** menu, point to **PHP**, and then click **Include** to open the **Select an include file** dialog box. In the dialog box, click **leftstuff.php**, and then click **Open**.

In the Code pane, only an *include* statement was added to your page's code, but Expression Web 2 displays the resulting HTML in the Design pane.

10. Save your page and preview it in a browser to ensure that it runs correctly.

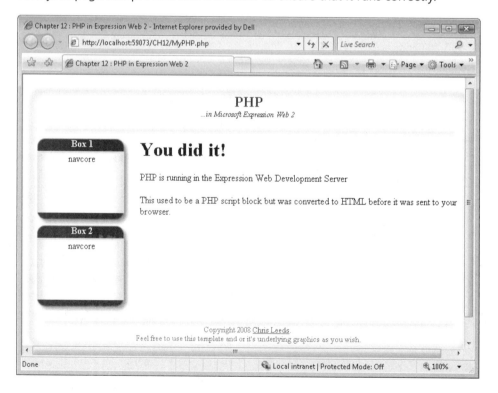

11. Close your browser window and return to Expression Web 2.

12. Repeat the steps above with the content of **<div#banner>** and **<div#footer>**, saving them also to the */inc* folder as, respectively, **banner.php** and **footer.php**, and including them into your page by using a PHP Include.

Script tag

13. In the Design pane, click the **Script tag** visual aid representing the PHP *echo* statement within the **<div#content>** area of your page, and then press ⌦.

In your Code view, between the opening and closing body tags, notice that there's very little HTML code. Besides having a clean page that's easy to insert content into, you can also protect more sensitive page areas from inadvertent modification.

```
Web Site   MyPHP.php*   leftstuff.php   banner.php   footer.php          ×

11  <body>
12
13  <div id="banner">
14
15  <?php include('inc/banner.php'); ?></div>
16  <div id="core">
17      <div id="leftstuff">
18
19      <?php include('inc/leftstuff.php'); ?></div>
20      <div id="content">
21          <p> </p>
22      </div>
23  </div>
24  <div id="footer">
25      <?php include('inc/footer.php'); ?></div>
26
27  </body>
28
```

14. Save your page and preview it in a browser to ensure that everything executes as expected.

BE SURE TO leave the *CH12* site open for use in the next exercise.

CLOSE any open files in Expression Web 2.

Using PHP includes in Expression Web 2 is a painless process that can be done in a completely graphical setting. The ability to see the content of a PHP include within the Expression Web 2 design surface is very helpful when designing a site that makes extensive use of them.

Using PHP Functions and Variables

As your use of PHP progresses in Expression Web 2, you will undoubtedly find yourself working in the Code pane more and more. Fortunately, Expression Web 2 has IntelliSense for PHP and some code completion tools that assist greatly.

In this exercise, you will use PHP functions and variables from both the Insert menu and in Code view by using IntelliSense.

> **USE** the *CH12* sample site you modified in the previous exercise.
>
> **OPEN** the *CH12* site if it isn't already open.

1. In the **Folder List**, expand the */inc* folder, and double-click **banner.php**, which you created earlier in this chapter. Set your cursor in the Code pane before the first HTML tag (<h1>).

2. On the **Insert** menu, point to **PHP**, and then click **Code Block**.

   Expression Web inserts a PHP code block into your page.

3. Enter the following lines inside the code block to set up some variables of your own, and then save the page:

   ```
   $Copy="Copyright &copy; 2007&#8211;";
   $CurYear= date('Y');
   $Holder="<a href='http://chrisleeds.com/contact'>Chris Leeds</a>";
   ```

   Now that you've declared those variables, you can use them anywhere.

4. In the **Folder List**, double-click **footer.php** in the */inc* folder to open it for editing.

   Next you will use a PHP *echo* statement to write the copyright line, based on the values set in the previous step.

5. Set your cursor in the Design view of the page, just before the first line of text. Then on the **Insert** menu, point to **PHP**, and click **Echo**.

   A PHP *echo* statement is added to the page.

6. Inside the *echo* statement, type the following code:

   ```
   "$Copy $CurYear $Holder";
   ```

   That line will take care of writing and updating the HTML in the page, based on what the actual year is.

7. Highlight the original copyright statement—everything between the closing PHP tag (?>) and the line break tag (<br />)—and press ⌦. Then save your page.

Preview

8. In the **Folder List**, click **MyPHP.php**, and then, on the toolbar, click the **Preview** button.

The browser now shows a copyright statement. It will update the current year auto-matically and if you needed to change the copyright holder or link, you could edit one location and have it automatically updated wherever the variable is used.

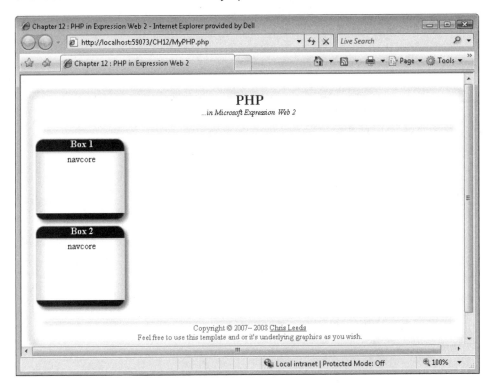

9. Close your browser window and return to Expression Web 2. In the **Folders List**, double-click **MyPHP.php** to open it for editing.

10. Set your cursor inside the <p> tag in the **<div#content>** section of the page. On the **Insert** menu, point to **PHP**, and then click **If**.

A PHP code *if* statement is inserted into the page.

11. With your cursor inside of the *if* statement, in Code view, enter an (, and then press Ctrl+L to reveal the IntelliSense choices. In this case, press F, and then press the ↓ key to select **file_exists**.

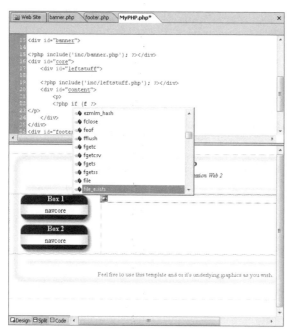

12. Press Enter to insert that variable. To see a tooltip for the variable, press Ctrl + Shift + Space .

13. As indicated in the tooltip, finish out the line of code by putting the file name in the syntax shown:

```
('inc/Untitled_1.php'))
```

> **Tip** You must always press Ctrl+L to display the IntelliSense window, and display the tooltips by pressing Ctrl+Shift+Spacebar.

At this point, you have successfully asked the server if a specific file exists by using PHP. In the following steps, you will add code to direct the server to write something into the page if that file exists, and something else if it doesn't.

14. Insert the next PHP instruction on the same line but begin and end it with a curly brace:

```
{echo "the file exists";}
```

15. Press `Enter` to break to a new line, and then type the following:

```
else {echo "The file does not exist";}
```

```
Web Site   banner.php   footer.php   MyPHP.php*                                    ×

13 <div id="banner">
14
15 <?php include('inc/banner.php'); ?></div>
16 <div id="core">
17     <div id="leftstuff">
18
19     <?php include('inc/leftstuff.php'); ?></div>
20     <div id="content">
21         <p>
22         <?php if (file_exists('inc/Untitled_1.php')){echo "The file exists";}
23         else{echo "The file does not exist";}| ?>
24 </p>
25     </div>
26 </div>
```

16. Save your page and preview it in a browser.

Notice that the server has written *The file does not exist* into the page.

New Document

17. Close your browser and return to Expression Web 2. Click the **New Document** arrow, and then click **PHP**.

18. Save the page. In the **Save As** dialog box, save it to the */inc* folder by using its default name, *Untitled_1.php*.

19. Return to *MyPHP.php* and preview it in a browser.

Because the file now exists, your statement executes differently.

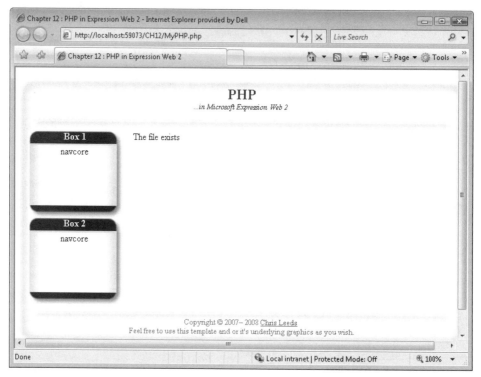

20. On the **Tools** menu, click **Page Editor Options.** Then in the Page Editor Options dialog box that opens, click the **IntelliSense** tab.

On this tab, you can enable or disable PHP function categories and customize the list to your preference. There are also features for PHP Global Variable Completion and PHP Parameter Information that you can enable or disable based on your preference.

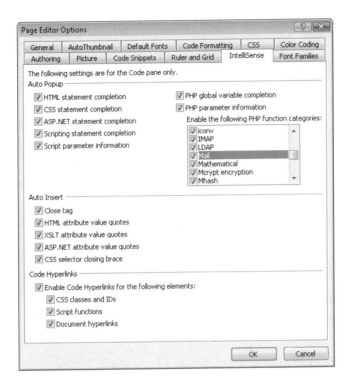

Page Editor Options

Tip You can customize the color scheme for PHP files on the Color Coding tab. There is a group of eight PHP items under the Display Items label that can be custom colored.

CLOSE the *CH12* Sample Site, and exit Expression Web 2.

Although the preceding exercise didn't have much specific meaning programmatically, you should now have a higher comfort level working with PHP in Expression Web 2, whether in Code view or Design view, and you should be familiar with how IntelliSense for PHP can help you write PHP code more quickly and with less potential for errors.

Additional Resources

If you'd like to learn more about PHP and how you can use it in your Web sites, you'll find a great number of resource sites on the Internet as well as in printed volumes.

Some very helpful online resources are:

- *php.net.* This PHP group's official site. Not just where you can download PHP executables to run on your computer, but a full site of documentation, help, and a full complement of developer resources.

> **Tip** If you're looking for quick information about a topic in PHP, you can enter the domain as such: *php.net/echo* or *php.net/include*. If there's a page for that topic, it will be displayed; if there isn't a page to display, you'll automatically see search results for the topic in question.

- *sitepoint.com.* This Australian site is full of practical examples for using PHP code. There are articles from both a design and a programming perspective. They also have several books on the topic of PHP.
- *php.resourceindex.com.* This is a very large index of "everything PHP," from completed scripts you can use, to communities of people using and learning PHP.

Key Points

- You can create PHP pages from scratch or convert an HTM/HTML page to PHP.
- PHP includes will show as an *include* statement in Code view, but render in Design view as you would see it in a browser.
- In order to use PHP to preview your pages locally with the Expression Web 2 Development Server, you must install PHP on your local computer.
- Commonly used PHP script blocks can be inserted from the Insert menu.
- Expression Web 2 uses IntelliSense for PHP, making it faster and easier to work with PHP in Code view.

Glossary

\<a\> An HTML anchor tag. When the tag includes an href attribute, it is a typical hyperlink. When it does not include an href attribute, it is a bookmark.

accessible A requirement that users with alternative browsers such as screen readers are able to understand and use a Web page.

ActiveX A set of technologies developed by Microsoft for enabling interactive content with multimedia effects and interactive objects.

Adobe Flash (.swf) A proprietary vector graphics file format produced by the Flash software from Adobe Systems. Flash files can contain animations and/or varying levels of functionality.

AdRotator An ASP.NET control that gets data from an XML file and rotates hyperlinked images in a particular place on an ASP.NET page.

AJAX Controls ASP.NET functionality that works within a free framework for quickly adding client-side scripting that works across all popular browsers to provide more interactive pages and enhance other ASP.NET controls. ASP.NET AJAX is built into ASP.NET 3.5. It is also available as a separate download for ASP.NET 2.0.

alt text The text contained within the *alt* attribute of an HTML \<img\> tag. The text is available to the browser.

Application Options A dialog box in Expression Web 2. You can open it by clicking Application Options on the Tools menu. In this dialog box, you can set broad parameters for how Expression Web 2 operates.

architecture In reference to Web site architecture, it is the basic folder structure of a Web site.

ASP Active Server Pages are a discontinued Microsoft technology that was very popular but has been replaced by ASP.NET.

ASP.NET A Microsoft framework for Web development that enables you to implement dynamic Web sites, Web applications, and XML Web services.

ASP.NET Development Server A server that installs with Expression Web 2 to enable users to preview ASP.NET pages and functionality in a browser. With it, users can preview ASP.NET functionality even in files in a folder-based site.

ASP.NET Image control An ASP.NET control that provides programmatic access to image properties.

ASP.NET Navigation Controls Controls that can be used to create menus and other navigational aids on ASP.NET Web pages. Introduced with ASP.NET 2.0, these controls include SiteMapPath, Menu, and TreeView controls.

.aspx The file extension of an ASP.NET forms page; for example, *default.aspx*.

best practices Industry-accepted preferred methodology for performing a specific task or operation.

block quotes An HTML tag (\<block\> \</block\>) designed to set a quote apart from adjacent HTML elements.

breadcrumb A navigational aid that shows the page a visitor is currently viewing along with the pages leading to it.

Byte Order Mark (BOM) A Unicode character mark that denotes the beginning of a UTF file. Generally unseen but desired for reliability, these marks can cause rendering problems on certain servers and in files that include PHP Server Side Scripting.

cascading style sheet (CSS) A standard for creating a separation of content and presentation. This technology is useful in Web design for a number of reasons, such as positioning elements for layout purposes, styling text, or applying backgrounds.

cell A component of an HTML table, represented in HTML code by <td> and </td> tags.

child pages Pages below a particular page in the architecture of a Web site.

Classic ASP Legacy Active Server Pages; a technology that has been replaced by ASP.NET.

clip art Prepackaged artwork for computer documents. The artwork originally existed in the form of clip sheets, pages of drawings that graphic designers could cut out and use in compositions.

code hyperlink A special hyperlink visible only in the Code view within Expression Web. Pressing Ctrl while clicking the code hyperlink shifts the work area's focus to the CSS style or other source code to which the link refers.

Code Snippets list The list of code, either supplied with Expression Web or user-customized, that resides in the Code Snippet tool in Expression Web.

columns Table cells arranged vertically in relation to each other.

comments An HTML element that a designer can use to make comments in the code of a page. The comments aren't visible when rendered in a browser; for example, `<!-- this is a comment -->`.

configuration file A file that contains certain constants that are used by server-side code or scripting. For example, a configuration file might contain a database connection string, the base URL of certain pages within a site, or certain elements like the site's name.

contact forms A form used to allow a site visitor to enter input for the purpose of initiating contact.

cross-browser compatibility The ability of a Web page or pages to appear similarly in various Web browsers and allow their functionality to be maintained regardless of the browser they are being viewed with.

cross-platform compatibility The ability of an application to function on multiple computer operating systems, such as Windows, UNIX, and Macintosh.

CSS class A cascading style sheet element that can be applied to multiple elements in a Web page. On the style sheet, the class name is always prefixed by a period (.).

CSS ID A cascading style sheet element that can be applied only once to an element in a Web page. On the style sheet, the ID name is always prefixed by a number sign (#).

Data Access Components ASP.NET components that enable interaction with various databases.

database A format for storing and retrieving information. Usually presented as a relational format where information within it contains references to other information within the database.

Database Results Wizard A feature in Microsoft Office FrontPage that enables users to create, read from, write to, and display data from a database.

DataView Controls A customizable view of a DataTable for sorting, filtering, searching, editing, and navigation.

default file A file on a Web server that is passed to the browser automatically if the browser requests a folder only and not a specific file.

definition list An HTML list similar to the ordered list and bulleted list but designed to contain terms and definitions.

Dynamic Web Template (.dwt) An HTML-based file that can contain settings, formatting, page elements, and editable regions.

disk-based site A Web site that resides in the folder structure of a user's computer instead of on a Web server.

\<div\> A block-level HTML tag for a division, often used in conjunction with cascading style sheets to apply formatting to the tag and its contents.

DNS (Domain Name System) The system that points a domain name to the IP address of the Web server where the site resides.

dock Refers to attaching a toolbar, pane, or other user interface element to a specific place within the application's interface.

DOCTYPE A declaration that allows a browser to know what kind of document it is displaying, and establishes what HTML rules are pertinent to its structure.

document title An important part of a Web page that resides in the HEAD element of the source code. The document title is what's visible on the browser frame, in the favorites or bookmark list, and gives search engines an idea of what the page is about.

domain control panel A Web-based tool provided by the registrar to enable the domain owner to make changes, such as to DNS records or ownership information. This term can also refer to facilities provided by a Web site's host that enable the site owners to make changes to their hosting parameters, set up e-mail accounts, or other changes.

domain extensions The domain extension is the .net, .com, or .org segment of the domain name. There are a large number of domain extensions available, such as .tv, .biz, .name, .mobi, and country-specific extensions.

domain name The name that a user enters into a browser to visit a Web site. The domain name resolves to the appropriate numerical IP address where the site is hosted; for example, the domain name *microsoft.com* will resolve to the servers that host the Microsoft Web sites under the microsoft.com domain.

dynamic HTML (DHTML) An arrangement of HTML, CSS, and JavaScript used to provide functionality within a browser.

dynamic site A site that retrieves and displays information from a database or other mechanism, such as XML data. Pages within a dynamic site may display different information or provide different functionality based on user interaction.

encoding A method to cloak or hide the true character value of data passed between a server and a client.

Expression Studio 2 Refers to the entire suite of Microsoft Expression applications packaged together: Expression Web 2, Expression Blend 2, Expression Media 2, Expression Encoder 2, and Expression Design.

Expression Web site A Web site created in or maintained with Expression Web, usually containing metadata to allow Expression Web to provide management capabilities.

Extensible Hypertext Markup Language (XHTML) A markup language similar to HTML but that conforms to the XML syntax. Because XHTML must be more tightly formatted than HTML, it is often used in conjunction with automated processing.

Extensible Markup Language (XML) A general-purpose markup language that allows its users to define their own tags.

File Transfer Protocol (FTP) The most commonly used method of copying files from a local folder structure to a Web server.

floating toolbar A toolbar that has been moved from its default location in a user interface and "floated" to another area, as opposed to being "docked" in a fixed location. See also *dock*.

fly-out menu A sub-menu that appears when you point to a DHTML menu.

font tags Deprecated HTML tags previously used to describe what font, font style, and color that text should be shown with.

footer The bottom element of a Web page, often applied uniformly to all the pages in a site.

form data Any input a user enters into a form that they submit.

form validation A method to ensure that form input meets certain parameters, such as specific fields not being empty or the value entered into a form field having certain characteristics. Form validation can be done by using client-side scripting such as JavaScript or on the server with a server-side scripting process.

FrontPage Link Bars A FrontPage feature that inserts a series of links into a page based on how the pages in a FrontPage site are defined in Navigation view.

FrontPage proprietary Technology that requires either FrontPage as an HTML code editor or that requires FrontPage Server Extensions.

FrontPage Server Extensions A software package installed on a server that enables FrontPage to communicate with the Web server and provides additional functionality for Web sites.

FrontPage Shared Borders A FrontPage proprietary method of writing common content into the top, bottom, and/or sides of each page in a group of HTML pages.

FrontPage Substitution A FrontPage proprietary method of changing content based on a variable within an HTML page.

.fwp The file extension for a Personal Web Package.

global elements A page element such as navigation or other elements that are present on all pages.

global.asa A file used in legacy ASP applications. The file extension .asa stands for Active Server Application.

graphical user interface (GUI) A graphical (rather than textual) representation of a computer's user interface.

Graphics Interchange Format (GIF) An image format, with an extension of .gif, limited to 256 colors.

header The top segment of a page's template. This element is often present and uniform on all pages in a site.

Help cursor A special cursor that gives the user visual feedback. It generally appears as a pointer with a question mark.

hidden folders Folders within an Expression Web site that contain metadata enabling Expression Web to manage the site. These folders are always preceded by an underscore (_).

hierarchical information Information relating to or arranged in a formally ranked order.

hosting A service providing space, bandwidth, and processing for a Web site.

hosting account An account from which a user manages one or more domains or Web sites.

HTML Markup component A FrontPage feature that allows HTML markup or other code to be placed into a Web page in a visual way and also protects the code from being changed by any FrontPage processes.

Hypertext Markup Language (HTML) The standard text formatting language for Web-based documents since 1989.

Hypertext Transfer Protocol (HTTP) The protocol used when using FrontPage publishing. It's also the most common protocol for browsing the Web.

IBM DB2 An IBM proprietary database technology.

image editor An application that is used to create or manipulate an image.

image swap A term used to describe replacing one image for another. Usually used as a visual effect enabled by JavaScript.

imported Refers to files and/or folders that have been brought into a Web site from an external location.

index file A file that serves as the default file of a Web site or "home page" file of a folder.

insertion point A visual indicator as to the location in an application where user input will be placed; the location in a document where users set their mouse pointer and click.

Interactive buttons A feature built into Expression Web that enables users to insert buttons that respond to user actions and provides a roll-over effect based on JavaScript and background images. The Interactive buttons can be used as hyperlinks or serve as the basis of further JavaScript functionality.

Internet Corporation for Assigned Names and Numbers (ICANN) A non-profit organization that has assumed the responsibility for IP address space allocation, protocol parameter assignment, DNS management, and root server system management functions.

Internet site A Web site on the World Wide Web that can be accessed by remote users with a browser and an Internet connection.

intranet site A Web site that exists on a local network and can be accessed by the computers and users connected to that local network.

JavaScript A scripting language designed to run within the browser of the visitor; also called *client-side scripting*. JavaScript has a wide variety of uses but is most commonly used to provide interactive properties to HTML elements.

Joint Photographic Experts Group (JPEG) A compression technique for color images. Although it can reduce files sizes to as little as five percent of their normal size, detail is lost in the compression.

layout The arrangement of a Web page's container elements, which provides order and placement for all of the page's content.

Legacy ASP See *Classic ASP*.

<li> An HTML tag for a list item, appearing within ordered (numbered) lists and unordered (bulleted) lists. Each line in a list is a list item.

link bars A series of links, usually image-based hyperlinks, which are arranged together to give the visual appearance that each link is part of a larger graphical object.

list item An individual item within an ordered or unordered list. It is always inside of a parent list and uses the <li> and </li> tags.

lists HTML elements that provide a basis to organize information. These include the Ordered List (<ol>) (also referred to as the *numbered list*), the Unordered List (<ul>) (also referred to as the *bulleted list*), and the Definition List (<dl>).

local folder A folder existing on the user's computer, as opposed to a folder on an intranet or the Internet.

local network A network of computers connected only to each other as opposed to computers connected to each other by the Web.

local site The copy of a Web site that exists on your desktop computer's file system instead of on a server.

log file The file that Expression Web creates that contains information about publishing operations for an Expression Web site.

long description (longdesc) An attribute of an HTML <img> tag that provides the user with a URL to a file that describes the image in detail.

maintainability The ability to maintain a Web site or level of efficiency in maintaining a Web site's appearance or content.

master page An ASP.NET 2.0 feature that provides for templating of pages.

Menu Control One of the ASP.NET Navigation Controls. This control provides a DHTML-type of menu in vertical or horizontal orientation.

menu group A group of related items within a common menu.

metadata Files that contain information about other files, folders, or groups of files and folders. Strictly defined, it would be data about data.

metafiles The actual files that contain the metadata.

Microsoft Developer Network (MSDN) A site and group of products and services to assist people who develop software within various Microsoft platforms.

Microsoft Office Access A program for visually creating, editing, and maintaining databases.

Microsoft SQL Server databases A database server designed for enterprise-level database performance.

Microsoft Visual Studio .NET A code-editing application designed to enable professional programmers to create programming code in a visual user interface.

MySQL An open-source relational database management system that relies on Structured Query Language for processing the data in the database.

navigation components Components available within FrontPage for page navigation, such as the next/back links and navigation bar. These components must be used in conjunction with a site that has been defined in Navigation view.

Navigation Controls ASP.NET 2.0 features, such as Menu Control, TreeView Control, and SiteMapPath Control, designed to provide navigation elements on Web pages.

Navigation view A view available in the FrontPage user interface that enables users to design the navigational structure of a Web site visually by dragging pages onto the work area. This FrontPage proprietary method of navigation structure design has been deprecated in favor of ASP.NET Navigation Controls.

network share A folder, drive, or drive partition available to computers and users on a local network.

node A segment of XML data that may or may not contain additional segments within it.

Oracle An enterprise-level database system.

ordered list An HTML element that uses the <ol> and </ol> tags to contain the items within the list, which are themselves contained in <li> and </li> tags. This type of list is usually presented as a numbered list.

Page Banners A FrontPage component that can be inserted into a page. It shows the name of the page in either a graphic or text format and must be defined in Navigation view.

Page Editor Options A dialog box in Expression Web 2. You can use this dialog box to set specific behavior characteristics for how Expression Web works with specific files. You can open the dialog box by clicking Page Editor Options on the Tools menu.

PHP A server-side scripting language that can be inserted into the HTML code of a Web page. When a PHP page is accessed, the PHP code is processed by the server the page resides on.

physical size The actual dimensions in height and width of a visual element, particularly the height and width of an image in pixels.

pipe character A keyboard character that looks like a vertical line (|).

port number The port number identifies what type of port a process is using and helps keep processes from overlapping by allowing each to use a specific port. For example, port 80 is used for HTTP traffic, port 21 is used for FTP, and various other applications and devices use other non-standard ports.

proprietary technology A technology that is the possession of a particular entity. Proprietary software technology usually dictates the environment that it can be used in or with.

Providers An ASP.NET module that provides a uniform interface between a service and a data source.

publishing The practice of copying an entire Web site or specific files within a Web site from one location to another.

Publishing Strategy A predefined strategy for efficiently working with a server-based and disk-based site. This strategy is generally user designed and helps to improve publishing times, data retention, and overall manageability.

registrar A company accredited by ICANN to engage in selling, transferring, and registering domain names.

remote Web site The Web site that is being published to. The remote Web site doesn't necessarily have to be server-based. It could be a disk-based site being published into from any other site. The key to what qualifies as a remote Web site is that it is the site to be published into.

Remote Web Site view A view in Expression Web that shows both the local site and the remote site side by side in the main work area. This is the default view when publishing a Web site.

roll-over The action that takes place when users pass their mouse pointers over an element that changes as a result of their interaction with it.

root folder The folder that contains all the files, other folders, and assets of a Web site.

rows A segment of an HTML table that contains cells along a horizontal axis. It uses the <tr> tag and must be within an HTML table and contain at least one table cell <td> tag.

save time A process that takes place when a file is saved on the user's computer, as opposed to a run-time method that takes place when the page is processed by the server or visitor's browser.

screen readers A special type of browser designed for people with visual impairments. This browser reads the content of a Web page aloud to the visitor.

script blocks Refers to blocks of server-side scripting contained within the language's delimiters. For example, in PHP, the delimiters would be "<?php" and ?>; in ASP, they would be "<%" and "%>". The script block consists of the beginning and ending delimiters and all the content within them.

scripts Code that provides functionality or instructions for the browser to carry out certain actions or processes.

search engines Tools that contain information about Web pages on the Internet. A user can enter a search query, and the search engine will return results based on that user's query. Search engines are responsible for the majority of traffic delivered to a typical Web site.

Secure Server Certificate A file installed on a Web server that identifies a Web site and provides for encrypted transfer of data from the server to the browser and vice-versa.

Secure Sockets Layer (SSL) A protocol used to do two things: validate the identity of a Web site, and create an encrypted connection for sending and receiving sensitive data.

selector Represents a structure that can be used as a condition, such as a CSS rule, that determines which elements a selector matches in the document. It can also be a flat description of the HTML or XML fragment corresponding to that structure.

semantic markup Elements that are appropriate to content meaning rather than its presentation, such as using HTML tags to describe and order the elements of a Web page based on their meaning rather than their presentation.

server An application or hardware device designed to process Web pages and pass them to browsers.

server logs A file or group of files that a Web server maintains. These files contain a broad range of information about the site, the files within the site, and the visitors who request the files.

server side Actions that take place on the Web server as opposed to locally or within a browser.

server-based site A site that exists within the structure of a Web server and can be accessed through the Internet as opposed to a site that exists within the folder structure of a desktop computer.

server-side scripting Scripting or programming code that must be executed by a Web server as opposed to client-side scripting, which executes in a visitor's browser.

shopping cart An application that runs on a Web server and enables e-commerce so that site visitors can order, pay for, and, in some cases, take delivery digitally of products.

SiteMapPath Control An ASP.NET 2.0 Navigation Control that provides a tree view menu similar to the folders pane navigational arrangement in Windows Explorer.

Site navigation controls See *ASP.NET Navigation Controls*.

slice To divide a larger image into multiple pieces. This technique is done in an image editor in order to prepare graphics for use in an HTML layout. The term can also refer to an image that is a segment of a larger image that has been sliced.

standards-compliant HTML code that follows the standards for its document type as established by the World Wide Web Consortium (W3C).

state The condition of a hyperlink or button, such as normal, hovered, active, and visited.

static pages Web pages based on HTML that provide the same information regardless of user interaction.

subsites A division of folders within Expression Web. A subsite is a folder that Expression Web treats as if it were a complete and independent Web site rather than as a subfolder of a larger site.

Table Head (<th>) An HTML tag that defines a table header cell in a table. The text within the <th> element usually renders in bold.

table-free A layout that doesn't require an HTML table for positioning of elements. The practice of table-based layout is deprecated in favor of CSS layout.

tables An HTML element used in Web pages. This element was originally intended to provide ordering of tabular data but was also used for graphical layout of Web pages, a practice that has been deprecated in favor of using cascading style sheets for layout and tables only for the presentation of data.

tabular Data calculated with or making use of a table; for example, logarithms.

template packages Third-party products that a designer can use to create a Web page or Web site layout. Generally, these packages come with source images and HTML files with the source images used in the layout.

templates A predesigned layout and set of pages from which to create a Web site.

templating system A system used in order to provide uniformity and improve maintainability within a group of pages.

<th> An HTML tag that defines a table header cell. By default, the text in this cell is bold and centered.

themes Refers to a FrontPage-proprietary method of applying uniform formatting to a group of pages. This method has been discontinued in favor of cascading style sheets and other technologies.

third-party FTP client An FTP application used to transfer folders and files to or from a Web server.

thumbnail A small image representation usually linked to a larger version.

tiling A term used to describe how a background image repeats over and over until it fills the background of an HTML element.

timestamps A reference in a file or in the metadata for a file denoting when a particular operation occurred; for example, publishing, editing, or creation.

timing out When a publishing operation takes longer than a server is configured to allow, the operation fails and the connection is reset.

tooltip A small text message that pops up when a users points to an element; it usually contains the name of a button or other information about an element.

transparent background The background of a GIF or PNG image that has no color information, and any element under it is visible through the background.

TreeView Control An ASP.NET 2.0 control that renders a folder structure type of navigation element similar to a folder list pane in Windows Explorer and is suited for large numbers of hierarchical pages.

<ul> An HTML tag that defines an unordered (bulleted) list.

undock To remove a toolbar or pane from a location in the user interface where it was affixed.

unordered list An HTML element used for the creation of a list that doesn't require a specific order. It is most commonly presented as a bulleted list and uses the <ul> and </ul> tags to surround list items.

URL (Uniform Resource Locator) The "friendly name" by which a user can locate a Web site.

user interface (UI) The conduit between a user and a computer program.

Visual Basic Editor A tool used to create, modify, and maintain Microsoft Visual Basic for Applications (VBA) procedures and modules in most Microsoft Office applications.

Visual Basic Scripting Edition (VBScript) Client-side scripting similar to JavaScript but much less common because it's not a cross-browser scripting language and therefore can't be used in all browsers.

Visual Web Developer A free application produced by Microsoft designed to help users write programming code in a visual user interface.

watermark A term referring to a Web background that does not move when the page is scrolled; it generally is a low-intensity color, and text appears directly over it.

Web Bots FrontPage proprietary code used in order to provide extended functionality of a Web page.

Web site templates An arrangement of page and navigation elements that can be used to quickly produce a custom Web site by taking advantage of the assets of the template.

Web-based Distributed Authoring and Versioning (WebDAV) A publishing method available in Expression Web that is a set of platform-independent extensions enabling users to edit and manage files collaboratively.

Web.sitemap An XML file that ASP.NET 2.0 uses to create the link elements in a Navigation Control.

Windows Media Video (.wmv) A proprietary Microsoft compressed video file format that was originally designed for Internet streaming applications.

Windows Explorer A tool built into the Windows operating system that enables you to browse, view, copy, and delete files.

World Wide Web Consortium (W3C) A consortium of organizations, programmers, developers, industry executives, and users that seeks to guide the future development of the Web and ensure that all Web technologies are compatible with one another.

XHTML See *Extensible Hypertext Markup Language*.

XML See *Extensible Markup Language*.

Index

A

B

E

F

About the Author

Chris Leeds is a long-time digital photographer and Web enthusiast who has been a Microsoft Most Valuable Professional (MVP) for Microsoft Office FrontPage for more than five years. He is also a member of the Microsoft Professional Accountant's Network (MPAN), commentator at Lockergnome (*www.Lockergnome.com*), and a software reviewer on BrightHub (*www.BrightHub.com*).

Chris developed a software product called ContentSeed (*www.ContentSeed.com*) with which users can create Web pages that can be edited and managed by using only a browser.

Chris was a technical reviewer for *FrontPage 2003 (The Missing Manual)*, the author of *Microsoft Expression Web Step by Step* (the previous version of this book), has developed several tutorials about FrontPage, and hopes to continue helping the user community through the Web site *www.ExpressionWebStepByStep.com*, from which he'll try to answer questions regarding the book and Microsoft Expression products.

Dedication

I want to thank the readers of my previous edition of this book, and the visitors to my support site (*www.ExpressionWebStepByStep.com*). I'd like to include a special thanks to Kathleen Atkins (Microsoft Press Project Editor), Kathy Krause (OTSI Project Manager), Dan Maharry (Content Master Technical Reviewer), Brittany Mihalchik (my testing and screen shot assistant), and all the people at Microsoft Press and Online Training Solutions, Inc. who really had more to do with the physical manifestation of this book than I did. Last but not least I'd like to thank the people on the Expression Web product team for their commitment to deliver a truly technology-agnostic Web design tool that makes modern, standards-based Web authoring so much easier than it used to be.

Thank you all!

–Chris Leeds

What do you think of this book?

We want to hear from you!

Do you have a few minutes to participate in a brief online survey?

Microsoft is interested in hearing your feedback so we can continually improve our books and learning resources for you.

To participate in our survey, please visit:

www.microsoft.com/learning/booksurvey/

...and enter this book's ISBN-10 or ISBN-13 number (located above barcode on back cover*). As a thank-you to survey participants in the United States and Canada, each month we'll randomly select five respondents to win one of five $100 gift certificates from a leading online merchant. At the conclusion of the survey, you can enter the drawing by providing your e-mail address, which will be used for prize notification only.

Thanks in advance for your input. Your opinion counts!

* Where to find the ISBN on back cover

ISBN-13: 000-0-0000-0000-0
ISBN-10: 0-0000-0000-0

00000

0 000000 000000

Example only. Each book has unique ISBN.

***Microsoft®**
Press

No purchase necessary. Void where prohibited. Open only to residents of the 50 United States (includes District of Columbia) and Canada (void in Quebec). For official rules and entry dates see:

www.microsoft.com/learning/booksurvey/